PICKED BY THE BILLIONAIRE

ERIN SWANN

ISBN-13: 978-1718111165

Edited by: Jessica Royer Ocken, Donna Hokanson

Typo Hunters: Michelle Bonner, Jean Marie Gard, Lynette Hamilton, and Renee Williams

The following story is intended for mature readers. It contains mature themes, strong language, and sexual situations. All characters are 18+ years of age, and all sexual acts are consensual.

Join Erin's mailing list and be notified when this book and others are available. WWW.ERINSWANN.COM/SUBSCRIBE

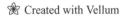 Created with Vellum

ALSO BY ERIN SWANN

The Billionaire's Trust - Available on Amazon, also in AUDIOBOOK

(Bill and Lauren's story) He needed to save the company. He needed her. He couldn't have both. The wedding proposal in front of hundreds was like a fairy tale come true—Until she uncovered his darkest secret.

The Youngest Billionaire - Available on Amazon

(Steven and Emma's story) The youngest of the Covington clan, he avoided the family business to become a rarity, an honest lawyer. He didn't suspect that pursuing her could destroy his career. She didn't know what trusting him could cost her.

The Secret Billionaire – Available on Amazon, also in AUDIOBOOK

(Patrick and Elizabeth's story) Women naturally circled the flame of wealth and power, and his is brighter than most. Does she love him? Does she not? There's no way to know. When he stopped to help her, Liz mistook him for a carpenter. Maybe this time he'd know. Everything was perfect. Until the day she left.

The Billionaire's Hope - Available on Amazon

(Nick and Katie's story) They came from different worlds. She hadn't seen him since the day he broke her brother's nose. Her family retaliated , by destroying his life. She never suspected where accepting a ride from him today would take her. They said they could do casual. They lied.

Previously titled: Protecting the Billionaire

Saved by the Billionaire – Available on Amazon

(Ryan and Natalie's story) The FBI and the cartel were both after her for the same thing: information she didn't have. First, the FBI took everything, and then the cartel came for her. She trusted Ryan with her safety, but could she trust him with her heart?

Caught by the Billionaire – Available on Amazon

(Vincent and Ashley's story) Her undercover assignment was simple enough: nail the crooked billionaire. The surprise came when she opened the folder, and the target was her one-time high school sweetheart. What will happen when an unknown foe makes a move to checkmate?

The Driven Billionaire – Available on Amazon

(Zachary and Brittney's story) Rule number one: hands off your best friend's sister. With nowhere to turn when she returns from upstate, she accepts his offer of a room. Mutual attraction quickly blurs the rules. When she comes under attack, pulling her closer is the only way to keep her safe. But, the truth of why she left town in the first place will threaten to destroy them both.

Nailing the Billionaire – Available on Amazon

(Dennis and Jennifer's story) She knew he destroyed her family. Now she is close to finding the records that will bring him down. When a corporate shakeup forces her to work with him, anger and desire collide. Vengeance was supposed to be simple, swift, and sweet. It was none of those things.

Undercover Billionaire – Available on Amazon

(Adam and Kelly's story) Their wealthy families have been at war forever. When Kelly receives a chilling note, the FBI assigns Adam to protect her. Family histories and desire soon collide, causing old truths to be questioned. Keeping ahead of the threat won't be their only challenge.

Trapped with the Billionaire – Available on Amazon

(Josh and Nicole's story) When Nicole returns from vacation to find her company has been sold, and she has been assigned to work for the new CEO. Competing visions of how to run things and mutual passion collide in a volatile mix. When an old family secret is unearthed, it threatens everything.

CHAPTER 1

LIAM

I PANTED RAGGEDLY AS I SLID OFF MELINDA AND ROLLED ONTO MY back, the final aftershocks of pleasure fading slowly away.

She nibbled my ear before laying her head on my shoulder.

I returned the favor by pinching her nipple.

She made her delightful little purring noise as I pulled her into my side, and she slid a leg over mine.

I was comfortable here, almost too comfortable. She was warm and soft against me as I stroked her long blond hair. She deserved some cuddle time while I caught my breath and let my cock deflate enough to be able to dress. The time would be shorter than she liked, but it couldn't be helped.

This evening Melinda Nixon and I had entertained Jeremy Sanders and his wife at the Boston Opera. It had been tolerable as such things went. Sunday nights were always less crowded. And thankfully tonight's performance of *Aladdin* had been in English.

I wanted to add an outdoor footwear line to the company and hoped to persuade the Sanders family to divest theirs. Buying their business would go a long way toward meeting our goals for this quarter.

A year ago I had thought it was merely a matter of spreadsheets and check-writing to acquire a business. Three consecutive failures had taught me how wrong-headed I'd been. Since coming to Boston, I'd learned evenings like this were a necessary part of the company courtship dance before making a formal offer——a sort of corporate foreplay.

Tonight had gone well. In particular, Mrs. Sanders had been quite taken with Melinda's knowledge of Arabian mythology.

The dim red numerals of the clock read one-twelve in the morning. An energetic session before the opera and now another after had thoroughly relaxed me. It was time to go home.

"Do you have to go so soon?" Melinda asked as I climbed out of bed.

I searched for my underwear. "Sorry, I have to meet Josh at six for squash." I discarded the condom and pulled on my clothes, not bothering with the cummerbund or my cufflinks. I kissed her on the forehead. "You did great tonight."

Melinda held my hand momentarily. "I had a good time too." She didn't ask me to stay; she understood. The rules were simple: I didn't spend the night. Not ever.

Reaching the door, I pulled a red velvet Cartier pouch from my pocket and left it on the front table for her: earrings with black pearls on white gold hoops, understated elegance. Flicking off her hall light, I closed the door behind me and latched the deadbolt.

Melinda served as intelligent and stunningly attractive eye candy when I needed a date for an event like tonight. In return, I accompanied her to a social event of her choosing every few months. She had looks, class, and also wicked smarts.

We fit well together, but we weren't exclusive or attached. I fucked other women when I found an appropriate target, and I didn't care if Melinda had other men. She understood our arrangement: no commitments, no entanglements, no expectations, and no relationship.

I replayed the evening in my head on my way downstairs. I felt good about everything except the appearance of the redhead.

Once inside my car, I punched the key fob in and the V-12 roared to life.

Eat your heart out, Daniel Craig. You get to drive an Aston Martin in the movies. I drive one every day.

I rubbed my ring finger. I had dared to love once, and lost.

The scar weighed on me every day.

∿

AMY

THE PURPLE AND ORANGE FEDEX ENVELOPE DOMINATED MY desktop. Why did they always arrive on a Tuesday?

I hung up my jacket before closing the door to my office. I needed quiet time to finish my presentation for Friday's investor meeting.

My phone vibrated with a text message.

VIV: See you 2nite

It had slipped my mind; I'd agreed to meet my sister, Vivienne, for drinks. She was my rock, even if she was off-the-wall crazy half the time. I had canceled on her last week and didn't dare invite her wrath by canceling again.

ME: Might be late

VIV: Then drink fast to catch up

THE FEDEX ENVELOPE WAS FROM THE DEVIL HIMSELF. I'D TRIED once to tell my assistant to stop signing for these, but it had only worked for a week. *He* had arranged for a process server to wait outside my office and added the fee to my bill.

My hand trembled as I ripped open the package and a single envelope slid out. It was an innocuous white; the return address was the problem. *Forrester, Forrester & Jenkins attorneys at law*: my ex-husband's choice of divorce lawyers.

Maximilian Forrester was the face of the firm. His ugly mug appeared on late-night commercials on every local television station. I doubted there was anybody in Boston who hadn't heard of Max Forrester, the divorce lawyer who specialized in handling the man's side of the case.

Translation: when you were done fucking your wife, and you really wanted to fuck her over in the divorce, Max was your guy. The man had no moral compass and knew no limits. Calling him a human shark was an insult to sharks. I shook hands with him once, and it took two applications of hand sanitizer to remove the slime. Just his name was enough to make me want to retch.

I dreaded what the letter inside would say. An envelope like this never brought good news.

Samantha Tiffany knocked on my door once as she invited herself in the way she always did. She reached my desk in three strides.

"Friday's investment meeting just got moved to tomorrow afternoon at two. I hope that's not a problem," she announced.

"Sure, not a problem." It would mean less time to prepare, but handling meetings like this was my job.

Samantha and I had started Tiffany's Fine Chocolates together three years ago. Her name was on the packages, but we were equals. Amy's didn't sound as sophisticated as Tiffany's, and T&A Chocolates didn't make the cut either.

Our specialty was organic, preservative-free, GMO-free, kosher confections for those who cared to spend a little more for the very best. She was a wizard in the kitchen we called our lab and concocted kick-ass chocolates with her bakery background. I handled the marketing side of the business.

Samantha noticed the envelope. "What's in it? Do I need to get my earplugs?"

The last time I'd gotten one of these fucking envelopes I had screamed bloody murder. It had scared our receptionist, Lucy, so badly she almost called 9-1-1.

I plopped my ass down in my seat. "Don't know, and right now I don't care."

"Maybe Matt remarried, and you don't owe spousal support anymore."

"That's about as likely as me winning the Mega Millions drawing." An actuary would disagree——it was even less likely than winning the lottery.

Matt Hudson, my worthless ex-husband, knew a good deal when he saw it and was too mean to let me off the hook easily. He would milk this for as long as he could. Hard work and Matt were not well acquainted with one another.

"If you want to leave early and get shit-faced, I'm up for it," Samantha offered.

With all the work we had piled up, she had to be seriously worried about my sanity to suggest leaving early, but I had to meet Vivienne anyway.

I shook my head. "Thanks, Sam, but no. I need to work on this presentation."

The evil-Sam grin overtook her face, which always meant something totally out there was coming. "We can make a little voodoo doll and stick pins in him." She giggled.

The doll didn't sound as good as going out with her to get drunk; the fun wouldn't last as long.

When I didn't go for her suggestion, she retreated. "I'll leave you to it then." She stopped before shutting the door. "You know, if you want to get back at him, Gary down in shipping has some pretty inventive ways."

The suggestion tempted me to laugh, but I didn't want to encourage her. "I don't even want to know how you know that."

Samantha closed the door behind her.

Knowing Gary, I imagined he might have perfected the exploding package of dog shit I'd seen on the internet.

I took a deep breath. The funding meeting, which was now tomorrow afternoon, was important——too important to jeopardize by taking time to feel sorry for myself.

I didn't have the emotional strength to deal with the bad news inside the envelope right now. So I slid it into my purse for later, preferably when there was nothing breakable within reach.

BEING TUESDAY, THE BAR VIVIENNE HAD CHOSEN WASN'T CROWDED when I arrived. She had gotten us a table with a good view of the place, as was her specialty. Deer hunters had blinds for hunting their prey. Vivienne selected tables similarly; she wanted a clear view of the field.

Yellow mush in a glass sat in front of my seat. "I got you a margarita to start." She was trying to break me of my habit of always ordering an appletini.

I pasted on a smile and took the seat across from her. "Thanks." I sipped the concoction slowly. These tended to give me a brain freeze if I wasn't careful.

"Okay, what's wrong?" she asked. "You've got that look again."

No matter how cheery I tried to be, Vivienne could always tell when I was hiding bad news. I pulled the letter out and placed it on the table. I'd opened it before coming over and confirmed the bad news.

Her face dropped, and she huffed. "What does the fucker want this time?"

I slumped in my seat. "Another hundred a month. This never ends. It's just not fair. And he's…"

Vivienne cocked an eyebrow. "He's what? Are you still trolling his Facebook?"

I stared down at my drink and took a long sip to avoid answering the question.

"Who is it now?" she asked.

I sipped more of my yellow mush.

"Never mind." She pulled out her phone. "I'll check myself." She fiddled with her phone for a few seconds. "Not MaryJo Mulvaney?"

I nodded. I had been checking Matt's Facebook using Samantha's phone. I'd uninstalled it on mine.

"This is great," Vivienne said with a laugh. "That slut's got, like, every STD known to man, and probably a few they haven't named yet."

I laughed. MaryJo never had been very picky. "You think?"

Vivienne leaned forward. "Serves him right. He'll be on antibiotics for a year trying to get rid of the warts on his dick."

I laughed. Vivienne could always cheer me up.

She pointed her finger at me. "You really need to get over this loser."

She was right, but it was difficult after devoting years of my life to trying to make it work.

Vivienne lifted her drink. "Like Oprah says, don't get mad, get even."

"She didn't say that."

"Who cares? It's still a good rule. You need to get yourself laid tonight and put him behind you."

"Shh, not so loud." Luckily the bar was noisy enough nobody seemed to have heard my crazy sister.

"How did the date with Jester go? Is he worth banging?"

She always harangued me about my dating——or often lack of dating——since my divorce from Matt.

I shook my head. "It's Jasper, and no, he was a waste of a dinner."

"Not that I'm counting or anything, but you're now oh for four-teen. You seriously need to up your game."

Of course she was counting, and if I had told her about Todd or Jerry last month, she would've known I was officially zero for *sixteen* since trying to dip my toe back in the dating pond.

"You can't have your vibrator be the only thing getting you off. Tell me I missed one and you've had at least one good fuck since your divorce."

I studied my margarita.

"Look, your vagina is like an ear piercing. If you don't put something in it every once in a while, it might just close up on you."

She was teasing me, but she was right. My vibrator and my fingers had been my only release since Matt.

The guys I had dated were not all bad, but I couldn't bring myself to take the final leap into getting hot and naked. Some, like Jasper, were complete losers, but with the others, as soon as the question had turned to his place or my place, I'd broken it off and powered up my computer to select another name from the list.

I hadn't been this picky in college. But now none of them seemed special enough to sleep with.

"It's tough. I'm just not ready," I told her, stirring my drink with the straw.

"Stop making excuses. Stop thinking and start acting," she said. "It's like riding a bicycle——once you've done it, you don't forget. It's only two people exercising together. You don't even have to do much of the work."

"But I haven't found the right guy yet."

"You're not marrying the guy, for Christ's sake. Any guy with more than a three-inch penis should be good enough to get it done. You need to pop that post-divorce cherry of yours and move past Matt."

My rational brain agreed with Vivienne——sex shouldn't be such a big deal. But these days, emotionally I was terrified.

"We agreed you would get past this," she continued. "Get over the hurdle with one guy, and the rest will be easy. Have a one-night stand. I know it's not your thing, but it's the easiest way to get over this phobia of yours and rejoin the human race. Trust me, everybody else is doing it, and not just once a month either."

I stirred my drink, contemplating her words. It seemed a big step to sleep with somebody other than Matt and accept that I had screwed up that phase of my life, accept that it was over. It made the mistake more real. Plus, I didn't want to make the same blunder again and become a pro at failed relationships.

"I guess," I said.

"He doesn't even need to speak English. Once his head is between your legs, it won't matter."

I clamped my thighs together at that visual.

"With your looks and that rockin' bod, you could land any one of the guys in this place tonight and get it done."

"You think so?" I didn't believe it for a moment. I wasn't homely, but I'd never put myself high up on the sexpot scale.

"Sure. If they've got red blood in their veins, they'll definitely go for you. Just let him do what comes naturally to a man. It's easy, and if you're too nervous about the whole thing, do the starfish."

"Starfish?" I asked.

Viv was always teaching me things I hadn't heard before. She was my younger sister, but in middle school she'd had to explain what Mickie had meant the first time he said he wanted me to *blow him*. He had laughed when I puckered my lips and made like his face was a birthday candle. I was too ashamed to talk to him again all year.

"Starfish. Just lay on your back, go spread eagle, and let him do all the work. It's better if you participate, but it'll get the job done. He gets his rocks off, and you get past this hang-up."

I took another sip of my now-thawed drink.

"Amy, I'm not going to stop bugging you about this. You have to get on with your life. I know you don't want to become a nun, so stop acting like one. So what if your marriage failed? A lot of them do. You don't have to be mental about it. You know Matt's been banging every chick in Brockton he can get his hands on."

Vivienne had warned me about Matt before I dated him, but had been polite enough to not remind me of that more than once after the divorce.

"But I'm not ready for that kind of relationship yet," I told her.

"That's the most fucked-up thing you've said yet. We're talking sex, fucking, boinking, not marriage. You don't have to be in a relationship with a guy to have sex with him. This is the twenty-first fucking century. Go have a random hookup, a good time with a stranger. You'll never see the guy again. You can let yourself go."

I shook my head and played with my glass.

"Didn't you have a one-night stand in college with that Arnie dude?"

"No," I admitted.

I had let guys get to second base on the first date, but never anything more. Arnie didn't even get that far.

"I don't know how," I said. I had never picked up a guy. They always made the first move. I had no clue what to do.

Vivienne grinned and took two swallows of her Moscow mule. "Good girl. The first step in recovery is admitting you have a problem."

"So what do I do? On the off chance I want to take your advice tonight…"

Her grin increased to a full-on megawatt smile. "Pick a guy, preferably one who's alone and looks like he showers on a regular basis." She scanned the room.

I waited for her advice. She was the expert at this.

Vivienne tipped her head toward the bar. "Dark hair, navy suit, looks like he showers regularly."

The man she pointed out was alone at the bar and had been there ever since I arrived. He was nursing a drink and seemed to be pondering the state of the world in the bottom of his glass.

"He's hot," Vivienne said. "But I can't tell if he's wearing a ring from here."

A quick chill ran through me. I hadn't considered that some men here might be married. I would not be a home-wrecker. "What if he just took it off to come in here?"

"Don't get all paranoid, sis. This time of year you'll see a tan line on his finger if he took it off. What I was going to say is, you can check for a ring first."

"Or if he had one on recently."

"Sure, that too. If it looks okay, then pick him up."

Those were all the instructions she was offering? Pick him up? If he was a pencil or a stapler, I could pick him up, but I was clueless on how to pick up *a guy*.

"But——"

"No buts. Go up and meet the guy."

"How?"

"Find a reason to get close to him, maybe look sideways at him, catch his eye. Talk to him."

"And just ask if he wants to fuck?"

"Of course not. Undo another button on your top."

I undid a button.

"That's not enough; you need another one."

"But I don't ever——"

"Trust me. Another button. This is advertising. You understand advertising, right?"

I undid another, and now you could see my cleavage and my bra.

"That's nice," my sister said. "Black lace——they go for black. Or red, that gets 'em too."

I might not be into her kind of *advertising*, but I liked nice lingerie.

"Now go do it." Her eyes bored into me. My sister would not let me back down. "Remember, you're doing this to get back at Matt for those damn alimony payments."

Her statement riled me enough to do anything. Matt had said I wasn't talented enough to land a marketing job at the tech startup, and he had scoffed at my and Samantha's idea of starting our confectionery company. I had been successful at both those things, and I could learn to do this too.

I got up, straightened my skirt, picked up my glass and started for the bar. I was uncomfortable having so much cleavage show-ing, but that's what my margarita was for. I sucked down the last of my liquid courage.

I can do this.

CHAPTER 2

*A*MY

I CAUGHT A HEEL ON THE WAY OVER, BUT MANAGED TO NOT FALL
on my face. It would have been a fitting way to get the guy's attention, though, looking like a complete dork. Maybe I could
convince him to take me to the ER for my bloody nose or twisted
ankle.

I decided I didn't need to talk to him if I lost my nerve. I went
beyond him, checking out his left hand discreetly in passing. Vivienne would be proud; I'd accomplished my first task.

He wasn't wearing a ring, and the finger had a consistent tan.
Bingo——a single man. My heart beat faster. I no longer had an
easy out. I leaned forward on the bar, my hands on the cold,
polished wood as I scanned for the bartender. I hadn't thought to
look for him before this.

"He'll be back, I'm sure," the guy said. He didn't have the
accent of a native Bostonian. He knew how to pronounce his Rs.

I got up the nerve to glance directly at him.

My God, he was handsome. His gaze fixed me in place.

I became a gazelle, stalked by a lion.

He grinned. "Hi."

I was lost. "Hi," I squeaked out.

Those caramel brown eyes pulled me in like a tractor beam. He could see right into my frightened soul. He had an imperfection to the bridge of his nose, which only seemed to make his face more perfect.

He swirled his amber drink. "Liam," he said in a smooth baritone before taking a sip.

"Liam," I repeated.

"No, I'm Liam."

I gasped. I jerked my hand to my mouth in embarrassment, hitting my empty drink glass on the way. It rolled toward the edge behind the bar.

He reached over and grabbed the goblet before it tumbled to the floor. "Careful there, Sunshine. This is where you tell me *your* name." He offered a hint of a grin and none of the laughter I deserved for being such an imbecile.

"Amy," I said.

This man mesmerized me——not just a guy in a bar, but a man with Hollywood looks. Dark brown hair to go with those eyes, and a strong, angular chin with enough stubble to make me wonder what it would feel like between my thighs.

God, I'm turning into Vivienne.

"Amy. That's a wonderful name. It comes from the French word for *beloved*. I like it."

A serious blush heated my cheeks. Nobody had ever said anything so charming to me on our first meeting. The timbre of his words sent a tingle racing through me. I could listen to this man recite the dictionary all night and be happy.

A voice from my left surprised me. "Sorry for the wait. What will you have?"

I turned to see the face that went with the husky voice. The bartender, an older gent with a goatee and graying temples, had returned.

"Russ, I'm treating," Liam said before I could get a word out.

"Whatever Amy and her friend would like, put it on my tab."

Russ nodded and looked my direction expectantly.

I pivoted back to the lion named Liam. "Taking a big risk there, Liam. What if I wanted a bottle of Macallan 18?"

His mouth curled up into a smile, melting me. "Not a big risk. They only sell that by the glass here." He held up his tumbler, now nearly empty. "It's quite good. Really."

My mouth dropped. The man knew his whiskey and only drank the best. Matt's taste hadn't extended beyond Fireball.

"Russ, two glasses of eighteen for the ladies, neat," he said in that smooth, chocolaty baritone of his.

"Belay that order, Russ," I said quickly. "We'll have more of the same."

"Ex-Navy?" Liam asked. He cocked an eyebrow.

"No. I just watch a lot of TV." I thought it sounded more authoritative the way I'd said it.

Russ paused a moment to see if Liam was going to overrule me. He didn't. "One margarita and one Moscow mule coming up."

"Turning down good whiskey?" Liam asked me.

I lifted myself onto the barstool. "I don't want you to think you can buy me that easily."

He cocked his head. "A principled lady. I like that. What shall we talk about?"

"Who said we're talking?" I asked.

"That's why you came over here, isn't it?"

The heat of another blush simmered in my cheeks. The man was a mind reader.

"You took a seat instead of walking back to your table with your friend, so I'm assuming that's an invitation to talk."

He made it all sound so logical, so transparent. I had meant to be subtle and failed.

"You first, Liam," I said. "What are you doing here? Drowning your troubles? Did she stand you up? Did your stock take a pounding today? Get fired?"

He laughed lightly. "No. Nothing like that. They can't fire me; I'm the boss, but it doesn't mean I have all the answers. I was just trying to think through a personal problem wrapped in a business one."

"Tell me the truth," I challenged him. "Why so glum?"

His brows furrowed. "Are we really going to play truth or dare?" he asked.

"You chicken?" It escaped my mouth before I had a chance to consider my words.

"Okay. I don't want a friend I work with to lose his job, and I'm not quite sure how to solve the problem."

"You're the boss, don't fire him," I suggested.

"The problem is more complicated than that."

Russ handed me my frozen margarita.

I moved my hand on the bar part way across the distance between me and Liam. "You're not from around here are you?"

He took another sip of his scotch. "California actually. What gave it away? The accent?"

I sipped my drink. "Well, you certainly don't know how to paahk yaah caah in Haahvaahd Yaahd." I said with my most exaggerated Boston twang.

"Yeah, the accent eludes me, so I guess I'll always be marked as an outsider."

"No doubt. Just passing through?" I asked, hoping for a yes. That would ensure we didn't meet up again if I ever got as far as Vivienne expected me to.

"Here to stay now. I'm just a few blocks away on Tremont." Tremont was an expensive neighborhood. It cost a lot to border the Common.

I sipped my drink, unsure what to ask next. Vivienne hadn't provided a script.

His eyes heated my blood again. "Your turn, Amy. What did you want to ask me?"

"I just wanted to get another drink."

"Liar," he said with a smirk.

He was right, but I hoped he couldn't guess the rest. His hand made the journey the rest of the way between us as he placed it atop mine.

The sparks from his touch ignited in me. I didn't pull back. His hand had welded mine in place.

"I dare you to tell me something honest," he said.

Truth or dare time had arrived.

I tried to look away but was unable to break free of the lion's gaze. "I think you're sexy," I blurted out.

His mouth fell open.

I quickly grabbed my drink, along with the one Russ had mixed for my sister, and retreated to our table before I made an even bigger fool of myself.

Those eyes. That voice.

My words had escaped before my brain-to-mouth filter could catch them. Well, at least it was the truth. I'm sure he'd been told the same by lots of women, but I couldn't believe I had said it. It was so un-Amy of me. It was a Vivienne line, my little sister with the unfiltered mouth.

Vivienne cocked her head as I sat. "From here it looked like it was going well. Why are you back? Is he gay?"

"What was I supposed to do? Pull up my skirt and bend over the bar?"

"Well, that's one way, but I was thinking something a little less direct." She attacked her drink and guzzled half of it.

I giggled. "I was pretty lame." I'd gotten his name and not gotten my head bitten off. It wasn't quite as scary as I had expected. The banter had been fun, right until I went all high-school.

"Well, at least you're smiling now that you talked to a man. Think how much brighter your disposition would be if you'd fucked him," she said with a grin. "You should have kept at it. I know you can do it if you try hard enough."

"Sex isn't the only thing," I told her.

It certainly wasn't going to make my alimony payments.

"Yeah, but good sex makes everything else better," Vivienne said, raising her glass to me.

"Well said," a man's baritone announced. The smooth voice that had entranced me minutes ago came from over my shoulder.

I looked back to find Liam standing behind me, and I wondered how much of our conversation he had heard.

"I think you're sexy too," he said, fixing me in place with those liquid caramel eyes. "And I think you should give me your number, Amy."

Vivienne quickly finished her drink. "Oops, I realized I'm late for an appointment," she said, grabbing her purse and standing.

"I'll come along," I said.

Liam placed a firm hand on my shoulder, keeping me seated. "No, you won't."

"I won't?" I asked like an idiot. I didn't need permission.

"You're staying here with me for a while. I'd like to learn a little more about Amy."

Vivienne's smile was ear-to-ear. "Sounds like a plan," she said before she scooted off.

And then I found myself alone with a man who was asking to hear about me instead of talking non-stop about himself, or the Celtics.

He took Vivienne's seat across from me with a smile that heated me all the way to my toes.

I recrossed my legs to quench the fire between my thighs.

❧

LIAM

THE PANIC IN HER EYES RECEDED QUICKLY. THIS WOMAN HAD A deep well of confidence, as she should have. Her eyes left her drink, and she scanned me, taking my measure.

I'd gone to the bar tonight to ponder the food-division problem

Josh and I had gotten ourselves into. It was screwing up our performance metrics big time. The undercurrent of my last several conversations with our lead investor, Syd Kovar, had made it clear his patience would wear thin before long, and it could cost us the company in the end if we didn't fix things.

The situation didn't sit well with me. Josh had suggested the strategy, but I'd bought into it, which made it a joint idea. So it was our problem to rectify together.

But sitting across the table from luscious Amy, the food division receded quickly to a tomorrow issue.

If I couldn't get into her pants tonight, she was hot enough to deserve a second attempt, and merely the memory of her pale green eyes framed by long, dark hair would be all I needed to jack off tonight if that's what it came to.

"We established that I'm not from around here. What about you?" I asked.

She looked down at her drink shyly before answering. "Grew up in the western part of the state and moved here after Brown for work."

"But you don't have a New England accent either."

"I work to avoid it. I'm in marketing, and I find it easier to talk with people across the country if I avoid the accent."

"That's very astute of you."

She blushed. "Thank you."

I'd had Russ freshen up my Macallan and took another sip of the smooth amber liquid. "Who do you do marketing for?"

She stirred her margarita. "Oh, just a company a friend and I started."

She didn't seem to realize how big an achievement that was. It seemed more like she was ashamed of it.

"You sound like an amazing woman to have accomplished that."

She tucked stray hair behind one ear. "Does that kind of line usually work for you?"

Women normally found me quite smooth——at least that's what I'd thought. "I meant it."

"I get that you're trying to get me in bed. I do. But you can't possibly know if I'm amazing or not after two sentences."

She was completely unfiltered. Completely refreshing. "Well, you're right about me wanting to seduce you. But Brown's not an easy place to get in to is all I meant."

She smiled. "Are you always this complimentary, Liam?"

"Only with a woman who deserves it. Starting your own company is quite a feat."

An immediate blush reddened her cheeks. Her smile as she played with the ends of her hair was totally disarming. I hadn't been this unnerved by a woman in a very long time.

"What if I come home with you…" she said before puckering her lips to sip on her straw.

The sentence alone jerked my cock fully to attention.

"And," she continued, "I turn out to be a disappointment?"

With that face and her body, it didn't seem possible. Not even remotely. I had stock answers to most women's questions, but hers stumped me for a second.

She stood. "Don't answer that. Let's go."

"Go?"

She hefted her purse. "Sure, your place. You said you only live a few blocks away on Tremont, right?"

I nodded. It wasn't supposed to be this easy. It normally took more time. Women with her looks required more time, more coaxing, and certainly a less-direct approach.

"How about your place?" I suggested.

"I didn't invite you to my place. You invited me to yours."

I had admitted to wanting to seduce her, yes, but I always went to the woman's place, never mine. Not even Melinda had been to my penthouse. It wouldn't be right. It was against my self-imposed rules.

The women generally preferred their home turf anyway, or a

hotel. Ever since *Fifty Shades* came out, they were all afraid I might have a dungeon of some sort.

"You change your mind?" she asked matter-of-factly, like we were talking about changing a wine order.

"I was just thinking," I said, stalling for time.

She put a twenty on the table for her tab. "About where you live? Give me your driver's license and I'll find it for you——or did you forget that too?" This girl had spunk.

"I think I can find it," I said, getting out of my chair.

"What? The license or the apartment?"

"Very funny, Amy." I was trapped. I didn't take women home, but here I was agreeing to take her up to my penthouse. I had one last option.

As we exited into the cool evening air, I leaned over and whispered. "If we go to my place, I'm going to fuck your brains out all night long and not let you go till morning." It was my last attempt at getting her to back down.

She grabbed my ass and squeezed. "Sounds like a plan."

My cock hardened even further. I took off my coat and wrapped it over her shoulders.

"Why thank you," she said in a very sultry voice. "Which way?"

There was no longer any face-saving way out of this. I placed my hand on the small of her back and guided her toward my building. The heat of her touch as she wrapped an arm around me set my blood boiling.

I sped up the pace. It wasn't far. She was sending my cock into overdrive, and I couldn't wait to get her naked. At least I wouldn't have to hunt for my clothes in the dark tonight.

She walked with an uneven gait.

"Shoes hurting?"

"Yeah, a little. They're made to look good, not be comfortable. The price we pay for vanity, I guess."

"I hope you don't want to kick them off as soon as we get inside. They'll look great over my shoulders."

She giggled. "I can be persuaded."

Somehow nothing I said got to this girl. I guided her to the left on Tremont Street. "I can hail a cab, if you like."

"No, I like to walk. The Common is pretty in the evening." The Boston Common was much smaller than New York's Central Park, but still a pretty space as downtown parks went.

I enjoyed walking on the Common as well. It was a cleansing thing to do when I needed to think. A block later, I stopped us outside my building.

"What's your apartment number?" she asked.

"The penthouse," I replied.

It didn't get the response I'd expected. She didn't seem impressed in the least. She took out her phone and sent a quick message.

"Checking in?" I asked.

"No, just telling Viv where they'll find the body if I don't turn up tomorrow."

I laughed. "Viv?"

"My sister. The girl you chased away."

"Why? Did she want to join us?"

"Don't get weirdo on me or I might change my mind about coming upstairs."

This was my opening to get rid of her. All I had to do was tell her I was inviting another girl to join us and it would be over.

But before I could say a thing, she walked past my doorman, through the door he held for her, and into the building.

This fox was going to make me break a cardinal rule.

CHAPTER 3

LIAM

As we rode the elevator, nervousness showed in Amy's body language.

We arrived upstairs, and I slid my key into the door. "Are you okay with this?"

"Yeah, totally," she said, not very convincingly. "I'm just a little nervous. Well, a lot nervous. This isn't my thing. I mean, I haven't done this before. Not the sex..."

She was talking more rapidly now, no longer the confident young thing who had propositioned me at the bar.

"I mean, I've done that before. Like, haven't we all. It's... I'm not sure how this is supposed to go. I know I'm saying too much. That's what I do when I get nervous, like a nervous tick. I haven't done this before. Oh, I already said that."

She sent me for a loop. The girl who'd invited herself here to get fucked, the first girl to talk me into letting her in here hadn't ever done this before? She was like virgin clay straight out of the package, just waiting to be molded into something.

"Maybe if you tell me what I'm supposed to do, how this goes, that might help," she finally said.

I took her shoulders lightly, so as not to scare her.

Frightened eyes looked back at me.

"It'll be fine. You'll be fine. We are going to have an enjoyable evening together."

She nodded. "That sounds good." Her eyes softened.

I knew what I told her was the truth; this was going to be fantastic.

"Amy, you'll be fine. Just trust me to tell you what to do."

"I've had sex before. I know how to——"

I stopped her with a quick finger to her lips. "Don't talk, just do," I said.

She didn't move. She didn't object. Her lips turned up seductively.

I took my finger from her mouth, removed my coat from her shoulders, and stepped back to take in her beauty.

She fidgeted as my eyes drank her in.

"You are stunning," I said quietly.

"Thank——"

I stopped her again. "Just do, don't talk."

Her eyes went wide as she took in a deep breath, but she didn't object.

"Give me your purse."

She took it off her shoulder, and I placed it over the back of a chair.

"Amy, take off your clothes, but not the shoes," I told her as I went to the wine fridge to pull out a bottle of champagne.

"What?"

A quick point of my finger silenced her. "Trust me. You want this to be good, so you have to trust me to show you how." I pulled the champagne out and undid the wire holding the cork.

This would be the test. Would she follow instructions and get undressed in the middle of the room with the lights on? Tonight would either be fantastic, or she'd bolt, and I'd be spared having to break my rule.

I popped the cork in the sink and retrieved two flutes. When I looked over, she hadn't moved.

She was torn, conflicted. She stared at me wordlessly as I filled the two glasses.

I started toward her with the champagne.

She decided to please me and began to unbutton her blouse. *Good girl.*

I could hardly walk with the raging hard-on in my pants as she slowly took off her blouse to reveal the black lace bra I'd gotten tempting glimpses of earlier.

Her tits filled the cups and overflowed into an alluring cleavage. I took a seat to watch, setting the drinks down for the moment.

She kept her eyes on me——hungry eyes, not scared eyes anymore. She unclasped her bra, looped her thumbs through the straps, and pulled it off to fall away.

I inhaled sharply at the sight of her marvelous tits, a perfect white inside the tan line. They bounced a tantalizing dance as she moved. Tight little knots of raspberry pink nipples pointed out at me, daring me to lick them, to nip them, to suck them, to twist them.

Her smile grew as she gathered the effect she was having on me. She understood the power of the striptease artist over the audience. She controlled the pace, at least for the moment.

My breathing became labored as she teased me, wiggling slowly out of her skirt, kicking it to the side, and slowly, ever so slowly, pulling down the black lace panties that matched her bra.

Her tits swung enticingly as she leaned over to glide her panties down to her ankles. Her tongue darted out to lick her lips and she held my eyes while she stepped out of them and kicked them aside.

My tension ratcheted up as she stood tall and naked except for those tall, red fuck-me shoes.

"Turn around. Turn around slowly," I instructed her.

She complied without complaint. Her long, dark hair cascaded down her back. The white of her ass matched the paleness of her tits.

I was going to enjoy grabbing that ass and caressing those tits. She had nice hips——hips made for grabbing. She hadn't shaved naked the way so many girls thought they had to today. She sported a trimmed landing strip of a bush, wider than most.

Her tits bobbed ever so slightly as she stepped around making her circle for me.

"You are gorgeous, Amy, perfectly gorgeous."

A quick blush rose from her chest to her cheeks. She smiled broadly, but wisely didn't say a word. She had said she'd started her own company, so she was obviously a confident, take-no-shit woman in the working world. Those kind were often the most willing to be compliant in the bedroom. They were confident in their minds and their bodies.

"Would you like a glass of champagne?" I asked.

She nodded, and I brought the glasses over. I handed her one, and she started to sip.

"Stand here, and don't move," I told her.

She lowered her glass.

"No, you can drink, just stay still."

She took another sip.

I took my free hand and traced under her breasts ever so lightly.

She gasped at my touch.

I moved to circle her tight little nipples.

She shivered under my fingers and tentatively sipped her drink.

I traced a line with a single finger down from her neck to her bellybutton and stopped. I moved behind her and traced the length of her spine from her neck to her tailbone and back up.

Slight gasps escaped her lips with the teasing of my fingertips. She finished the bubbly.

I walked the empty glasses back to the kitchen. "Go to the window," I told her.

After a short hesitation, she strode to the glass, which looked out over the Boston Common twenty-six floors below, and turned to face me.

She was unusual for sure. With her body, she needn't be ashamed of a thing, but not many girls exhibited her raw confidence. Melinda was confident in bed, but she would never consider standing naked in front of a window.

I knew nobody on the Common could see anything without a telescope——I had checked——but Amy didn't know it. There was a dangerous wickedness to being naked in front of the glass, but she seemed fully prepared to deal with it.

I couldn't control my cock much longer. I approached her. The temptation to taste her and feel her was destroying me. I'd tried to drag this out, to make it last for both of us. But the wait was becoming unbearable.

~

AMY

I HADN'T EXPECTED ANYTHING AS PROVOCATIVE AS THIS DANCE WE were performing around each other. I had thought it might be a quick fuck and out on the street again. I'd envisioned being on my back as soon as the door closed.

The ritual he'd had me perform started out as uncomfortable to say the least, but it had become teasing, playfully erotic, and sensual beyond description.

I looked out into the darkness completely naked, backlit by the room. Anybody on the Common could see me against the window. This was more dangerous than anything I'd ever done, and my nerves tingled as goosebumps covered me——not from cold, but from the excitement, the danger.

I reached out to touch the huge bulge in Liam's trousers as he returned from the kitchen.

He swatted my hand away. "Turn around."

I faced the window. Following his command was a simple choice, the only choice.

"Spread your legs, put your hands on the window, and don't move them until I tell you to."

Liam was one-hundred-and-ten-percent dominant male. He probably chewed people up and spit them out on a routine basis at work.

The tenor of his voice encouraged obedience, and I had no will to resist. My inner thighs were slick with my juices. I was more wet than I had ever been, and all without anything more than the electric touch of his fingertips.

He came up behind me, the bulge of his arousal against my butt. His arms encircled me, and I gasped as his fingers slid up my saturated folds and traced the length of my slit from my entrance to my clit and back.

I jerked as a single finger slowly entered me, retreated and moved to circle my clit, sending sparks through my whole body.

"Still, Sunshine. Stay still. And you can't come until I say so," he whispered into my ear, just before he licked it.

The words sent a spasm to my core. He gently blew into my ear, and all my functioning brain cells flew out the other side.

The finger attack on my swollen little bud started again as his other hand found my breasts and tweaked my nipples one by one.

I had come up here to be fucked, to get his cock inside me, but he was denying me, instead torturing me with unbelievable pleasure using his hands and lips. This was so much better than I'd imagined it could be.

He nibbled on my ear and rubbed his fabric-covered erection up against me.

I took a hand from the window and grabbed for him.

He forced my arm back to the window. "Behave yourself, or I won't let you come."

Behaving myself hadn't been on tonight's agenda, but at this point, going home without an orgasm would be the ultimate punishment. I relented and concentrated on the hot trail of sparks his fingers left as they caressed my breasts and trailed up and down my sides before returning.

Matt had been rough with my breasts, but Liam caressed them as if he worshiped them, except when he tweaked my nipples and sent a quick shock through me.

His relentless onslaught of my clit continued with renewed vigor as he found exactly the right motion and pressure to make me moan, and to take me to the edge of my orgasm. I'd never come close so quickly with a man.

I started to shake with all the built-up tension in my body, but he pulled away before I reached my release.

"Please," I begged him.

His fingers darted into me and then back to my tiny bundle of nerves as he rubbed his cock against me harder.

I wiggled my ass against him as his fingers circled my clit again. I was getting closer. My breath caught with each gentle touch of his fingers. He pushed me nearer to the precipice with each second. I couldn't keep my legs from shaking.

His fingers pressed harder, and his pace increased. "Come for me, Amy. Come now," he said with a jagged breath. He was almost as close as I was.

With another pinch of my nipple and pressure to my clit, he pushed me past my limit. Dynamite exploded in my veins as the spasms overtook me and my body dissolved in a pool of pleasure.

The shockwaves slowly ebbed, and I would have fallen if he hadn't held me up.

He picked me up and carried me past the couch into a bedroom where he laid me on the bed, high heels and all, without another word. Mr. Talkative he was not, but with fingers like that who needed vocal cords?

He kicked off his shoes and removed his shirt. He had taken me to the moon and back, and he was still clothed.

I had no idea what a one-night stand was supposed to be like, but if this was it, I needed to sign up for more, lots more. I was exhausted from the experience, and we hadn't even gotten to the "fuck me senseless" part he'd promised.

He had flicked on the lights as we entered the room. Apparently he was not an in-the-dark lover, which was another new experience for me.

He pushed me up farther on the bed. He still had his pants on as he spread my legs.

I was completely open to him and surprisingly uninhibited about it.

"You have a beautiful pussy, simply beautiful," he said as he lowered his face to my crotch.

Nobody had ever told me anything so naughty, but most of my experience had been with the lights off. Matt had liked my boobs, but he'd never said anything else about my body.

I tensed as his tongue traveled the length of my drenched folds and darted around my clit.

"Relax, just lay back," he said. "No. Play with your tits for me," he said with his chin against my clit.

That was another new request, but I went along and pushed my breasts together, fingering my nipples lightly.

"Show me how you want me to handle them," he demanded. His tongue circled and darted at my clit as he watched me fondle myself and pinch my nipples.

I thought he'd done a masterful job, and I wasn't showing him anything new, but his eyes conveyed the opposite.

The combination of his tongue on my clit, the scratch of his stubble, and the lust in his eyes sent fire coursing through my veins as he quickly ramped me up again, nearing the cliff.

A finger, followed by a second entered me as he kept up the attack with his tongue and lips.

The sensations crashed over me in ever-increasing waves, and I was unable to keep my eyes open.

"Don't stop," he said.

I had lost myself to his fingers and his mouth and neglected my breast-stimulating duties. I squeezed myself more roughly, as I anticipated he would do, and I pinched my nipples the way he had earlier, with a light twist.

I couldn't catch my breath as he worked me more rapidly, and the stars exploded behind my eyelids.

His mouth licked and sucked my tender bean. My nerves went into overload as his fingers crooked up and stroked my G-spot.

With a sudden shiver, my spasms began, clamping my channel around his fingers, and my thighs took his head in a vise. The rush of pleasure rolled over me as my body shook and slowly melted into the mattress.

That made two incredible orgasms, but who was counting? I had yet to see his cock, had yet to touch it, or feel it inside me.

He shifted himself and came up to claim my mouth with his. This was the kiss I had expected earlier——the kiss I'd hoped for, the kiss I needed.

I wasn't disappointed. I opened to him as his tongue sought entrance. Our tongues circled each other in the tangled waltz of lust. With his lips still wet with my juices, he tasted of whiskey, raw sexual power, and me. The scent of old leather entered my nostrils as I speared his hair and pulled him to me. We traded breath and yearning with our lips and our hands as I was finally able to touch him and feel his chest against my breasts as he settled down over me.

He rolled us to the side, and I was able to pull his belt and work to get access to the cock behind the bulge, the target of my craving now.

He slid off the bed and pushed his pants down, along with his boxer briefs.

I didn't have a lot of experience, but what popped out was the largest piece of man meat I had encountered.

He grinned as he took in my expression. "Don't worry, I'll be gentle."

I shuddered at the sight. I might not be able to take him in. Matt hadn't been small, I'd thought, but the tool Liam brought to the party was XXL for sure. It was probably a good thing I hadn't seen it earlier, or I might have chickened out. How do you go to the ER and explain that a man split you in two?

He retrieved a condom from the nightstand and handed it to me, also a new experience.

I giggled. In college, my boyfriends had always *handled* this. It took me two tries to tear open the package with my teeth. I figured out which way was up and started to unroll the condom over his cock.

The groans started. The sounds of pleasure I elicited stroking the latex down his cock were like an aphrodisiac, urging me on. Knowing I had this power to turn him on was exciting, intoxicating. I alternated between fingering his balls and slowly rolling the condom down his length.

His breath hitched with each squeeze of my fingers.

He joined me on the bed and positioned himself over me.

I still wasn't prepared for the sensation as he pushed in and stretched my walls.

LIAM

SHE WAS COMPLETE, UTTER TEMPTATION. THE WAY SHE HAD responded to my every touch or lick had been pure delight.

Amy was sexual napalm waiting to be ignited, and I was the man with the match.

Now was my payoff. I had longed for her touch since the moment we hit the street outside the bar, and even before.

The way she'd looked as I made her come was now seared into my memory. She tasted divine and had been so responsive. Like a parched rose desperately in need of a little water, she'd blossomed under my tongue and come on my mouth with incredible intensity.

I stroked my tip the length of her pussy before gently pushing in a bit, receiving a moan of pleasure from her. I retreated and then pushed in farther.

"Okay?" I asked.

She nodded with clenched teeth, but then wrapped her legs behind mine and pulled me in deeper with those red fuck-me heels.

With each stroke I pulled more of her wetness out and then pushed in deeper, deeper into her tightness, her incredible fucking tightness.

"You're so fucking good. So perfect," I told her with uneven breath.

As I reached the root and buried myself completely in her, she had me wound so tight I dared not move for fear I'd come too quickly with the immense pressure behind my balls. God, she was good.

I took her legs and put them over my shoulders, lifted her ass, and moved my thumb to her clit.

The gasp she let out was heavenly. "I can't take it."

Those words were my cue to keep manipulating her clit. I stayed still with her core contracting on me with each movement of my thumb on her love button. Her pussy trembled around my cock as I thumbed her.

She milked my cock as she came ever closer to her undoing.

I didn't let up. I tweaked her nipples the way she had done with my free hand.

Her breathing became erratic, and only short, staccato words escaped her lips as her eyes clamped shut.

"Jesus…"

"Oh, fuck…"

She clawed at my arms.

"I'm…"

"I can't…"

Her hips bucked into me as her walls clenched down on my cock.

"Oh, God…"

"Holy fuck…"

The rhythmic spasms of her orgasm threatened to milk me dry as I began to thrust.

She slowly relaxed as she floated down from her high.

I pounded her for all I was worth.

The sight of her marvelous tits bouncing back and forth with each thrust took me past my limit as I tensed up and erupted inside her with a final push.

I collapsed beside her on the bed, spent, at least for the moment.

"I can't move a muscle," she said.

I pulled her to me and her head settled on my shoulder. "Then don't."

We lay there, both catching our breath for a few minutes, before she got up to use the bathroom.

I discarded the condom while she was away.

She came back and settled under the covers with me.

I had broken my rule: I never had women in my penthouse. Now, one was here under the covers with me.

She mumbled something.

"What?" I asked. I thought maybe she might have asked for more champagne.

"My sister was right," she said sleepily.

"Right about what?"

Some women didn't make sense even before they were exhausted by sex, but Amy wasn't one of those.

"She said it wouldn't be bad, and she was right."

Where had that come from? Her sister had thought sex with me would be bad?

"The sex?" I asked.

"Yeah."

"You expected sex with *me* to be bad?"

"Of course not. This was my first post-divorce sex. Viv said I just needed to get it done. She was right. It's no big deal."

Not bad and no big deal?

My balls shriveled up. I thought it had been pretty damned

good. I'd given her three orgasms to my one. I thought that was me doing a pretty fucking fantastic job.

I'd never asked a woman why she'd slept with me, and none had ever volunteered it until now. Tonight I was the man she'd used to get over a post-divorce hump.

Normally we would be at her place, and I would be leaving right now, and not having this conversation.

Instead, I checked my nightstand.

I had a brief panic attack. I might be out.

Finally I located them at the bottom of the drawer. I pulled another three condoms out and put them on top, to be within easy reach for later.

I was going to spend the rest of the night convincing Amy I was more than *no big deal*.

CHAPTER 4

AMY

I'D TEXTED VIVIENNE THIS MORNING WHILE WALKING FROM LIAM'S Tremont Street building to the MBTA station at Park Street, telling her things had gone well and I was still alive. No need to send a search party to look for my body.

If you measured a random hookup by how many Advil you needed in the morning to walk normally, it had been a great night. I'd popped the pills in the elevator, and now I was doing my best to imitate a normal walk until they kicked in. The man had more stamina than I could keep up with, and I was going to be a very good customer of Starbucks this morning. Dragging a futon into the office for a nap was also likely, if I made it to the afternoon.

Vivienne's message came shortly after I boarded the Red Line train home for a shower and a change of clothes.

VIV: How well?

ME: Very

My phone rang with my sister's smiling face on the screen.
"*Tell me about it. I want to hear all the details,*" she insisted.

A crowded MBTA train was not a place to be discussing my sex life. "No way. I'm on the train home right now. I'll tell you later."

"*Call me when you get home,*" she begged.

"No, I'm running late as it is."

"*Tonight, back at the bar then.*"

I adjusted my grip on the rail as the train turned a corner. "I'm pretty tired, and I have an important meeting to prep for. I can't make it tonight."

"*That good, huh? Then I absolutely have to hear.*"

I got her off the phone by agreeing to consider meeting her tomorrow night.

Things at our company had been going fairly well——better than fairly, actually, because we were outgrowing our cash flow.

Taking on extra retail outlets was straining our capacity. Since we guaranteed that everything was freshly made when we shipped it, we had to have enough spare capacity for the peak times, unlike the big companies that made extra during the slack times and stored it in warehouses.

The big challenge coming up for us was signing on with World Foods. Getting on their shelves would put us in the big leagues. But, they were not known for being flexible on delivery dates.

The train's wheels squealed as we rounded a corner.

We had talked to a manufacturer of organic bamboo clothing who'd been taken on by World Foods, and it had broken the company. They'd ended up losing not only World Foods but half their other distribution outlets when they couldn't handle the volume and fell behind.

We couldn't afford to repeat their mistake. This wasn't baseball. One strike and we would be out——out of their stores, and possibly out of business. We had worked too hard to screw this up now.

It was my job to convince this afternoon's investor that we represented a good enough opportunity to have him give us what we needed. The bank line of credit wasn't big enough, and we had struck out on getting it expanded.

The bank's vice president, Clyde Woolsey, had told us we didn't have a long enough operating history. In this area, that seemed to mean we hadn't been around to witness the Boston Tea Party.

Asking how a new business could be expected to grow enough to become an established old business without sufficient credit had only warranted a yawn from the man. Evidently, our problems weren't his problems.

As Woolsey had viewed it, the only problem worrying him was where he could find good scampi for lunch.

The train came to a screeching halt at my stop, and I hobbled off.

∾

LIAM

I'D FINISHED MY GRANDE EXTRA SHOT MOCHA IN THE ELEVATOR, and I desperately needed another. My cock still tingled, and I smiled to myself, remembering how Amy had felt clamped around me for the last time this morning.

She had exhausted me, but I'd refused to let it show until the door closed behind her. If the sounds she made were any indication, she had enjoyed herself as much as I had.

"Good morning, Mr. Quigley," my assistant, Veronica, said flatly.

She'd been with me a little more than six months and had proven to be an exceptionally organized hire. Aside from her lack of social skills when she was trying to protect me, her biggest drawback was her refusal to call me Liam. It wasn't the way she was brought up, she had explained. I'd learned to live with it.

"Morning," I managed on my way past her desk.

She had needed this job to provide for her sick mother, she'd explained in her interview, and I needed her organizational skills. Since starting, she had mellowed some, and if her progress continued, she would work out well.

I cut her a lot of slack, given my personal understanding of how hard it could be caring for a family member with cancer.

The alluring Amy had caused me to break my second rule in twelve hours. I was late to work, and I was never late——well, almost never.

"You look like shit," Josh said as he followed me through the door into my office. "What happened?"

My chair squeaked as I slumped into it.

His name was also on the letterhead, but technically Josh Fulton worked for me. He was also my best friend. I owed him a debt I could never repay.

He helped himself to a seat opposite me.

I threw my coffee cup in the trash. "Don't you have someone else to harass?"

He picked up the little red squeeze ball I kept on my desk. "Nobody that deserves it as much as you."

My doctor had prescribed the ball as one of five exercises to keep my elbow from getting worse. Who knew there was such a thing as squash elbow?

"Blow me," I said.

I didn't need any harassing this morning, and I certainly hadn't done anything to deserve it from him.

"And fuck you too," he replied.

I buzzed Veronica.

She poked her head in. "Yes, Mr. Quigley?"

I smiled. "I could sure use a double espresso about now."

"Right away," she replied as she closed the door behind her.

One of the perks of being the boss was the ability to buy a top-of-the-line espresso machine for the office without anyone questioning my judgment. When I'd worked for Dad in California, he'd thought the expense was too frivolous. If a simple Mr. Coffee was good enough for him, it was damn well good enough for the rest of us.

Josh tossed my squeeze ball from one hand to the other. "So?" he asked.

"I got used for sex last night, I think."

He laughed. "And that's a problem?"

"She said she just had to get it done. Her first sex after her divorce."

After she had said that, I couldn't get over feeling like I was just a means to an end.

"It's every guy's fantasy to be used for sex, so what's the problem?"

"Seriously?" I asked.

I used women for sex, not the other way around. At least I had always thought so.

"Yeah, sounds pretty fucking awesome to me. Give me her number if you don't want to provide the service." He laughed. "I'm up for that kind of work any night."

"Fuck you. You've already got a girlfriend. Or did you piss her off too?" Josh had recently been seeing someone named Brinna who I hadn't met yet. He had gone through quite a few girls—— not because it was his style, but because he always managed to screw it up somehow. Foot-in-mouth disease, I called it.

He sucked in a breath. "No. We're just going slow." This was news. The way he talked about her, I'd thought they would be further along.

He put my squeeze ball back on the desk.

"Slow?"

"Fuck you. You just got laid, and now you're hassling me because all she wanted was your body and not your mind. You're fucked up, you know that?"

I didn't respond. I had always thought the women I bedded wanted to fuck *me*, but was I merely providing a service? Was I an unpaid male prostitute?

"Look, she really got to you. I get it. Stop being a dickhead and give her a call, ask her to dinner."

I frowned. I didn't do dinner dates. It was a surefire way to get a girl's mind on the relationship track, and I wasn't boarding that train again. Not ever.

Josh sighed. "So not dinner. Yeah, it's against your principles. Just give me her number and I'll take her to dinner and ask her what she saw in you. I'm sure it'll be a short conversation."

I rolled my eyes. "Very funny."

"Was she at least pretty?"

"Gorgeous enough that she wouldn't give you the time of day."

Gorgeous was putting it mildly. Amy's beauty had taken my breath away, and we'd had an unbelievable night together.

"You know, refusing to see a girl like that a second time just proves you're an idiot."

I tilted my head. "Blow me," I repeated.

I had no intention of sharing women, Amy or anyone else, with Josh or any other coworker. Bumping into them again would be more than awkward for everybody.

Josh didn't move. "Tell me what went wrong at the opera with the Sanders. Your text was pretty cryptic."

It was a fair question.

Josh had been out yesterday, so I'd only seen him at squash since the opera evening and had been too busy whooping his ass to tell him.

I leaned forward and picked up the squeeze ball. "I saw her again."

"The redhead?"

"Yup. She took some pictures of us during the intermission. With Jeremy Sanders there I couldn't very well go chase her."

The same short little redhead had popped up at several places over the last several months, always taking pictures of me, and I'd never been in a position to chase her down. Not yet.

"Still no idea what her game is?"

"Not a clue."

Veronica's timing was excellent as she interrupted us to bring in my espresso. I was done with this conversation. Dwelling on the way Amy had made me feel wouldn't help me get any of today's work done, and there was plenty of it on my desk.

I thanked Veronica and shooed Josh out.

Not even Veronica knew how much I owed Josh.

CHAPTER 5

LIAM

I DIDN'T MIND BURNING THE CANDLE AT BOTH ENDS SOMETIMES, but my all-night marathon with Amy had made me more than a little drowsy this morning. I finished off my fourth espresso, feeling so wired, my leg wouldn't stop trembling.

The text surprised me.

MELINDA: I have to go out of town

She hadn't mentioned anything about this last Saturday night at the opera, and it was going to put a kink on my plans to entertain the Schmulians. Hubricht Schmulian ran Springbok Foods and was one of two companies we were considering adding to the Quigley-Fulton stable in the foods division.

ME: How long?

Her reply was immediate.

MELINDA: Visiting family

She hadn't answered my question, but right now, with Josh back in the room, wasn't the time to deal with this.

MELINDA: The earrings are nice

ME: How long?

I PUT MY PHONE DOWN AND TURNED MY ATTENTION TO JOSH.

"Some of this can be explained by the summer quarter," he said. "It's always the weakest for this business. It should improve in the fall."

We were preparing for the conference call due to start any minute now with our lead investor, who was traveling in Europe somewhere today. I tried to focus on Josh's spreadsheet.

"You try that on Syd and he'll rip you a new one," I told him.

Syd Kovner had been our early lead investor, and together with Craig Barnett, he represented the entirety of the second-tranche investors we'd added last year.

Josh hadn't learned yet how excuses didn't cut it with Syd. It was like Yoda said, *"Do or do not; there is no try."*

To grow the company, we'd needed additional capital, and Syd had pulled it together for us. The fly in the ointment at present was that we'd agreed to allow the second tranche to pull out later this year if we didn't meet our metrics. Currently we were behind the eight ball on profitability, given the poor results of the food division. We also needed another large acquisition, or two smaller ones, to meet our overall growth target.

Josh had been the one to suggest getting into the organic food business, but so far it wasn't meeting our expectations——or anybody's expectations.

I put down the spreadsheets. "Well, this just proves what we knew already. We don't have the scale yet to have this make sense."

Melinda's reply arrived.

MELINDA: A few months maybe

This was perplexing, but then I didn't know much about Melinda's family, only that she had grown up in Texas with two brothers and could turn on that melodious accent whenever she wanted. Not having her around was going to put a serious crimp in my plans. She was key to the corporate-foreplay component of our deals.

Veronica poked her head in. "The call is set up, if you're ready?"

I nodded and punched up the call on my desk speakerphone.

If there was one thing I understood about Syd, it was never to delay giving him the bad news.

"Hi, Syd," I started. "You're on speaker here, and Josh is with me. We want to go over the preliminary numbers for the foods division with you."

"Hi, Josh. Craig isn't with me today. He's off to Corsica with his latest wife," Syd laughed.

"How many does that make?" Josh asked.

I rubbed my ring finger nervously.

"Four now," Syd answered. As the CFO of an internet startup, Craig Barnett had become quite wealthy, even by my standards, and had decided to spend his money accumulating ex-wives.

It was just as well that Craig wasn't on the call. As a previous CFO, he liked to get a little more into the details of the numbers than I cared to go. Syd and I tended to agree that long-term strategy and our progress toward it was more important than quarterly key results. But Craig often reminded us it wasn't the CFO's job to see it that way.

Josh fidgeted in his chair. I kept telling him Syd's bark was worse than his bite, but it didn't keep the bark from scaring him.

"*Well, the summer is a bad time of year for that business isn't it?*" Syd asked.

"That's what I was just telling Liam," Josh offered.

"*And how bad is it right now?*" Syd asked.

Josh opened his folder. "The preliminary numbers say we'll be about negative twenty percent for the quarter."

"*And how much is that in total?*" Came back over the speakerphone.

"Forty million in round numbers," Josh answered.

Syd whistled over the phone. "*Wow, eight hundred Suburbans is more than we were talking about a few months ago.*"

Syd had taught me that talking about numbers in millions made them seem smaller than they were, so he liked to talk in clearer terms: how many Chevy Suburbans you could buy if you rounded the price to fifty thousand per vehicle.

Josh was sweating this, so I answered for him. "Yes, it is." There was no sense in trying to sugarcoat this. We hadn't projected it would be this bad.

"*And how much better will it be in the third and fourth quarters?*" Syd asked.

"We should be able to about halve the number," Josh told him.

"*Liam, you guys said last time that the basic problem was one of scale, and I assume you have a suggestion.*"

"We've been pursuing the solution to this problem," I said. "The only quick way out of this is to be more aggressive on the acquisition side."

"*Didn't we say that last quarter?*" Syd asked.

"We did," I answered.

"*Then go ahead and get more aggressive,*" he said. "*But you have to make your numbers.*"

"Thanks, Syd," I told him. "We're moving on it. We have two candidates in mind already."

We finished the call with the requisite goodbyes.

Josh shook his head. "Well, that was clear."

"Crystal," I concurred.

"Yeah, and those reminders about meeting the numbers, do you think that's just a negotiating ploy?"

I shifted in my seat. "Possibly." I didn't tell him I was virtually certain tha Syd would pull out if given the option.

Josh's expression fell. "Sorry I got us into foods," he said glumly.

"Don't sweat it. We're in this together. Let's just fix it."

He managed a weak smile.

I stretched my shoulders. "When's the Tiffany's meeting?"

"Two at their place. I can come along if you want. I'll introduce you to Sam Tiffany."

"No, I don't need any help. Thanks."

"Just saying, this is important and if you're not feeling a hundred percent, I——"

I stood up. "I've got this."

Taking my cue, he rose from his chair. "This should be easier than the Schmulian deal."

He didn't need to remind me that the biggest impediment to capturing the Schmulian business was the old man's feelings about my lifestyle.

"Blow me," I said, giving him the evil eye.

He raised his hands in surrender. "Okay, already. I get it. You can't admit the chick has you off your game."

"Fuck you, and go figure out some of that strategic marketing shit I pay you for."

He was good at the marketing crap, I had to admit. He was also good at calling me on my bullshit, but I didn't care for it right now.

Josh's one-liner grin appeared, the one that usually preceded a good-natured poke at me. "Hope you can stay awake that long." He shut the door on his way out.

What I needed to do was salvage the mess he'd gotten us into, and that was best done without him in the room.

He and Martin from finance had met with the Tiffany's people before to get preliminary numbers from them. I'd instructed them to be clear about our intentions, but with Josh in the room, marketing-speak often bent the truth.

Martin had confided in me after the last meeting that the Tiffany's people weren't keen on selling, but had suggested we invest in their company for a partial ownership stake. Josh, of course, never wanted to shut down any line of inquiry and had told them we might be persuaded to consider it.

Nothing could have been further from the truth. So now it was my job to get the discussions back on track before it was too late. We didn't take minority positions in other companies. That rule was inviolate.

With the Tiffany's spreadsheets in front of me, I needed some lunch to counteract the caffeine jitters, but first I had another task.

I dialed Syd back.

"Have you given any more thought to the Chameleon deal?" I asked.

Chameleon Therapeutics was a biotech I wanted to acquire, but I had gotten pushback from both Syd and Craig.

"Liam, I understand why they appeal to you, but I couldn't help raise the money for that in the current climate."

"I know I can make them successful for us," I countered.

Syd took an audible breath on the other end before continuing. *"No, Liam. We have to maintain our focus, and a business that's not turning a profit doesn't fit the mold. Nobody will buy in."*

Don't fit the mold, meant *no fucking way* in Syd-speak. He didn't get it. He didn't understand the importance of their work.

"Look, maybe next year after you've digested this organic foods push it'll make more sense."

I could tell he didn't really mean it. It was an easy way to put me off and put some of the blame in my court because we hadn't performed well in foods yet. This conversation wasn't going to get me anywhere it seemed.

"Yeah, okay, Syd. Maybe I can find one that isn't chewing through cash."

"Sure. We can talk about it when you do."

Translation: fat chance.

"*Don't forget you need to hit your numbers*," he repeated.

The message was clear.

I was going to have to go it alone on Chameleon. I felt in my bones that they had the talent and the right approach to make a serious dent in the cancer epidemic.

Every company was mimicking the other's work. Chameleon had a completely blank-sheet approach to the problem.

My biochemistry degree gave me enough of a background to understand the basics of their approach the minute they'd explained it. It gave me an advantage over the financial whiz kids that dominated the Wall Street crowd. All they ever understood were spreadsheets. Anything beyond dollar signs, digits, and commas was a foreign language to those nerds.

And the financial weenies like Craig and Syd were a bunch of sheep, too cowardly to stray far from the crowd. That was why the venture capital community hadn't yet appreciated the opportunity Chameleon represented. Group-think won out over intellect and punished the outliers.

I had promised to make a difference, and I always kept my promises. Syd or no Syd, I would find a way.

For Roberta's sake, I would find a way.

CHAPTER 6

AMY

I HAD CHECKED AND RECHECKED MY SPREADSHEETS AND DATA.
We'd gotten ourselves into a situation where we needed this investment badly. It certainly would be the key to success. It might end
up being the key to survival.

Samantha and I had put a lot of our blood, sweat, and tears into
this place, and it wasn't only us. We had over a hundred committed
employees. We needed to be successful at this or we'd put all those
families' futures in jeopardy.

At my last job, I'd had an *influence* in marketing. But what I
accomplished here was likely to make the difference between
success and failure, or at least it seemed so today.

I made a quick pit stop in the restroom to check my makeup.
The investor group was due any minute now. The visage looking
back at me from the mirror wasn't horrible, but it certainly wasn't
my best. Today was not a good day to have gone without sleep.
But once the night had started with Liam, I hadn't been able to stop
myself. I squeezed my thighs together, recalling the sensations.
Down, girl.

It was time to get serious. A touch-up with some more foundation powder improved the situation. A swipe of lipstick and I was ready to go.

I double checked the coffee and water in the boardroom. Grace Lloyd, our controller, poked her head in my office to tell me the investors had called to say they were running about fifteen minutes late.

Grace was joining me in the meeting, and our strategy had been that Samantha would not be in the room——although she had been in the previous two meetings rather than myself. We couldn't have all the decision-makers in the room at one time. If things got too difficult, we needed to have a reason not to commit one way or the other.

With nothing left to occupy my time, my thoughts drifted back to last night. Sex with Liam had been completely different from any I'd had with my ex-husband, Matt, or anyone else for that matter. Was sex with a virtual stranger better or somehow different? It didn't make any sense. But nothing about last night made any sense. My first try, and I'd hit a home run——or found a home-run hitter was more like it.

I'd never had a more thrilling night. The only disappointment now was that by definition, a one-night stand meant one night only.

My loss.

I had no last name, and no number. But I did know where he lived, if I dared.

Grace's knock interrupted my reverie.

"They're here. I put them in the boardroom, if you're ready."

"How many?" I asked, gathering my papers and notepad.

"Just two. Martin Fullbright, their finance guy——he was in the previous meetings——and another I haven't met yet."

That was a disappointment. I hoped we weren't dealing with a lackey who had to call back to the mothership for permission to take a leak.

"Okay, let's do this." I took a cleansing breath, put on my game face, and turned the handle to open the door.

Just another meeting.

"Gentlemen, welcome to Tiffany's..." I froze mid-doorway.

I blinked, hoping that doing so would erase what I saw in front of me, but it didn't.

He had a face you wouldn't forget, whether you saw it on the street or over you in the bedroom.

Liam.

The man who'd made me come a thousand times last night. The man with the dangerous cock that had almost split me in two. The man with the devilish tongue and wicked fingers——and those eyes.

Grace urged me forward with a hand at my back.

Liam's smile broadened as he scanned me and offered his hand. "Liam Quigley. Miss?"

And that voice.

"Amy, Amy Hudson," I squeaked out. "A pleasure to meet you, Mr. Quigley."

His hand was warm, and his shake firm. "The pleasure is all mine," he said.

The same baritone that had entranced me last night reverber-ated in my bones. His eyes fell briefly to my chest before returning to my face with a raised eyebrow and what could have been a wink.

I felt like the goat being picked from the herd to be cooked for the feast. How was I going to do this without thinking he was visual-izing me naked every minute of the meeting? He'd seen me completely nude last night, and with the lights on, no less. On my back with my legs spread, on my stomach with my ass in the air, bent over the couch, against the window——I couldn't count the ways.

I willed my face to maintain a calm, businesslike smile. Unsuc-cessfully.

Liam reluctantly released my hand when Grace offered hers.

"This is Grace Lloyd, our controller," I managed.

Grace handed Liam her card as I introduced myself to his associate.

"Grace," Liam said, accepting her card. He flashed the signature smile. "I believe that comes from the Latin word for *charm*. What a lovely name. I like it."

Grace broke out her biggest grin.

He had used virtually the same line on me last night, the jerk.

"We were expecting Sam Tiffany as well. Will he be joining us?" Liam asked.

His coworker, Martin, furrowed his brow, but didn't correct him. Obviously you didn't correct the boss.

"No, Samantha and I are co-owners, and *she* won't be joining us today."

His face showed a brief moment of regret at his mistake before regaining his confidence. He nodded.

This was definitely no longer just another meeting. He had found all my weaknesses last night, and now I was supposed to negotiate our company's future across the table from this man?

Opening my folder, I slid over copies of the two-page term sheet I had prepared. "I put together a quick summary of what we've been discussing."

Martin appeared to study the sheet in some detail.

Liam merely glanced at it before holding me captive in his gaze again. His eyes were performing the same magic they had last night, freezing me in place without a syllable spoken. His mouth opened slightly, and he lazily licked his lips.

The simple gesture sent a rush of liquid heat to my lady parts. The memories of his stubble scraping my thighs and what he could do with his wicked tongue flashed in front of me.

This was ridiculous. I had fucked up my first and only one-night stand. The whole point of doing it was to never see the guy again, to have no regrets, and here he was the next day, throwing me off my game.

Liam set the term sheet down. "I think we may have gotten off on the wrong foot here." He glanced between Grace and me.

"How so?" I managed to say, almost bumbling those two simple words.

"I'm not here to negotiate an investment in your company today."

What the fuck?

It was exactly what I'd been afraid might happen. This was just a fucked-up negotiating ploy on their part, and it was pissing me off. They thought because we were women, they could take advantage of us.

"Well then maybe you should have sent somebody who actually has authority." I gathered my papers and stood, ready to leave this joke of a meeting.

"Miss Hudson, please sit down for just a moment."

I wasn't in his apartment anymore, but his voice carried the same determination as it had last night.

I took my chair again. "It's Ms. Hudson."

"I meant no offense, Ms. Hudson," he said in the most empathetic voice. "Let me clear up more than one misconception. My name is Quigley. My name is on the door of Quigley-Fulton. I assure you that as the CEO, I don't have to call anybody for authorization for anything."

I felt myself blushing. I'd misjudged the situation.

"As I said earlier," he continued, "I think we've gotten off on the wrong foot. I must apologize for my employee's misleading you if you believed we intended to invest in your company at this meeting. It's just not the way we do business."

He'd said it all. Quigley-Fulton was a dead end. We would have to look for money elsewhere.

He tapped the papers in front of him. "This does not go far enough. I think we should expand the discussion beyond a mere investment in your company. It looks to me as if you and Ms. Tiffany——and of course Grace here and all the others——have done a magnificent job building Tiffany's up so quickly."

His words took me instantly from despair to simple bewilderment. I enjoyed having somebody appreciate what we had accomplished so far.

I closed the folder in front of me and concentrated on what I had just heard. "Expand in what way?"

He picked up the term sheet. "I see here that your offer——if I can call it an offer——was twenty million for one quarter share in Tiffany's? Is that right?"

Valuing our company at eighty-million dollars was a bit aggressive, actually quite aggressive. But it made a good place to start the negotiation.

I turned to the second page of our term sheet. "Yes, that's what we consider fair at this point in our growth. If you go to the second sheet, you'll see our historical numbers. Our growth rate quarter over quarter has been substantial and quite consistent."

Both Liam and his assistant studied the page for a moment.

"Quite impressive for such a young company," Liam offered.

I put my papers down and smiled. "Thank you. We are quite proud of it."

"And so you should be," he continued.

This was turning into a giant mutual admiration society meeting. He still hadn't explained what he meant by expand the conversation.

"What, then, is it you think we should be discussing?" I asked him.

Liam placed the papers in front of him and steepled his hands. "I think a quarter of your company is worth more than twenty million."

His associate shifted in his chair, perhaps not totally in agreement with his boss on this.

This negotiation had gone completely off the rails. Since when did the investor suggest the price was too low? Liam hadn't had any more sleep than I had. Perhaps that explained it.

I eyed him, unable to guess his game. "Perhaps you should explain further."

Liam shifted forward in his chair. "I would like to discuss buying more than twenty-five percent of Tiffany's."

I tried once more to read his expression. "How much more were you considering?"

His eyes bored into me. "All of it, for one hundred twenty million," he said calmly.

I did my best to control my voice. "You want to take my company away from me?"

"No, I didn't say that. I'm offering to buy you out at a significant premium to your suggested valuation of the company."

I worked to slow my breathing. "But Sam and I built this company. We're not about to walk away."

Now I understood his game, and it was not one I wanted to play. This was our baby. We had started with a vision and created the reality. No one was going to take it away from us. I didn't even have to ask Samantha about it; the answer was crystal clear.

"I understand and appreciate that," he said calmly.

It was clear he didn't appreciate anything. He had no idea what we had put into this company and what it represented to us. To him it was merely a series of numbers.

"I'd like you to stay on, working for Quigley-Fulton as we fold our businesses together," he said.

I stared him down. "We started this business to be in charge of it, not to be pawns on your chessboard." Bile rose in my throat. I didn't intend to work for somebody else again, and neither did Samantha. We had discussed this. It had been our dream to start a company and not have to justify ourselves or our actions to anybody else.

"That's not an option," I told him.

Out of the corner of my eye, I could see Grace relax a bit. She was probably quaking in her boots at the prospect of working for these jerks——and men at that.

Liam folded the papers I'd given him and placed them in his pocket. "It seems then that we're done for today."

"We would consider a forty-percent investment, if that would make a difference?" I told him, trying to salvage the discussion.

He stood. "Thank you very much for your time. I really think you should consider our proposal. It would meet all your capital needs, and you'd still be in charge of your business, only as a subsidiary under the Quigley-Fulton umbrella." He made it sound almost warm and fuzzy, like being safely out of the rain.

But I understood how conglomerates worked. You had autonomy to do what you wanted until the day you didn't. Which was ten seconds after they decided it was in their interest to cut you out of the equation. I wasn't signing up for that life, not for any amount of money.

"Ms. Hudson, call me if you change your mind," he said as we shook hands. He walked out the door without looking back.

Our best prospect, with the fattest checkbook, had just walked away.

CHAPTER 7

LIAM

"HOW DID IT GO?" JOSH ASKED AS SOON AS THE ELEVATOR DOORS opened on our floor.

I marched toward my office and ignored him.

"That bad, huh?" he asked, following me.

Except for seeing Amy there, the meeting had been a disaster. She'd been the one bright spot.

I strode into my office, with him in my wake.

He just didn't get how sometimes I didn't want him to follow me around.

I closed the office door. I didn't relish announcing the outcome of the meeting to the world. "It was a waste of time. They aren't at all interested in selling."

He sat down in the chair opposite my desk as I took my seat. "Did you mention the higher valuation?"

I pulled the paper they'd given me out of my pocket. "Do I look stupid to you? Of course I did. But you read them all wrong. There is no amount of money that's going to budge those women."

I wasn't certain the statement was entirely true, but it was true enough for our purposes. There was no *reasonable* amount of money that would budge them, in my estimation. I'd seen this before——entrepreneurs who couldn't be separated from their companies any more easily than they could be separated from their children.

"I'm going to have another go at them tomorrow, but I don't hold out a lot of hope," I told him.

He sat back in his chair. "So it's on to Plan B, I guess?"

Plan B meant approaching Hubricht Schmulian of Springbok Foods again, and it hadn't gone so well the first time we'd attempted it.

"You remember Springbok?" he asked.

"How could I forget?" I shot back.

I'd gotten my own front-page spread in the local tabloid right after the meeting, which had blown the whole deal. Hubricht Schmulian was pickier than most——well, pickier than anyone I'd ever met, when considering who he might sell his business to.

"It just means you have to put on the charm offensive," Josh said.

"That's sort of an understatement, isn't it?"

"Well, maybe he's cooled off a bit. You haven't exactly been front-page news lately."

The tabloid story had been about how I'd been seen at three different clubs over the course of a weekend, with three different women, of course. I wasn't exactly the stable family man Hubricht Schmulian wanted to entrust his business to.

I appreciated how he treated his employees as family. We tried to do the same here at Quigley-Fulton, just perhaps not with his intensity. He was also a bit of a moralist. Schmulian viewed my lifestyle with more than a smidgen of disdain.

I didn't see the problem with entertaining multiple women, so long as I treated them well and they enjoyed themselves. He didn't agree.

Josh left my office, and I sat my head down on the desk after closing the door he'd left open.

A bit later I heard a commotion outside.

"But I need to see him," the woman said——a voice I couldn't place, muffled by the door.

Veronica was in protect-the-boss mode and refusing to let her in.

"But it can't wait," the woman tried to explain.

I rushed to the door and opened it to find Mirabella from payroll, a woman I hadn't had much interaction with.

"I'm sorry, Mr. Quigley, I tried to explain——" Veronica said.

I stopped her mid-sentence with an upraised hand. "Mirabella, isn't it?" I asked.

"Yes, Mr. Quigley. It'll just take a minute, I promise."

I motioned for her to enter the office. "Certainly. No problem. Thank you, Veronica. But this is okay."

I closed the door after her and motioned to the chair opposite my desk. "Mirabella, what a lovely name. I think it comes from Latin and means *wonderful*, if I remember correctly. I like it."

She beamed a full-face smile as she took her seat.

I rounded my desk and sat. "How can I help?"

"It's Timmy. He broke his leg yesterday playing in a tree, and——"

"Is he okay?" I interrupted. I recalled Timmy as a very energetic young boy at our last company picnic.

She nodded. "But he has a cast, and he has to stay at home, and he's so young, and I can't, I just can't... And Mr. Fulbright, he said——"

I leaned forward and raised a hand. "Slow down, Mirabella. How long do you need to take care of Timmy?"

"He said I could only take two weeks," she continued, ignoring my question.

"Don't worry about that," I told her.

The panic in her eyes receded slightly.

"How long do you need?" I asked again.

"His cast needs to be on for six to eight weeks."

I picked up the phone and dialed Martin in finance.

He picked up quickly.

"Martin, I've got Mirabella here," I started.

"*I'm sorry, Liam. I tried to explain to her that the policy is two weeks,*" he said.

"Yeah," I said. "That was the old policy. It's been revised to two months in the case of family medical emergencies." I left out that I was modifying the policy on the fly. "Could you please arrange for her family medical leave to start today and run for two months? Please bring in whatever temp help you need to fill in during the interim."

Mirabella smiled.

"*Certainly. I'll get right on it.*"

"Thanks, Martin. Keep up the good work," I told him before hanging up.

"Mr. Quigley, I can't thank you enough," Mirabella said tearfully.

I stood. "Please call me Liam, and no thanks necessary. We look out for each other here."

She continued to thank me profusely, but did switch to my first name.

I escorted a beaming Mirabella out of the office and asked Veronica to arrange a taxi to take her home right away.

I closed the door and lay down on the couch, resting my eyes. Last night had taken its toll.

∼

Amy

Samantha looked up from her desk as I entered her office. "From your expression, I gather it didn't go well."

"Nope."

Samantha shook her head. "Maybe we should have bought the used ovens instead of the new ones last month."

"That wouldn't have made much of a difference, Sam, and without them you wouldn't have the temperature control you need. Our whole selling proposition is based on quality, so we honestly didn't have a choice."

I closed the door. "The previous guys they sent never told us they were only interested in buying the whole company."

Samantha's brow creased. "What are we talking about?"

"It was the strangest meeting I've ever had," I told her. "They started by telling us our valuation was too low."

She perked up at that. "Too low?"

"Yeah. He suggested a company value of one-hundred twenty million. But only if we sell out to them and become a subsidiary."

Samantha slumped in her chair. "Fat chance with that." Her attitude hadn't changed. "Where does this leave us?"

I sat. "Between the proverbial rock and a hard place. We are going to have a cash crunch, and although this won't put us out of business, it means we won't be able to grow for squat next quarter. As far as raising money goes, that's almost as bad as being out of business. With a flattening growth curve, it can be very hard to attract additional investors in this environment."

My phone buzzed. I'd put it on silent for the meeting. Checking it, I found a text.

VIV: Can't make it tomorrow night - needs to be tonight

Naturally she couldn't wait to debrief me about last night, and if I didn't agree to meet her, she'd probably be pounding on my door later.

ME: OK

～

LIAM

. . .

A KNOCK AT THE DOOR WOKE ME. "YEAH?" I ANSWERED.

Josh walked in. "Napping?" he asked.

I checked my watch. It had been over an hour since I resolved the Mirabella situation.

"I've got it set up," he said.

"You've got what set up?" I asked. He wasn't making sense.

"The meeting with Schmulian, of course," he said.

I still didn't understand what he was talking about. "What meeting with Schmulian?"

"We already talked about this. We have to get busy with Schmulian if the Tiffany's deal is a no-go."

The conversation finally came back to me.

"It'll be fine," he said. "He's looking forward to meeting your new girl."

"What new girl?"

"Melinda, of course. I didn't tell him her name. You can introduce her when you get there. I think if you go schmooze him enough with Melinda, you may be able to convince him you've turned over a new leaf——his kind of leaf."

"That's not going to work," I said.

"Why not?"

"Melinda's left town for a while, and she's not available."

"I thought you two just took the Sanders to the opera Saturday night."

I got up from the couch. "We did, and that went well. You and Martin should be able to finish things up with them pretty quickly. But since the weekend, Melinda's had to leave town."

"For how long?" he asked.

"I don't know?"

He glowered at me. "Did you do something to piss her off?"

I was pretty sure I hadn't, but it wasn't any of his business. I ignored the question and took my seat behind the desk. "Like I said, she's not available."

Josh smiled at me. "No problem then. Recruit one of those other women you've been seeing."

"It's not that simple."

He didn't understand the problem. Except for Melinda, I had never seen one of them a second time until I met up with Amy today. I made a point of discarding their phone numbers, if I got them. A second meeting would seem like a date, and a date would seem like it should lead to a relationship, and I wasn't going there.

"Why not?" he asked.

I put my head in my hands. "I'll figure it out," I mumbled.

"You better, because Tiffany's and Springbok are the only additional candidates I see out there right now. If we can't merge one of them in with the food sector business, then the numbers from this morning aren't going to get better very quickly."

"Tell me something I don't know."

How vital Melinda had been to this whole process was now clear. We were toast. *Josh* was toast if we missed our numbers this quarter, and I couldn't let that happen. I owed him my life, and I couldn't let him down. Sanders was in the bag, but I definitely had to take one last run at Tiffany's, because Springbok without Melinda would be impossible.

"I'll call before the end of the day and set up another meeting with the Tiffany's people, but don't hold your breath."

I needed to think of something inventive before we met again.

AMY

PULLING OPEN THE HEAVY WOODEN DOOR, I ENTERED FORTINI'S. I scanned the interior. Apparently I'd beaten Vivienne here, so I got to choose a quiet booth near the back. I told the nice waitress we'd start with two glasses of the house white. I hoped it wouldn't put me to sleep in my current state.

Vivienne arrived before the wine did. She waved from the door and hustled over.

She slid into the booth across from me with eager eyes. "Tell me all about it. How'd it go?"

"It started okay, but it got all screwed up," I confessed.

She cocked her head. "You chickened out? Don't tell me you chickened out and didn't go with him?"

I shook my head. "No, I went."

Our waitress arrived with the wine, temporarily stopping the inquisition.

"Well, what then? Did he not bring a full set of equipment to the party?" Vivienne asked.

I caught a giggle halfway out of my throat but couldn't contain my smirk as I recalled the size of Liam's equipment.

"No, let me guess. Did he have trouble getting hard enough? You know they have pills for that."

I shook my head. She had always enjoyed twenty questions, so there was no reason to give her a quick set of answers.

"No, nothing like that." Liam's cock had been hard as steel.

"So he wasn't hung? Too bad. I thought his hands were big enough that it shouldn't have been a problem."

"No, he was hung all right. Like a horse——no change that, more like an elephant."

Vivienne laughed. "So too big. I hear that can be painful."

"Big, but not *too* big. I can tell you any girl who says size doesn't matter hasn't had the right size yet."

Vivienne laughed. "Speedy Gonzales then?"

I shook my head. "He took his time. Boy, did he take his time."

"I'm sorry, Amy," Vivienne said. "If he couldn't make you come, don't worry. There are plenty of men out there that can do it right. Now that you've gotten past this mental hurdle of yours, you can go find the right guy, a guy who will treat you right."

I smiled, remembering how he'd made me come with just his finger and then with his tongue before I'd even seen him naked.

"I know that smile," Vivienne said. "You're holding something back on your little sister. So he *did* make you come?"

"Yeah," I admitted, crossing my legs.

"You're still holding back. Okay, how many times?"

"Lots." I couldn't remember the exact number, but it had been plenty.

Vivienne's jaw dropped. "I don't frigging believe it. How can you call that a failure? Give me his number. I'll take a ride on that train any day."

I rolled my eyes.

"So, he spends his time, he gets his rocks off, and you get satisfied. Where's the problem?"

I took a deep breath. "He came to my office today."

Vivienne gasped. "Amy, you're not supposed to tell him where you work, and you're damn well not supposed to invite him there."

"I know that." I took a sip of my wine. "I didn't tell him where I worked. He just showed up. It turns out he works for, scratch that, he *runs* Quigley-Fulton. We've been talking to them about investing in the company, and he came over today for the meeting. I swear I had no idea."

"That must've been awkward."

Awkward didn't begin to describe it. "I almost passed out when I saw him."

She raised her glass. "Maybe it will work to your advantage."

"What? Like I offer to blow him and get a better deal? No way. It doesn't matter anyway. They don't want to invest; they were only interested in buying the whole company, and that's not on the menu."

I should have chosen a better word than *menu*. I had been on the menu last night, and I'd enjoyed it.

"I was just thinking that meeting a hot bazillionaire sounds pretty damn good. You might want to give him a call sometime and get back together."

I couldn't contain my smirk in time.

"You didn't. You already called him?"

"No, he called before I left and insisted we meet again tomorrow."

"Well, you certainly don't need any advice from me then. It sounds like you go on this date and see where it leads."

"It's not a date."

At least I didn't think it was a date. He'd said he wanted to discuss the deal we weren't going to come to agreement on, if that made any sense.

Five minutes later, I'd managed to steer the conversation away from my botched one-night stand by asking about Vivienne's work for the fourth time.

She filled me in briefly before commiserating with me about my latest letter from Matt's fucking lawyer.

I took a moment to look up the origin of the name *Liam* on my phone while Vivienne and I shared a plate of lasagna. *Strong-willed warrior*——it seemed to fit him.

After dinner, I begged off early. A warm, soft bed was calling me. And I already knew who I'd be thinking about as my head hit the pillow: a tall, dark, and handsome strong-willed warrior.

CHAPTER 8

LIAM

WE NEEDED——I NEEDED——THIS DEAL WITH TIFFANY'S TO come together. It seemed such a natural fit. If I could persuade them that they'd have enough autonomy to suit them, perhaps they would see it as well.

Veronica popped her head in the door of my office. "Reception called to say Miss Hudson is on her way up."

"Ms. Hudson," I corrected her.

Veronica rolled her eyes. "I stand corrected."

A few minutes later, I rose as Veronica escorted Amy into my office. She was dressed in a blue business suit with a not-too-short skirt and a light pink blouse, her dark hair up in a French twist—— the epitome of a successful businesswoman.

I rounded my desk quickly to shake her hand. "Thank you for agreeing to meet me again." The warmth of her touch brought back memories of our evening together. I pushed those aside. "You look lovely again today."

An instant blush filled her cheeks. She nodded. "Thank you. A very nice office you have here, Mr. Quigley." She looked out through the window at the view.

"Liam, please. I insist."

She nodded. "Okay, Liam. What am I here to discuss?"

I guided her to a seat on the couch. "Your company, of course." I took the chair opposite her.

She tucked her skirt under her crossed legs. She was delectable.

Averting my eyes, I suppressed the urge to join her on the couch and take up where we had left off the other evening. This meeting needed to be all business. I couldn't let my concentration waiver.

Her eyes narrowed.

This was where it got tricky. "I thought we might talk a little further about your objectives for Tiffany's, and how we might work together to meet both our goals."

"If that's code for 'you want to take my business away from me', the answer is still no."

She wasn't going to make this easy.

"It's not code for anything, Amy. Just tell me more about what you and Samantha would like to accomplish."

She cocked her head, and her eyes appraised me cautiously. "It's very simple. We started the company with the mission of creating the best possible chocolates and candies we could with only the best organic and GMO-free ingredients——no preservatives to make simple, pleasurable confections."

"That sounds good. Please tell me more." I needed more information——not what I could read in a brochure, but what she could tell me from her heart.

"That's pretty much it. We know how to pay attention to what the customer wants, and that's what we deliver."

"And so how's it going so far?" I asked.

She shifted in her chair. "Why are you asking me all this?"

"I would like to understand your vision better."

"You said you want to meet both of our goals. For me, for us, that means landing an investment in the short term. We've grown so rapidly that we're outrunning our capital," she explained. "Our growth rate going forward is going to be cash constrained."

I leaned forward. "What if I told you I could supply all the capital you needed?"

"That's what we were discussing yesterday. And as I recall, you walked out, saying you weren't willing to put money into the company."

"Perhaps we misunderstood each other," I said. "What I was proposing was to bring Tiffany's under the Quigley-Fulton umbrella.

Her eyes hardened.

"We'd like you and Sam to continue doing the good work you've done in growing Tiffany's. With our capital and your determination and ideas, I think Tiffany's can be quite successful."

She slid back on the couch, her mouth a hard, thin line. "What is it about *no* that you don't understand? We are not interested in being under anybody's *umbrella,* as you put it."

"What's so bad about having our capital at your disposal, and free reign to run the business as you see fit?"

Her countenance softened. "Complete autonomy?"

"Within reason," I responded.

She huffed. "You see, that's the problem. You and I are never going to agree on what *within reason* means. I'm afraid our organizations are just incompatible."

"What makes you think they're incompatible?" I asked in a voice raised more than I'd intended.

"Do you have on-site daycare?" she shot back.

She had me there. I shook my head. I had to get this dialed down. "No, I'm afraid we don't. But that doesn't mean we can't," I added.

"Do you have a private nursing room for women with infants?"

I had to shake my head again.

"You see, Sam and I are running a women's business——run

by women for women——and that's just the beginning of the incompatibility."

This was too important an opportunity to let go so easily. "Those both sound like extremely good ideas. I'd be happy to implement them here."

"You say that now, but if we sell to you, you and your board will be in charge, and we won't. We've come too far to give up our independence."

"It doesn't have to be that way at all."

"And what guarantees do we have? Huh?" Now she was the one getting agitated. "I've seen how big companies operate."

"Not ours."

"That's what they all say, but in the end, the corporate machine steamrolls over any objections, and the people from outside that don't fit in get riffed. My previous job was at a startup that got bought out, and it wasn't pretty. Six months later, half of us were out of a job."

I needed to keep this from deteriorating further. "I can understand your reluctance, but that's not the way we operate."

"So, you happen to be the one tiger that knows how to change his stripes?"

I pulled out my coin and rubbed it between my fingers under the table.

I leaned closer. "Amy, trust me. I understand."

"But that's the crux of the problem. Don't you see? You're also a mere cog in the machine. You can't make any guarantees that bind your board."

She'd hit the nail on the head. I was in charge up to a point, but I could be overruled. There was no way to argue my way out of her statement.

"What if we up the price?" I didn't hold out a lot of hope, but it was worth a try.

"You don't get it. The price is not the issue. We've started something important to us, and we intend to see it through. This is more than a business for us. This is our life, it's our adventure, and we're not willing to give it up."

Her passion was palpable and admirable. No matter what, these women were determined. As she'd said, price was not going to sway them.

There was only one option left: Josh's plan B.

Amy stood and hefted her bag. "It looks like we're done here."

I stood as well, replacing the coin in my pocket. "Sit down. We're not done yet."

She stared at me blankly and started for the door.

"Please, Amy, I may have a solution to this impasse."

She reached for the door handle and turned, with a hint of a forced smile. "Thank you for your time, Mr. Quigley."

∼

AMY

"DON'T YOU OWE IT TO SAMANTHA TO HEAR ME OUT?" HE ASKED. "And it's Liam."

My hand was on the door handle. The meeting had been a giant waste of time, but his challenge struck a nerve. He was right. I had a duty to keep listening to his bullshit if there was the slightest chance it could lead to something helpful. I owed it to Sam and everyone else at Tiffany's.

Spending any more time in this man's office was not high on my list. He had seen me naked, for Christ's sake. But I strode back to the couch.

"I'm listening." Though he made it impossible to concentrate.

He took a deep breath. "I'd like to invest in Tiffany's," he said, as if it hurt him to admit it.

"So you're willing to take a minority stake? Why didn't you say that earlier?" Now things were looking up.

He cocked his head. "No, not with company money but my own."

That came from left field. I tried to process what he had said. "You personally?"

He smiled. "Don't be so surprised. I come from a very wealthy family."

Wealthy was one thing, but somebody who could write a check for tens of millions of dollars after two meetings with us was a completely different level of rich.

"Couldn't that be a problem with your board?" I asked. "Getting in the middle of a transaction that was supposed to be for the company?"

"Let me handle that. Since it's clear you won't sell the entire company, it's no longer a viable option for Quigley-Fulton."

"Do you still have that term sheet I gave you?" I asked.

A smile tugged at the corners of his lips. "Yes, but I think the terms need to be reset."

Well, there it was. The deal wasn't sweet enough for him.

"Let's be honest. You desperately need a cash infusion, and you're not going to get anywhere near the price you're asking from anybody else you're talking to."

"That's not——"

He raised a hand to interrupt me. "Amy, I have plenty of sources in this town. I know you've reached out to at least a dozen investors, and none of them has been willing to go any higher than about half of what you're looking for. The bank won't extend your line of credit, and without additional capital, your growth rate is going to tank——and with it your valuation."

He was certainly well-informed. We had been to fourteen investors and the best offer we'd gotten outside of his was sixty percent of the valuation we were looking for. He was also right about the implications for our growth rate if we didn't raise additional capital soon.

"I take it you have a proposal?" I asked. He had the upper hand here.

He steepled his hands. "I do. I'd be willing to invest twenty million for the twenty-five percent you were looking for, with one or two slight changes."

I let out the breath I'd been holding. This was sounding better and better. I had been afraid he would use the opportunity to squeeze us for a larger share and less cash.

"Let me continue. I propose making the investment in two stages: ten million now and another ten upon completion of a milestone."

The idea of a milestone for payment hadn't been one of our talking points earlier. This put us in completely new territory, but ten million certainly got us a long way toward where we needed to be. It would buy us a lot of time.

"What milestone? And how long?" I asked.

"Three months max."

I waited for the gotcha.

"This is going to sound a little off the wall…" he said.

I took a deep breath and steeled myself for the unexpected. He had surprised me at the bar and again at his penthouse, and in the most pleasant of ways. He had surprised me yesterday when he showed up at our meeting, and he was doing it now.

He leaned forward. "I want you to consult for me, Amy, to help me close a deal to purchase an alternative company to Tiffany's."

It was certainly odd, but it didn't sound as bad as he had prepared me for. "I'm not sure what I can do that you can't get done with any one of a hundred people you have working here."

"No, it has to be you," he said firmly. "First, let me say that my investment would be a passive one. I'd give you proxy rights to vote my shares as you wish," he continued.

It didn't make any sense. Private equity investors didn't ever give up their voting rights. It was their one source of leverage. I searched his eyes for any sign of deceit and came up empty, but there had to be a catch.

It no longer appeared I had a choice in the matter, without jeopardizing the future of our company. And, after signing the paperwork, I might look forward to some more time with Liam. There was something electric about his presence. He was daunting, annoying, and alluring all at the same time. Nothing with him made any sense.

"How much time will you require for this consulting? I do have a full-time job at Tiffany's, you know."

He smiled. "Not very much, I hope——mostly evenings over a few weeks, perhaps a month or two. Like I said, three months max. We have a secondary acquisition target. I'm going to need your help to close the deal."

Perhaps this was the catch. "And what happens if you don't close the deal?"

"*We* close the deal," he said. "That's a good question. If you put forward your best effort, then you will have satisfied our agreement, regardless of the outcome."

Yes, this was the catch. Everything was dependent upon his assessment. "And if you don't think I've done well enough?" I asked.

His eyes bore into me. "I promise you, I'll be objective."

"And I'm supposed to just trust you?"

His eyes narrowed. "Amy, I always keep my promises. You can take that to the bank. But let me reiterate that I'm willing to make a ten-million-dollar investment tomorrow in Tiffany's. The remaining ten million is only dependent on you making your absolute best, full-faith effort to help me close this deal. Nothing more."

His voice and his eyes conveyed determination and truthfulness. I had given my body over to him a few nights ago, trusting him completely. He hadn't let me down, and I sensed he wouldn't now. I had nothing to go on other than instinct, but there was something about him that engendered my trust. This was also the best deal that had come along, even if we only got the first half of the money. It would be most of the fifteen to eighteen million we needed right now.

I squeezed my thighs as our evening together came back to me.

"If I agree, what kind of consulting help do you need to close the deal?"

A smile grew slowly on his face. "Pretend to be my girlfriend for the duration of the negotiations."

Girlfriend?

CHAPTER 9

Liam

I closed the door and locked it. The knock came less than two minutes later, followed by another.

Leaning back in my chair, I closed my eyes, ignoring the sounds. The meeting hadn't gone quite as I would have liked. Finding common ground to purchase Tiffany's would have been ideal, but that wasn't in the cards. At least I had an option now to work on Springbok.

Amy had been shocked by my suggestion, but what woman wouldn't be? I replayed the conversation in my head, visualizing her reaction to my words, looking for clues, aspects I needed to put more thought into before we talked next. I didn't come up with anything important.

But I had to come up with the words to sway her.

Five minutes later, the knock returned, and I rose to open the door.

As I opened it I found Josh, looking like a puppy that had been locked outside all night.

"You make any progress?" he asked, walking past me.

I hadn't made any progress buying Tiffany's, which is what he meant. "No. It's not gonna happen. They're just dead set against having to report to anybody else."

Josh took a chair, inviting himself to stay as usual. "Didn't you explain all the benefits of joining us?"

I glared back at him. "Blow me. Of course I did." I sat behind my desk. What I didn't need right now was more inane commentary.

Josh took a deep breath. "They'll be back when they find out they can't get anywhere near the price they'd like from anybody else."

I knew that wasn't going to be the case, but I couldn't explain why to Josh right now. He didn't need to know I'd offered to put my own money into their company.

"That won't be happening. We need to move on to Springbok."

Josh brightened. "Good thing I set up the meeting then. You're scheduled for dinner with them Saturday night."

Way too soon for me. "Saturday?"

"We agreed that Springbok was Plan B, and we need to get moving. They'll love you."

I nodded silently. Amy hadn't committed, and if I couldn't convince her, I would be out of options.

~

AMY

"CAN YOU SAY THAT AGAIN?" SAMANTHA ASKED. "SLOWER THIS time."

I slid off my shoes. I had walked back from the Quigley-Fulton office to our building to try to compose my thoughts, and my feet were reminding me how bad an idea it had been.

"Liam Quigley, the head of Quigley-Fulton," I repeated slowly, "is willing to invest twenty million of his own money in us. On top of that, he'll give us a proxy for his twenty-five percent voting rights."

Samantha's eyes lit up. She understood how important that would be going forward, and also how unusual. "That part I understood. It all sounds great, but you said something about a condition."

She was not going to understand this any more easily than I had when he'd first said it.

"The condition is…" I started, unsure exactly how to say it without getting laughed at. "I have to be his girlfriend for a few months." It almost sounded normal when I said it out loud, but of course it wasn't.

Samantha's mouth dropped. "I can't let you prostitute yourself like that."

My first reaction had been pretty much the same. "No, it's not for sex——"

"That's what they all say," she interrupted.

"He needs me to help him close an acquisition."

Samantha cocked her head. "And you believe him? It's the screwiest thing I've ever heard."

That was certainly a legitimate question.

"Yes. I do." He'd promised me.

By any objective measure, I didn't know him well enough to judge his truthfulness, but my intuition told me I could trust him, and what choice did we have?

"You sure he doesn't need you to tie him up and whip him or something equally kinky?"

I laughed. She couldn't know how well I understood Liam's sexual proclivities, and they didn't go in that direction. I was at least certain of that.

"I'm quite sure. Look, I understand it sounds odd. I couldn't believe it when he told me. But, I trust him. And even on the downside, if this doesn't work out, we still have ten million and the voting rights. We'll still be free to go out and sell another piece of the company to one of the other investors we've been talking to. But the terms won't be as generous as his——that much I can tell you."

Samantha nodded thoughtfully.

I had pondered this on my walk back, looking for a hole in my logic. So far I couldn't find one. And, the more I thought about it, the more I was looking forward to spending time with Liam. He was the most unusual man I had ever met, to say nothing of being perhaps the sexiest, even if I had insisted that sex was not to be part of the deal.

"So you're up for doing this prostitution thing?" Samantha asked with her brow furrowed.

"I haven't committed yet. I'm leaning that way, but you have to stop calling it that. I'm doing *consulting* for him. Nobody else can know about this arrangement. You have to promise me that, Sam. Just you and my sister, Vivienne, of course." I couldn't keep this from her even if I tried.

Samantha nodded. "I still don't like it. But you're a big girl, so it's your decision."

"I can handle myself."

I hope.

I needed to repeat that a few times mentally to convince myself. This was going to be an unusual few weeks for sure.

Liam had been right when he'd pointed out how we——I—— didn't have a choice. In retrospect, Samantha and I should have tried to raise money sooner. This was something I had to do for her and all of our employees and their families. Failure was not an option.

～

LIAM

. . .

I LOOKED UP FROM THE PAPERS ON MY DESK AND CHECKED MY watch for the hundredth time. I hadn't been able to get Amy out of my mind last night and hadn't slept well as a result. It had been a full day since I'd proposed investing in her company, and it shouldn't have taken her this long to decide.

Perhaps I should have explained it differently? If I didn't hear something soon, I'd need to call her. Like an idiot, I'd forgotten to give her a deadline.

A real rookie move.

I turned around to contemplate the skyline. I went over the conversation in my head, looking for a mistake on my part.

"Ms. Hudson and Ms. Tiffany to see you," Veronica's voice came from behind me.

I rotated to face the door. "Thank you. Send them in."

The lovely Amy entered, followed by a shorter redhead, whose likeness I recognized from the Tiffany's packaging.

Amy closed the door behind them. She wore a conservative, light gray suit today, but more importantly, a smile graced her face. A very good sign.

I rounded the desk to greet them. "Good to see you again, Amy." I shook with her first.

"A pleasure, Mr. Quigley."

"Liam, please," I reminded her.

"And you must be the company namesake, Samantha Tiffany," I said, offering my hand to the redhead. She had a firm handshake.

"Guilty as charged."

"Samantha," I said as she released my hand. "I think that comes from Aramaic, meaning *listener,* as I recall. What a lovely name. I like it."

Samantha rewarded me with an ear-to-ear smile. "Amy said you were a charmer."

"Did she now?"

Amy's face flushed.

I motioned to the chairs and returned to my side of the desk, sitting after they had.

Amy could have declined over the phone. Arriving here with her partner meant they either intended to accept my offer, or they wanted to negotiate. I smiled and waited for one of them to begin.

Amy crossed her legs and shifted in her chair. "Liam, I think we need some clarification on the terms you're offering."

My mouth turned dry. "Yes?"

Samantha shot a quick glance at Amy. "We don't have anything in writing, so perhaps you could spell out your terms for us?"

I opened my desk drawer and pulled out the simple two-page contract I'd prepared yesterday after our meeting.

"I can remedy that." I rose to hand them the two copies I'd made over to them.

Samantha studied the papers intently.

Amy finished her scan quickly. "This looks like what we discussed," she told Samantha.

Samantha looked up as she finished. "To be clear, you don't expect any other *services* from Amy besides consulting?" She was clearly here to protect her friend's honor.

I'd expected this. "I think Amy and I are clear on the boundaries."

Amy nodded.

"There will need to be kissing, hand holding, that kind of thing, but no sex. Completely professional. This is a business transaction," I continued. "Nothing else."

Samantha relaxed into her seat.

I shifted forward. "I can have the money available today, if the terms are acceptable."

They glanced at each other, a smile passing between them.

"I do need an answer," I said.

Samantha nodded to Amy.

"It works for us," Amy said.

My heart sped up. I now had a path to success with Amy's help. I pulled out a pen and handed it over the desk to her.

They silently signed, one by one.

I added my John Hancock, and with that, we had a deal.

"We can start the discussion this evening over dinner if that works for you," I said to Amy.

"Sounds good."

Their smiles told me I wasn't the only one happy about this.

CHAPTER 10

AMY

WARM, MUGGY BOSTON EVENING AIR GREETED ME AS I EXITED THE door of our building and turned onto the sidewalk. There was still plenty of summer daylight left, and it felt good to be out from underneath the florescent lighting of our office. This was the earliest I'd left the building in at least a month, and I would've felt guilty if my next task wasn't work related.

Liam had suggested Holmby's Grill, a steakhouse near our offices for dinner. It was time for my consulting to begin. I'd walked by the place a few times but never ventured in. It was a few blocks away, and with fifteen minutes before our scheduled meeting, I would be on time. I hated being late.

Calling this dinner a business meeting was a little odd. The business of the meeting was more like a date——a first date, an evening to learn enough about each other to pull off seeming like boyfriend and girlfriend for a while.

I shook my head. I couldn't afford to think like that. This was a job, a consulting job——or rather an acting job I had to nail. My whole company depended on me.

I'd trolled the internet for information on Liam Quigley and hadn't come up with much. He was a smoking hot bachelor billionaire, a stepbrother to William Covington, the CEO of Covington Industries, and had a different woman on his arm every time he was seen out, according to the tabloid articles I'd found. Otherwise, the man kept a low online profile. No Facebook, Twitter, Instagram, nothing——an online hermit of sorts.

And surprisingly for someone of his rank in the Boston business establishment, he hadn't granted any interviews I could find. The company bio on him was equally brief.

I pulled open the heavy oak door to Holmby's and was greeted with a rush of cool, dry air. As my eyes acclimated, it struck me as a perfect place for our conversation: dark, secluded, and quiet. The walls were dark mahogany, with booths and chairs upholstered in maroon leather. A wooden bar along one side sported a brass footrail. It looked like a scene out of a 1930s mystery.

Liam waved from a booth in the far back corner, his smile widening as I approached. "So good to see you again, Amy," he said as he stood.

"You too, Liam." I extended my hand to him.

He surprised me with a quick hug and a kiss on the lips. It was short and sweet, but a definite boyfriend-style kiss with my breasts pressed lightly to his chest.

"Sunshine, what kind of girlfriend are you that you shake your boyfriend's hand? If you act like that, it'll be over before we even get started."

I laughed. "I hadn't expected to be in character yet. Jitters, I guess." I set my purse down and slid into the booth, my insides warm from the contact with him.

He took his seat after me. "You're going to have to be in character all the time we're together, Amy."

I nodded. "Of course. It won't happen again."

He reached across the table to place his hand on mine. The touch sent sparks shooting up my arm. "No worries, and you look lovely this evening."

I could feel the heat rising in my cheeks. I was reacting like we were naked again, and we had just started talking.

"Let your hair down. It's so beautiful; it's a shame to keep it up."

"But——"

"Please" was all he said.

And that was all it took to convince me. I pulled the pins out and shook my hair free, wishing I'd packed a brush today.

"That's better," he said.

The waiter came by, breaking the awkwardness of the situation with a breadbasket and waters for us.

"So how was your day, honey?" I asked.

He smiled. "Oh, just the usual, Sunshine. I had one boring meeting after another, with a few pleasurable interludes where I was allowed the time to think of you and look forward to this evening."

The heat of a blush rose in my cheeks. "Stop it," I complained. This man could charm my clothes off any day of the week. "If we've been seeing each other for a while, you're not going to be so gushy sweet all the time."

His eyes held me hostage. "Well, it's the truth."

The words didn't do anything to cool down my blush.

"How about you?" he asked with a wicked grin.

"It was just a humdrum day." I cracked a smile. "I didn't think of you once," I lied. I had thought about this evening a dozen times. "Oh, and we got a ten-million-dollar wire transfer today. The same as any other day."

"Sounds pretty good. Is Samantha going to be okay with this… arrangement?" he asked.

I nodded. "She's protective is all."

The waiter arrived once again, and Liam sent him away with an order for a bottle of sauvignon blanc and the garlic shrimp appetizer.

We each spent a minute studying the menu. I decided on the swordfish, and Liam chose the Kona-coffee-crusted New York strip steak. Armed with our answers for the waiter's next intrusion, Liam leaned forward.

"Amy, you can't know how much it means to me for you to be here tonight."

His soft, genuine expression of gratitude sent a flutter through me. I caught myself having first-date jitters all over again. This was supposed to be a simple business transaction, but nothing with this man was simple. The look in his eyes was hard to decipher.

Those eyes fell to my chest for a moment as his wicked smile returned.

I clenched my thighs together to ward off the tingling. "And it means a lot——" I started before being interrupted by our waiter again.

He was back with our wine, which he poured with a flourish before disappearing again, no doubt to reappear at the next inconvenient moment.

"I was going to say, thank you for the investment. It means a lot to everybody in our company."

From a business perspective, it was bad form to admit how desperate we had been, but on a personal level, I needed to thank him. We were going to be faux-dating for a while, and I had to get used to telling him what I thought, without the company-to-investor filter in the way.

He raised his glass to me. "To our joint success."

"To success," I said as we clinked glasses and each took a sip. "Maybe now would be a good time for you to fill me in on your plan, and why you need my help."

Wonderful-smelling garlic shrimp arrived before he could say anything.

Liam took a deep breath. "Honestly, we have profit and growth targets we need to hit. We were hoping to merge your company in to hit those targets."

I waited for the punch line. I still didn't understand why he needed my help.

"Springbok Foods is the objective now." He let the words hang there for a moment.

Springbok was larger than we were, and since we didn't directly compete, I was only peripherally aware of them. "And how do I help you with that?"

The waiter reappeared and took our orders for dinner.

After he departed, Liam took another sip of wine before answering. "We had some preliminary discussions with them earlier and ran into a something of a snag. It's a family-run business, and a bit unique. Hubricht Schmulian doesn't think I'm the right person to sell to." He swirled his wine around. "He thinks I've been...shall we say...too cavalier in my social life. He believes strongly in his version of family values. If we can convince him that I've settled down and I'm not the playboy type that he thinks I am, we have a shot at completing the deal. It sounds odd, I know, but that's the reality of the situation."

I caught a giggle mid-throat. "So, convince him you don't do things...things like Tuesday night?"

He stifled a laugh. "Something like that."

Now I understood his predicament. He had to lie his ass off, and he needed a girl to do it with.

"But why me? You must have a hundred women in your little black book you could call."

A frown appeared. "Not even close."

"Then thirty or forty."

"Try zero," he said, peering into his wine. The sparkle had left his eyes.

Something I'd said had upset him.

"Amy, trust me when I tell you I think you're very special. That's why I've picked you."

He picked me.

His voice conveyed nothing but sincerity as the blush returned to my cheeks. This man had a way of saying the most charming things at the most unexpected times.

I swallowed hard, once again caught in the gaze of the lion.

"So, how long have we been dating?" I asked as soon as I regained control of my vocal cords.

"How about six——no, let's make it seven months," he offered.

"Okay, so around Christmas time then," I replied.

A broader smile returned to his face. "Yeah, that sounds about right. It was love at first sight for me."

Not that I didn't believe in that, but it seemed too perfect. "Well, maybe for you, but not for me. I blew you off, and we didn't hook up until later."

He chuckled. "You resisted me, but I was persistent, very persistent."

"Yes, that sounds like you," I said. "And two months later, I agreed to go out with you."

He put his wine glass down. "And we've been a pretty steady thing since then."

"What do you mean *pretty steady*?" I asked. "I wouldn't spend months dating a guy who wasn't committed to the relationship."

"You're right, Sunshine. A very steady couple since then." Now it sounded better, more realistic for a girl like me, but it was worrisome that I'd had to correct him on something so simple.

I snagged a piece of bread from the basket. "Liam, tell me about your family. I know you're a Covington, but that's about it." Not exactly the truth, but I wanted to hear it all from him.

He shifted in his seat. "That will take a while. Let's see… My mother married Wendell Covington when I was young, which explains my last name being Quigley. But I consider myself a Covington nonetheless. Wendell Covington was the only real father I ever had."

"What happened to him, your biological father, I mean?"

He looked down at the table and paused. "He was never a father. I think of him as a sperm donor, and I've built my whole life around not growing up to be him. The man was abusive to both me and Mom. One night I tried to stop him from hitting her. After a dozen stitches in the emergency room, we got a hotel room for the night. We left the next day while he was at work, and I haven't seen him since." His voice conveyed both hurt and horror.

I couldn't imagine enduring something like that. My family had always been loving and supportive, and I couldn't understand how a family could be anything else.

It must have been awful for him, and his mother. I waited silently for him to process his feelings and continue.

"When Mom married Wendell, everything changed. He was my real father. He taught me what family was all about." He choked on the last few words and took a moment.

I had learned in my online research that Wendell Covington had passed away, the victim of an automobile accident, so I didn't ask any questions about that sadness. Clearly, Liam had endured physical and emotional traumas much worse than anything I'd experienced. My breakup with Matt had been angry and hurtful, but nowhere near the devastation of losing a parent, or the horror of an abusive upbringing.

"Anyway, I have an older brother, Bill," Liam said after a moment. "Who, as you may know, runs the family business. I also have two younger brothers and a younger sister. My sister, Katie, went to business school and is in the process of getting her CPA now in Los Angeles."

I finished chewing a piece of bread. "I hear that's difficult."

"It's never stopped Katie before. She's very determined when she sets a goal for herself. Patrick, my middle brother, is working in LA. He did negotiations and acquisitions for Covington on the west coast before setting up a consulting business. The youngest of us, Stephen, pursued a law degree of all things, and has moved up to San Francisco with his wife, Emma."

Liam paused as the waiter approached with a tray. Our salads had arrived.

"So you don't get to see your family much?" I asked.

"No, that's the price of venturing out of California. What about you? You said you grew up west of here?"

I stabbed at my salad. "I grew up in Greenfield, which is at the western end of the state, a little below the Vermont border. If you take Route Two out through Concord, you'll get there in a little over two hours."

"A country girl then?" he asked.

"Not anymore. I went to college at Brown and have been up here ever since. You couldn't get me back to Greenfield now. I've been converted to a city girl."

"And your parents?"

"Both alive and kicking in Greenfield. They'll never leave that town," I lamented.

"The girl you were with the other night," he said, "your sister, Viv, is she your only sibling?"

"Just the two of us. Viv is a year and a half younger than me. She lives in Cambridge, which allows us to get together pretty regularly."

He chuckled. "To pick up strange men?"

"No. Usually we're lamenting the lack of good men in this town. But not anymore, now that I've met you."

This brought a grin to his face. "A true compliment, coming from a lady such as yourself."

"It was meant as one."

"You mentioned the other night you were divorced," he said. "Can you tell me about it?"

I wanted to say no, but it wasn't an option in our circumstances. In months of dating, this certainly would've come up.

He waited patiently while I organized my thoughts.

I'd told the story a dozen times to other women at work. Why was it so hard now to tell him?

"His name was Matt Hudson. It ended two years ago. We met in college and were only married for a short time after that."

"But you kept his name?" he asked.

"It sounds better than my maiden name, more professional."

He studied me quizzically. His unspoken question hung in midair.

I hated admitting this. "I prefer Amy Hudson to Amy Hoare, and that's H-O-A-R-E by the way." There. I said it.

He controlled himself and avoided the laughter that commonly erupted after I said my maiden name out loud. "You must've had a very tough time in high school."

"Incredibly hard, for both me and my sister, but now she embraces it."

"I can understand why you were in a hurry to get married and change it."

Now I was the one who laughed. "It turned out to be the one and only upside to marrying Matt."

"No kids, I take it?"

"No, all I have left from the experience are a puke green couch he bought and alimony payments."

He cocked his head. "You're paying him?"

"I have a job, and he's going to school, or so he says. He never did get a full-time job while we were married."

"If you were only married a short time, why the alimony?"

"Good question," I told him. This part still seemed incredibly unfair to me. "If Matt had filed for divorce in Massachusetts, my alimony payments would have ended. But no such luck. His scumbag lawyer filed in Rhode Island and convinced the judge to extend the payments for another four years while Matt supposedly goes to school."

Liam reached over to touch my hand for a moment. "That still doesn't sound fair."

"Yeah, well, I've learned the hard way that the justice system is long on system and short on justice. I only found out that the judge and Matt's scumbag lawyer went to law school together after it was too late to complain. Just my luck."

"He's still not working?" Liam asked.

I was pretty sure of my answer to that based on my Facebook stalking. "Not since the divorce."

"Is that what caused the breakup?"

I sipped some wine before answering. "That probably would've caused a problem later, but he moved to go to school, and we couldn't handle the distance."

"That's tough," he said sweetly.

I couldn't hold back. "The cheating was the hardest part," I admitted.

Liam reached across to lay his hand on mine. "I'm sorry, Amy. You don't deserve that."

I nodded and blinked back tears. I agreed with him whole-heartedly.

The waiter saved me by arriving with our dinner. The food looked great and smelled even better.

Unsure where to take the conversation after our discussion of Matt, I dug into my food.

Liam took a bite of his steak, slowly chewing it and eyeing me with another one of those looks that heated me up.

"This tastes great, but not as good as Tuesday night." A wicked smirk splashed across his lips.

The comment instantly melted my panties as the sensations of his tongue on me filled my brain. I took a deep breath to calm myself and filled my mouth with swordfish.

I needed to steer away from Tuesday night if I had any chance of avoiding combustion.

"How long do we have to prepare before we meet with the Springbok people?" I squeaked. I sipped my wine to cool the fire he had lit within me.

He speared another piece of his meat and held it up before answering. "The first meeting is set for tomorrow night."

I coughed and spit some of the wine back into my glass, luckily not getting it all over the table. "That's not enough time. You have to move the meeting out."

"That's all the time we have. Josh set up the meeting a while ago, and one thing we know about old man Schmulian is that it would be unwise, to say the least, to try to reschedule on him." He went back to his dinner, apparently not understanding how important it was to have enough time to get to know each other if we were going to pull this off.

I leaned forward. "You have to move it out. You're jeopardizing the success, and that means you're jeopardizing the second ten million for my company, and that's not fair——not fair to me, or the other hundred and ten people that work at Tiffany's, not to mention their families."

He finished chewing and put his fork down. "I meant what I told you," he said firmly, fixing me in place with his gaze and a broad smile. "I'll judge you by the effort you put in, not our results. I understand this makes it difficult, but we don't have a choice. Josh's job depends on it, and I can't let *him* down."

"What do you mean you can't let Josh down? Who's Josh?" There seemed to be more going on in this transaction than I understood.

Melancholy wrote itself across his face. He didn't respond.

I waited, giving him time to compose his answer, but it didn't come.

"This won't work if you won't talk to me," I told him. "What is the deal?"

CHAPTER 11

LIAM

I'D UNDERSTOOD THE SUBJECT OF ROBERTA WOULD COME UP, AND I knew I would need to discuss it with Amy, as painful as it was. I wasn't ready, but unfortunately I'd screwed up and mentioned Josh.

In order to protect him now, I had to open up about the one episode in my life I didn't discuss with anybody. Melinda knew I'd been married before, but we'd never discussed it or the aftermath.

I found myself rubbing my ring finger as I chewed another piece of steak and composed my thoughts.

Across from me Amy waited patiently, somehow understanding not to push.

"I was married once before as well," I started. "Her name was Roberta. We'd known each other since high school, and we dated in college. We never talked about it, but I'd known for a long time we were destined to get married."

Across the table Amy's eyes regarded me kindly as she waited to hear the story, unaware of how the ending would shock her.

"She got a job out here in Boston, but I had to stay in L.A. I had promised Dad I'd go to work in the family business, and I

95

couldn't convince Roberta to stay. Needless to say, that put an end to the relationship. We both knew long distance wouldn't work for us." I could still recall the day she told me she planned to leave.

"I'm sure that must've been hard for both of you."

I paused to take a bite of mashed potato. "It was a real gut punch. Up until then, I'd had my life pretty well planned out. I always knew I would go to work for Covington, and I always knew I would marry Roberta. Then one day everything changed."

Amy put down her wine. "Did you consider following her out here?"

"That wasn't an option," I explained. "I learned two things from Dad——well, a lot more than two, but two really important ones. First, family is not just the most important thing in life, it's the only thing. *Family comes first* was his motto. He even made us all wallets with FCF stamped on them to remind us every day."

Amy nodded. "Family really is everything, isn't it?"

I took a sip of wine. "The other thing he taught me was that a man is only as good as his word, and a gentleman always keeps his promises. Always. That was a rule Dad lived by, and I honor him by following it as well."

It was truly my primary rule. I was careful not to overpromise, because underdelivering on a promise was utterly unacceptable.

I pulled out my coin. "Dad gave me this to remind me. I carry it everywhere."

She reached out, so I handed her the coin. "It's beautiful," she said, turning it over.

"It's a 1918 Lincoln half-dollar minted in Illinois. They only made a hundred thousand. Dad wanted me to remember to live my life every day as Lincoln lived his."

She handed the coin back. "That's quite a high standard to set for yourself."

I rubbed the familiar surface of the silver coin before pocketing it again.

"You're a good man, Liam Quigley," Amy said softly. "If you told your father how you felt about Roberta, wouldn't he have released you from your promise to stay and work for the company?"

I contemplated that for a moment. "I didn't, though. I'd promised my dad, and that was that. And secretly, I thought she'd change her mind, or that she'd hate the weather out here and return to California, or any one of a number of things that would have let me both have her and keep my promise to my dad."

"But you said you did marry her, right?"

This is where the story took a turn. "Shortly after my dad died, Roberta called, and I came out to see her." I took a deep breath. "She'd gotten sick, really sick. That's when I married her and relocated. I did all I could to help. The doctors tried, but it was too late, the cancer had progressed too far."

Amy reached across to me. "I'm so sorry, Liam. You don't need to tell me any more."

She didn't understand that this wasn't the end of the story, and I did have to continue.

"I felt terrible about it. I just know that if I'd been out here with her when the symptoms first started, we would've caught it early enough. So in a way, her death is on me."

"You don't know that, and you can't think that way. You can't take the whole burden on yourself."

"She hated going to the doctor," I countered. "If I had been here, I would have made her go, and it would have made the difference." I looked down at the table. "It's my burden to carry. I just wish I'd been here to change the outcome."

Amy's eyes met mine when I looked up. "It's wrong to blame yourself."

Shame wouldn't let me hold her gaze. I looked down at the table again, considering how to put the rest of my story.

"I took it really hard," I explained. "I started drinking, and I stopped going into work. I was in a completely self-destructive downward spiral. I didn't have anybody around but Josh at the time. He kept coming over to my place, trying to cheer me up, sober me up, get me outside. After a time, he got me back to work. That's all you need to know for now."

"Sounds like a really good friend," Amy said. After a moment she spoke again. "I'm still not sure I understand why his job is on the line. You're the boss, after all."

"It's an issue with our investors. They've so much as told us that if we don't meet our projections, they'll pull out. If they do, we lose the company. I have resources, but Josh loses everything."

"You're a good friend, Liam Quigley."

A questioning look overtook her face. "One more thing, after you lost Roberta, why didn't you go back to work in the family business?"

I took a sip of water. "When Dad died, Bill took over. I ran the east coast operations here for a bit, but that didn't work out. So, Josh and I started Quigley-Fulton. And eventually I plan on becoming a doctor."

"A doctor?" she asked. "Why would a titan of industry like you want to become a doctor?"

"Seeing what Roberta went through in those final days, I promised her I'd become a doctor and heal people. If I couldn't save her, perhaps I could help some others." I sighed. "But so far all the medical schools have a different idea. I've applied to seven and gotten seven rejections. To say my MCAT scores were not impressive is being kind. So, that's likely off the table."

Amy took the wine and poured a bit more for herself. "You can count on me, Liam. Now, we best get busy and focus on the task at hand. My favorite color is red. What about you?"

We spent the rest of dinner and more than an hour afterward trying to fill each other in on details we thought we should know before the Springbok meeting. After working through lots of minutia, I decided to delve a little deeper before our evening ended.

"What did you want to be when you grew up?" I asked. "Did you always want to make chocolate?"

"God, no. I wanted to be a nurse. That lasted until Viv got a nasty cut when I was seventeen and I passed out from the sight of the blood."

"Yeah, that could be a problem." I laughed. "Tell me, Amy, if you could have changed anything about your childhood, what would it have been?"

She didn't have to think. "I wish we could have taken a family vacation, all four of us, before Viv and I left for school. We never did, because the life of a dairy farmer is a continuous, seven-day-a-week job. My daddy never had a vacation the whole time I was growing up." She lost her smile looking down at her plate.

"Wow, a dairy farm. Sounds like hard work."

"Two milkings a day, and you can't ever miss one or the cows get sick."

I reached across to take her hand. I didn't know how to ease her pain. "Maybe you'll get a chance at that vacation someday."

She shook her head. "Daddy doesn't trust anyone else to take care of his cows for even a day."

We chatted easily, exchanging relevant details and memories for nearly another hour, so when I paid the bill, I added a generous tip for having taken the table for so long.

Amy gathered up her purse. "We should spend some more time on this tomorrow. Can we meet in the morning?"

I shook my head. "I can't. I have another commitment tomorrow I can't break."

It'd taken me a month to get the meeting set up with Chameleon outside of normal business hours, so I wasn't about to cancel. I was getting a rare chance to meet and pick the brain of their founder and chief investigator, Ryan Westerly. The keys to their approach seemed to revolve around his work, and I was anxious to learn more.

"I wish I could," I reiterated. "But this will have to be good enough."

Amy had attacked the problem of learning as much as we could about each other with gratifying determination, and the evening had gone by quickly. In the end, the dinner with her had been a refreshing interlude.

Leaving the restaurant, we turned right, the route to the MBTA station for her train ride home.

"Liam," she said, letting my name hang in the air.

"Yeah, Sunshine?"

"I want to be honest with you."

Fuck.

This is where bad news usually started. When a woman says she wants to be honest, it's always because she has some bad news to lay on you. I waited for the bomb to drop. This was the same woman who had told me flat out that sex with me was "*not as bad as she expected*" three days ago. I doubted whatever she had to say now could be as devastating as that.

"I had a really good time tonight."

I waited for the *but* followed by the news that she couldn't go through with it, or something equally bad. We walked along silently for another few steps, and she didn't add to her statement.

She snaked her arm around my waist, leaning into me as we walked.

The warmth of her hip against mine brought back images of Tuesday night and stiffened my cock. I had vowed to keep this fake. It wasn't money for sex, I'd told her, it was payment for consulting, for acting, and I needed to keep it that way.

I put my arm around her shoulder, and she relaxed into me as I shortened my stride to keep our feet in sync.

"Me too," I told her honestly. Telling her about losing Roberta, and my self-destructive aftermath, had been cleansing. I had kept it hidden for so long.

She hadn't judged me as I'd expected, but had been genuinely supportive. For over a year I had held it in, ashamed of the weakness I'd displayed, the lack of self-control.

"Thank you for helping," I added.

"You can thank me when it's done and you're writing Tiffany's another ten-million-dollar check. It will be a great help to the two hundred and forty-one people who depend on us," she said, giving my waist a squeeze.

"I thought you had a hundred and ten employees."

"We do," she said. "I had HR tally up the count including family members. Two hundred and forty-one, until Jessie Camino in Accounts Receivable gives birth. She's expecting twins, which will make it two hundred and forty-three."

Her summary emphasized another thing I admired about Amy. She viewed her work as a team effort, and her employees as an extended family. I hoped she and I would make an equally good team on our project.

We reached the MBTA station a block later, after waiting for the light. As we approached the glass doors of the station entrance, she turned to me and raised up for a goodbye kiss.

As I kissed her I pulled her closer, and held her tighter and longer than I should have. She tasted so sweet, and I breathed in the cherry scent of her hair. I broke the kiss. Any longer, and I would have been tempted to hoist her over my shoulder and carry her back to my penthouse for a do-over of Tuesday night.

"I have something for you."

"I can tell," she said playfully, rubbing her thigh against the bulge in my pants.

I laughed. "A reaction to your beauty."

"You have the oddest way of saying nice things."

I fished the Cartier pouch out of my pocket. "No, I really do have something for you." I pulled her to the side to get out of the path of the crowd coming up the escalator and exiting the station.

Her eyes widened as she noticed the velvet parcel I had retrieved. "What is that?"

"A small token of my appreciation."

The breadth of her smile increased second by second as she pulled the small red jewelry case from the pouch and opened it. "My God, Liam, you didn't."

"I thought the green would go well with your eyes tomorrow night."

I knew the first time I saw her that emeralds would complement the green of her eyes and look spectacular on her. The box
contained emerald stud earrings and a matching necklace. The
necklace's stone was a rectangular-cut, eleven-carat, almost flaw-
less emerald——all from Cartier, my store of choice.

"But I can't accept these."

"If you don't like the color, we can change them out for something else."

She gasped. "No, they're beautiful. I just can't... These are too
expensive."

I gazed into those wondrous green eyes of hers. "Don't worry, I
saved money by having them put all three in one box. And as my
girlfriend, you wouldn't wear anything less."

"I'll give them back after tomorrow night, then."

I glared at her. "I thought your parents raised you better than
that. Returning a present like this would be downright rude where I
come from."

She sighed and nodded. "Thank you, Liam. They're beautiful."
She closed the box, returned it to the pouch, and placed it in her
purse.

She surprised me with a sudden bear hug. "Thank you."

"You said that already." I grabbed her ass and squeezed hard,
eliciting a delicious little yelp from her. "I'll pick you up at five
tomorrow."

She released me. "But you don't know where I live."

I had done my research and already programmed her address
into my phone. "I have my sources."

She smiled as she backed toward the glass doors of the station.
"See you at five then."

The feeling of her ass under my hand stayed with me the whole
walk back home.

CHAPTER 12

LIAM

I POWERED UP MY PHONE AS I HEADED DOWNSTAIRS TO MY CAR THE next morning. I'd missed a call from Uncle Garth——an important part of Covington Industries and the person I could always turn to for help. If he couldn't get it done, he knew somebody who could.

I returned the call via Bluetooth after settling into traffic for the drive.

"Yes, please find everything your sources can get on Matthew Hudson, two Ts," I told him. "He currently lives in Brockton, Mass, and he was married to Amy Hudson, now divorced."

"Would I be correct in assuming that this has something to do with the young lady?" Uncle Garth asked.

"That would be right. How fast can this be done?"

He took a loud breath. *"Is this life and death?"*

I couldn't say yes to that. "No. Just informational at this stage. I don't suspect anything dangerous right now."

"I will put the Hanson firm on it, but working from three thousand miles away, it could take some time. Still, being patient always leads to the best results."

Patience was not one of my strong suits. "Thanks, Uncle Garth." He had much better contacts for this kind of work than I did, so all I could do now was wait.

"Will I have the opportunity to meet the young lady soon?" he asked, letting the inference hang in the air.

"Let's not get ahead of ourselves," I told him before we said our goodbyes.

It wasn't long before Siri told me my destination was ahead on the right. San Diego had their Biotech Beach area, San Francisco had Biotech Bay, and Boston had Genetown, mostly centered in Cambridge. I congratulated myself again on arranging a weekend meeting at Chameleon Therapeutics' nondescript facility.

Chameleon was being run by Anton Sarkissian, a gun-for-hire CEO. He'd been brought in to provide *adult supervision*. The founders of startups were often technical geniuses, but lacking in administrative skills. When that was the case, the money men brought in people like Sarkissian——temporary executives who moved from firm to firm. They were organized, but being itinerant, these temp CEOs often didn't share the vision of the founders. They were by nature driven by short-term goals and working to please their masters on the board who'd hired them, rather than building the best company for the long term.

But, Sarkissian was a problem easily solved. If we bought Chameleon, we'd be able to put somebody more fitting in place for the organization.

Today I would speak with the man who actually mattered: Dr. Ryan Westerly. Sarkissian's support was inconsequential; Westerly's support, however, was crucial.

Although we had a mutual nondisclosure agreement in place, I couldn't rely on it alone. Loose lips sank deals, I had learned. I didn't want to telegraph my interest in Chameleon to others in the Boston investment community——hence the unusual meeting time. The venture weasels who weren't out playing golf or tennis would be nursing hangovers on a Saturday morning, so I stood zero chance of running into one in Chameleon's lobby.

The parking structure wasn't full, but it did contain several dozen cars. I pulled in and chose a nice empty space away from the building, where I was unlikely to get a door ding.

The numerous cars present were a good sign. At this stage of their development, it was important for a company to have motivated employees, willing to take time out of their weekends. I wouldn't invest in one that didn't. A nine-to-five, weekday-only mentality that took hold before the company's success was guaranteed, often led to failure. Fortunately, Chameleon's employees seemed to believe in their work and cared enough to put in extra effort.

The glass door leading to the lobby was locked, so I pushed the button labeled *after-hours* next to the employee badge reader.

A petite brunette in a security uniform came through the door from the inner sanctum to let me in.

"Can I see some identification, sir?" Her badge read *Wanda*. Her cool demeanor and the Taser on her belt said *don't mess with me*.

"Certainly." I pulled out my wallet and found my driver's license. This was unusual——the first time one of these companies had asked me to prove who I was.

She studied the card for a moment and pulled out a UV flashlight to check it as well. This was impressive, equivalent to what the TSA put me through at the airport.

"Thank you, Mr. Quigley," she said, handing back the plastic card. "If you'd please sign in, sir, I'll escort you to Dr. Westerly."

The visitor's log was open on the receptionist's counter. I slowly retrieved a pen from my coat pocket while I scanned the names and companies who had signed in. None of them caught my eye.

My short security guard wasn't watching, so I entered my initials *LAQ* on the next open line, and *QF* in the company column.

"Your phone, please," she said when I'd finished. "We don't allow photography inside."

Another point to Chameleon for thorough security.

I handed her my phone, and she locked it in a drawer at the receptionist station.

She guided me through a series of cubicles to an office near the back.

I'd expected Ryan Westerly to occupy the corner office with two large windows or at least another one of the offices near the front. Instead, his windowless office was against the back wall.

Wanda motioned me inside. "If you wait here, he'll be right back."

The office was overflowing with paper——on top of the desk, on the floor, on the shelves, on the credenza, and even in the seat of the single guest chair facing the desk.

I waited inside in one of the few open spaces that wasn't in the direct path to his desk. This man didn't seem interested in recycling.

Ryan Westerly appeared from around the corner. His nametag said only *Dr. Westerly*. Everybody else's I'd come across, including the guard's, had their first name, but not his.

"I've got it from here, Wanda," he said to my diminutive escort.

She seemed uncertain whether it was safe to leave me alone with the boss or not. "But, Dr. Westerly, the manual says——"

"Wanda, I told you I've got it."

Seeming to sense it wasn't wise to argue with the founder, Wanda retreated.

Westerly extended his hand. "Mr. Quigley, nice to meet you. Why don't we use the conference room? It's a little less crowded in there."

I shook his hand. "Sure. Please call me Liam."

I followed him around the corner into a conference room with a large table and a whiteboard full of scribbles in red, black, and blue.

He didn't offer to have me call him Ryan. He took a seat on the long side of the table near the corner and motioned me to take the seat at the end. Another unusual move. The heads of these companies invariably chose the power seat, the one at the head of the table, but Ryan Westerly did the opposite. I liked him already.

He checked his watch. "You've got two hours. I don't normally talk to investors; I can't spare the time. It's Anton's job to talk to you guys and raise the appropriate money. My job is to move our technology forward as fast as possible. Talking to people like you is a waste of my time and sets the whole company back."

I'd understood from our previous phone conversations that Westerly was a no-nonsense man. He didn't mean to be rude; he was merely trying to be efficient. Laying out ground rules for a discussion was his way to focus our time.

"Thank you for taking the time, Dr. Westerly. I appreciate it, and I hope this can lead to a productive investment for me, and provide capital to allow you to accelerate your projects. A win for both of us."

"To be frank, Liam, the reason we're talking is I found your thoughts on osmotic filtration from our last discussion to be useful."

That was quite a compliment. Ryan Westerly was not only at the top of his field, he was probably several steps ahead of anybody else. He did Nobel Prize-caliber work, except he might not ever be recognized for it because he refused to publish. As he saw it, publishing took time away from his experiments. I'd probed his thoughts on problematic areas of his work, which had led to a discussion in which I suggested a few different alternatives he might consider.

I checked my watch and started the timer. If Westerly said he would allocate only two hours, he meant it, and I'd have to be cognizant of the time if I wanted to cover all of my subjects.

"Shall we start with the area of organometallics?" I suggested.

"I'd rather spend a few minutes on osmotic filtration again," he said. "And then move on."

Westerly ended up giving me exactly the two hours he'd promised. He was an exacting perfectionist if nothing else, and a driven workaholic if ever I'd seen one.

As I exited the building, Wanda returned my phone as promised. The meeting at Chameleon had gone well——actually better than that, exceedingly well. I was more sure than ever that Ryan Westerly and his crew were on to something big. Equally important, he seemed at ease with me, thanks to my technical background. It helped that I had reviewed several recent papers on osmotic filtration in the last few days.

I scanned the log again as I signed out.

On a previous page were the entries I'd been searching for. Two people from the Winterbourne firm had visited, including Damien Winterbourne himself. Not good news for me. They were the one local competitor I thought might be brave enough to separate from the pack and consider Chameleon. They had screwed up several other deals for me in the last six months.

Fuck.

Now we crossed paths again.

CHAPTER 13

AMY

THE DOORBELL RANG AS I WAS PREPARING FOR THE DINNER WITH Liam and the Schmulians.

I checked my watch. Four-twenty. Fuck, he was early, and I wasn't ready yet.

"Just a minute," I yelled as I tightened up the bathrobe I had on to do my makeup.

Being late was inconsiderate, but this much early was worse. I would hate having Liam watch me get ready, making me more nervous than I already was.

I swung open the door, ready to complain.

"Surprise," Vivienne said as she waltzed past me into my apartment.

I closed the door behind my unexpected guest. "Viv, what are you doing here? I have to go."

She turned and a Vivienne-only wicked smirk burst across her face. "I'm here to help you get ready for your date," she announced.

"It's not a date."

"The hell it's not." She pointed at my feet. "You got your nails done."

Busted. "I was due," I lied.

I'd had my hair blown out too. I was as nervous about this evening as I had been for my high school prom. Liam, not to mention *my* whole company, was depending on me. I needed to make a good impression as a convincing girlfriend. How hard could it be?

My stomach lurched, answering the question.

Vivienne followed me back into the bathroom. "So how are we going to put your hair up? How about a chignon? A horizontal one this time?" She grabbed a hair brush and started to brush out my hair behind me. "I watched this cool YouTube video, like, four times. I've got it down."

"Not today."

"But you always do a French twist. Be adventurous. Try something different."

The last adventurous thing she'd suggested had led to my all-nighter with Liam, so it wasn't a bad idea.

"No, I'm going with it down tonight."

She stopped brushing and put her hands on her hips. "So who are you, and what have you done with my big sister? You always wear it up for important dates."

"I told you this is not a date." I didn't admit I was wearing my hair down tonight for Liam.

Vivienne huffed. "And I'm going to lose ten pounds next week. You're having dinner with your bazillionaire boyfriend——"

"Fake boyfriend," I shot back.

"And this other couple. Who are they? The…"

"Schmulians," I told her.

"Right, and you're sitting here agonizing over your makeup because you're only going out to get hot dogs with, like, the most eligible bachelor in Boston, right?"

We had talked last night, and she already knew the answer to the question. Liam was taking us to Mooo, one of the nicest, most expensive restaurants in town——a few dozen steps above hot dogs.

I put down my makeup brush and glared at her reflection in the mirror. "You can leave, Viv, if you're just going to hassle me."

"And miss my chance to meet Mr. Wonderful? No way. Since you seem so intent on pushing him away, let your little sister get in line to be next on his list."

I rolled my eyes.

She'd wanted to stop by the restaurant last night to meet Liam officially. My mentioning I would throw a fork at her if she did had stopped her from carrying out her evil plan. But obviously, persistence ran in our family.

After I finished my makeup and slipped on my dress, I pulled the Cartier box from the drawer and added the gorgeous emerald earrings Liam had given me last night. Then I slipped the necklace around my neck, but I couldn't manage the clasp.

Vivienne came up behind me. "Here, let me." She wrestled with the clasp and was successful in the end.

Her jaw dropped when I turned around. "Where did this come from? It looks so real."

"Pretty sure it's the real thing," I told her. "Liam gave it to me, and also these earrings. You like 'em?"

I knew perfectly well if it came from Cartier it wasn't costume jewelry.

Her eyes widened. "Love them. They look great on you, matching your eyes and all."

That was exactly what Liam had said.

"You know, you're wearing about two years of salary around your neck."

I wasn't an expert in jewelry, but she had to be about right. The earrings were at least three carats each, and the necklace stone was a monster. Wearing these was akin to dressing up as a fairy princess when I was young, and it made me just as happy tonight.

I pulled my tall heels out of the closet. I didn't plan to put them on until the last moment, as they were beauty and pain all in one

package. I had chosen a nice black cocktail dress for this evening
——not too short, but still sexy. And Vivienne's comment Tuesday
night had sent me out looking for a nice red lace bra for this
evening. I decided it was what Liam's girlfriend would wear, even
if it wouldn't be visible. I intended to play tonight's part to
perfection.

By the time the doorbell rang, I was ready. Liam was right on
time, and it was my cue to slip into the heels.

Vivienne rushed to beat me to the door. "I'll get it."

She opened the door slowly, and there stood Liam.

Liam offered his hand, the other holding flowers. "It's nice to
see you again. Viv, is it?"

Vivienne shook his hand and held on like she wasn't ever going
to let him go. "Vivienne. It's a pleasure to see you again, Mr.
Quigley."

"Call me Liam, please." He finally extracted his hand from her
grasp. "Vivienne, that's such a lovely name. It means *lively*, I
believe. And I must say, you're even more beautiful than I
remember from our last brief meeting."

He was laying it on pretty thick, but it was cute.

Vivienne blushed fire engine red, falling under his happiness
spell just as I had. "Lively, yeah, that's me."

"May I come in?" he asked.

In her schoolgirl-like trance, she had blocked the door. "Oops,
sure thing," she said, moving out of the way.

Liam reached me in a few quick strides and pulled me to him
for a not-so-quick one-armed hug and kiss. It took my breath away,
once again, and ended before I was ready to let him go. But in
front of Vivienne, short was better than long, or I would never hear
the end of it.

He was dressed in a charcoal gray, pinstriped suit with a pale
blue shirt open at the collar, no tie. He looked even better than last
night. But maybe it was the lack of alcohol playing tricks on me.
Or it could have been the daylight and the way it played on his hair

as he walked in. Whatever it was, he looked delectable, and his smile topped it all off perfectly.

He stood back and devoured every inch of me. "Sunshine, I must say you look stunning this evening." His eyebrows raised ever so slightly as his gaze paused at my chest. "And I love the shoes."

I had decided on the same red heels I'd worn to bed Tuesday night, hoping he'd like the gesture.

The lion was back, and I couldn't control the heat he ignited in me. It rose quickly from my chest to my face. I froze for an instant, uncharacteristically at a loss for words.

"Cut that out, and you look quite..." I didn't have the right word in my vocabulary for the way he struck me. *Good* was too mild, and *handsome* was too mundane. "...suave yourself," I added. *Suave* and *sophisticated* were the perfect descriptors, I decided.

At first it had appeared he was carrying a large bunch of roses, but it turned out to be two separate bouquets.

He handed me one. "Lovely flowers for a lovely lady."

I accepted them and sniffed. The aroma was divine. "You didn't need to."

"Nonsense. And this other set..." He turned to Vivienne. "... was to be for your office, so you could be reminded of me all day long. But tonight these go to your lovely sister." He handed the second batch to a giddy Vivienne.

"They're beautiful," she gushed.

"I'll have another arrangement delivered to your office Monday morning," he told me.

"You don't need to do that," I protested.

"They're a gift. What did I tell you before about refusing gifts?"

Properly admonished, I stayed quiet. I would have to figure out how to deal with work later. "I'll put these in water." I went to the kitchen to locate a vase.

Vivienne stayed with Liam, eyeing him in a way that made it

obvious, sister or no sister, that she was itching to take my place as his fake girlfriend——or not-so-fake girlfriend.

I finished with the flowers and joined them again.

Liam grinned as he zeroed in on the emerald necklace he'd given me last night. "You changed the chain for a shorter one." The man didn't miss a thing.

I had changed it out to raise the stone. I thought it hung too low, drawing the eye too embarrassingly to my cleavage for a business dinner.

"Good choice," he said. "For tonight. But when we're alone, you should wear the longer one." He winked as he motioned toward the door. "Are we ready to go?"

"One quick thing." I rushed to the bathroom for a Kleenex. My lipstick had rubbed off on him. I reached up and gently cleaned it from his lips.

He stood still while I fussed over him. "Thanks. We wouldn't want people getting the wrong impression, now would we?"

Vivienne giggled.

Exiting my building to the street, I saw that some jerk had parked his sleek sports car in the yellow loading zone and left it there.

Liam walked forward and pushed a button on his rectangular key fob. The sports car unlocked. He opened the passenger door for me. The low-slung silver car was my ride for tonight, and its shape literally dripped sex appeal.

"Holy shit, Liam, this yours?" Vivienne exclaimed.

Liam nodded with a smile.

"Amy, this is a fucking James Bond car," Vivienne said, informing me of something I already knew.

We had seen *Casino Royale* together, twice. The *DBS* stitched into the headrests was a dead giveaway. This was a three-hundred-thousand dollar James Bond Aston Martin with a gazillion horsepower V-12 engine and the looks to turn heads all over town.

I had dreamed of getting a chance to ride in one. Now here it was, and with a driver every bit as ruggedly handsome as Daniel Craig. My dream was coming true tonight.

"Liam, it's beautiful," I said, hanging on his arm.

He turned and spoke in my ear. "Only half as beautiful as you."

Vivienne's smirk told me she heard him.

My cheeks heated again. I had to get him to stop embarrassing me.

"Liam, when can I get a ride?" Vivienne asked as I lowered myself into the leather seat.

"Maybe next weekend," he said.

"It's a date," she responded quickly. "Well, not a date, but you know what I mean."

Liam closed the door firmly and walked around to the driver's side.

My nostrils filled with the faint scent of expensive leather. I fastened the seatbelt and waved to my excited sister as she stood back.

Liam buckled in, pushed the key fob into a slot in the dash, and the engine rumbled to life.

So cool.

The burble of the exhaust was a low growl at the curb. Once Liam pulled out into the lane, he punched it, throwing me back into my seat. The engine sounds grew from a roar to a scream. We hurtled down the street, the loud mechanical music of the beast warning everyone to get out of the way——this monster owned the road. Liam braked before the next intersection, throwing me forward against the belt and bringing us back from mach one to a sane city speed.

I laughed, giddy from the excitement. "This car is fucking awesome."

"Not nearly as awesome as you tonight," he said looking over with a smile.

He had done it again, complimenting me needlessly.

"You have to stop that. It's embarrassing."

"Isn't that what a true boyfriend does?" he asked as we turned onto Somerville Avenue, toward downtown.

"Not any boyfriend I ever had." I tried in vain to recall anytime Matt had been so complimentary more than a week after we'd married. Gushy sweet compliments hadn't been his thing, not ever.

Liam patted my thigh. "I'm sorry you never had a decent boyfriend, then. Trust me, it is the way a proper gentleman treats a lady."

"Maybe in California, but not out here."

He laughed. "What? Are the laws of chivalry dead in Boston?"

"If you do it again to embarrass me, I'm going to get you back...somehow."

"You need to lighten up, Sunshine, and learn to accept a compliment like a lady."

He was probably right. But I wasn't a lady in his sense of the term. Not by a long shot. But the argument wasn't one worth having right now.

I amused myself by watching the pedestrians we passed turn to look at the car as it announced itself with the unmistakable growl of a powerful V-12.

As Liam accelerated away from a light, the effect happened farther and farther ahead of us. People were drawn to the sound and watched this car. We passed an old man who didn't turn his head. His hearing aid battery had probably gone dead.

In no time, we crossed the Charles River into Boston proper. Liam hadn't spoken since I'd scolded him for being nice to me.

I turned to him. "I'm sorry. You're right. I'll try to be more understanding of your west coast quirks."

He smiled. "No worries, Sunshine. I know you're really a lady, even when you don't act like one." He had done it again, telling me off and being complimentary at the same time.

I put my hand on his crotch and stroked.

He squirmed as the weapon in his pants started to stir. "What are you doing?"

"I told you I'd get you back if you kept it up. I dare you to go to this dinner with a hard-on."

He grabbed my hand and pulled it away. "Behave yourself, Sunshine. Boundaries, remember?"

"Right," I said, ashamed that I'd already screwed up.

"I'll try to restrain myself, okay?" he asked.

"Deal," I replied. I stopped struggling, and he let go of my hand. I had won this round. "What's the strategy for tonight?"

"No strategy. This is a meet and greet, an opportunity for them to get to know us a little. The only key to convey tonight is that you and I are serious about each other."

Now I was concerned. I had moved up a notch from girlfriend to *serious* girlfriend, and we'd only had time to learn the superficial things about one another.

"How serious?"

"Serious enough. We've been seeing each other for seven months now."

I knew I should have cut off his wine last night. He was already forgetting details. "You've already screwed up, Mr. Bigshot. It's only been five months. I blew you off for the first two remember?"

"Right. Most painful two months of my life."

This is going to be a disaster.

I knew Matt hated cauliflower as much as I despised brussels sprouts, and that he brushed his teeth before breakfast. I didn't know any of those things about Liam. How could I have agreed to this charade? It had sounded so easy at first. Hold hands, smile at each other, bicker a little but not too much. Now we were about to be tested, and we were woefully unprepared.

The enormity of the task hit me. Two hours from now, I might be explaining to Samantha how I'd blown it for all of us at Tiffany's.

CHAPTER 14

LIAM

As we pulled up to the XV Beacon Hotel adjacent to the restaurant, I contemplated how I was going to get Amy to be more comfortable accepting the compliments she truly deserved. Nothing came to me... I would have to work on it later.

The doorman opened Amy's door for her.

She stepped out while I passed the key to the valet.

Amy waited for me on the sidewalk as I instructed the valet in no uncertain terms how I expected him to treat my car.

I may have overdone it; the young man was ashen white as I left him.

Amy's brow creased. "What did you say to the poor guy?"

I placed a hand at the small of her back and guided her toward the hotel entrance. "I merely told him the car belonged to my boss, Carmen Dinunzio, and to take good care of it."

"And he is?" she asked as we walked to the entrance.

"The current head of the Boston Mob."

She gasped. "How do you know that?"

We waited for a couple exiting the hotel. "Wikipedia, naturally, and they must be right. The guy nearly pissed his pants when I told him."

Amy bumped against me. "You're terrible."

"Whatever works," I told her as I held the glass door open. My gut tightened as I caught sight of my little redheaded shadow across the street, watching us. I followed Amy inside, controlling my urge to chase the little camera-toting minx. Instead, I guided my date to the elevators and punched the up button.

Amy hesitated when the door opened. "I don't think I'm ready for this."

"You've totally got this. Don't worry," I told her.

We moved aside, making room for another couple to take the elevator.

The doors closed with her still looking terrified. "What if I blow it?"

I pushed the button to call another car. "Don't worry, Sunshine. I have faith in you."

The second set of elevator doors opened shortly after, and Amy entered the car with me following. "I thought we were going to Mooo. Isn't it next door?"

"Yes," I told her. "But they also have private dining rooms upstairs in the hotel, and this was Schmulian's idea.

She shrugged her shoulders at my answer. "What kind of name is Schmulian anyway?"

"They're originally from South Africa."

After we arrived upstairs, I located the door and knocked.

Hubricht Schmulian opened the door and welcomed us in.

I was immediately nuzzled by a large yellow Labrador with a vigorously wagging tail. I knelt down to greet the dog.

"That's Zeke. Don't worry, he's harmless," Hubricht told us as the dog finished licking my face and went over to sniff up Amy's skirt.

Smart dog.

I rose to shake Hubricht's hand. "Thanks for having us."

"My pleasure, son. Zeke seems to approve of you, a point in your favor. He's an excellent judge of character."

"I'll take it as a compliment," I said. "Hubricht, I'd like to introduce you to my girlfriend, Amy Hudson."

"A pleasure, and please call me Hue," he replied, taking Amy's hand as she fended off Zeke.

Hue introduced us to his wife, Felicia.

"Felicia, what a wonderful name. It has a Latin origin, if I recall," I told her. "It means *happiness*. I love it."

Felicia blushed. "Why thank you, Liam. I didn't know that."

"And what does my name mean?" Hue asked me.

"He with a bright heart," I told him. It was one I'd had to look up before coming over.

A proud smile grew on the old man's face. "So how long have you two been seeing each other?"

One minute inside the door and the inquisition had begun.

"Seven months now. Christmas roughly," I answered.

Hue turned to Amy. "I asked for this private room so we could bring Zeke along. I hope that's okay. Sorry about his manners."

Amy touched his arm gently. "I love Labs. We had two of them when I was growing up. He's really nice. And don't worry, he's better behaved than Liam is half the time."

Hue laughed and went to the sideboard. He picked up the phone and asked for the waiter.

Felicia took Amy aside. "Amy, I have to say your necklace is simply stunning,"

Amy glowed. "Why thank you. Liam got it for me."

Felicia glanced at her husband, who was still on the phone ordering appetizers and wine for us. "I'm so envious. I wish Hue would get me something half as beautiful."

"I heard that," he said from across the room. "Liam, you're making me look bad."

"Sorry, Hue, when I look at Amy, I can't control myself. I just thought it would compliment the beauty of her eyes."

Hue joined us and got a nudge from his wife. "You could learn a thing or two from this man, Hubricht."

"I keep trying to get him to stop that," Amy told Felicia with a warm blush rising in her cheeks.

"Stop what?" Felicia asked.

"The gratuitous compliments. He's always trying to embarrass me," Amy complained.

"We could trade problems," Felicia suggested. "Then you might miss it."

Hue chuckled, but wisely nodded and avoided responding. Instead, he welcomed us over to the window to take in the view of the city. The hotel wasn't tall enough to get a really good view, but it beat out street level.

Amy put her arm around me. "Liam tells me you're originally from South Africa. I hear it's a breathtaking country."

"Yes, it is," Felicia answered. "But we haven't been back in thirty years. This is our home now."

Amy held me tight. "But you must still love it. You named your company after the national animal of South Africa."

Amy had surprised me with something I hadn't known.

"We thought the name was a good one," Felicia said. "The springboks are quite lovely. And quite unique. How much do you know about our springboks?"

"Correct me if I'm wrong," Amy said, "but I understand they're the fastest of the gazelles. And as I recall, both the males and females have horns, which is quite unlike our native elk or deer in North America. But what I find most fascinating is how they get all the water they need from the plants they eat and can go all year without drinking."

"That's true." Felicia nodded. "I'm impressed. The average American doesn't understand anything about African wildlife, outside of lions and elephants." She beamed a broad smile.

"There's nothing average about my Sunshine," I chimed in.

Amy nudged me in the ribs. "I just have a particular fondness for animals and try to remember these things when I hear them."

She was clearly winning Felicia over. Amy innocently stepped on my toe for a brief moment, not catching anybody's attention but mine. It was another warning to stop the compliments.

A knock came at the door, and the waiter from Mooo arrived with our wine and appetizers.

Hue beckoned us to the table, which had been set elegantly with a starched white tablecloth and an embroidered runner down the middle. I sat opposite Hue, with Amy at my side opposite Felicia.

Hue had ordered shrimp, meatballs, calamari, and something else I couldn't quite identify.

Apparently noticing my confused expression, Hue pointed to the fourth dish. "Burgundy escargot."

I was game for most anything so long as it swam, walked, or flew, but I drew the line at eating something that slimed its way across the ground. I took samples of the other three as they were passed around.

Amy was braver than I. She scooped a snail onto her plate.

Hue leaned toward me. "I don't like the snails either," he confided. "Felicia makes me order them."

"How can you say that, Hubricht? You've never even tried one," Felicia said.

"And it's staying that way," he responded.

Felicia put down her wine glass. "How did you two meet?" she asked us.

Amy fielded the question. "It was a Christmas party, or so I'm told."

Both the Schmulians raised their eyebrows at her answer.

"Liam came on to me at the party," Amy explained. "But I wasn't very receptive. I didn't actually agree to go out with him until February."

Hue's brow furrowed. "Liam, I thought you'd been going out for seven months now."

"Absolutely right," I answered. I took a sip of wine. "It's been seven months since I first saw this beautiful woman." I turned and placed my hand over Amy's. "From that moment on, I knew she was the one for me. She's been the only one on my mind since that evening. I knew she was destined to be with me, but it took me two months to convince her. The longest two months of my life."

The blush in Amy's cheeks was bright and obvious. She was going to get me back for this later.

I pulled my hand away and took a forkful of calamari to shut myself up before I got in deeper trouble.

Felicia raised her glass, proposing a toast. "To true love."

We all clinked glasses, and I turned to Amy.

Her eyes sparkled as she held mine, and we repeated the toast.

With the waiter hovering, Hue suggested we decide on our dinner orders.

I chose the pepper-crusted sirloin, and Amy decided on the beef Wellington.

Felicia and Amy started discussing additional South African animals, while Hue wanted to talk about the prospects for the Patriots this year, and bemoan their draft choices.

Hue was not a fan of drafting running backs——too fragile, he thought. Our team had taken two with our top-round picks.

I disappointed him by not having much of an opinion on the matter.

The women moved on to discussing rescue shelters for dogs and cats.

Dinner arrived, halting the conversations for the moment.

I took the opportunity to admire Amy. I had told her she was stunning when I picked her up, and I now decided it was an understatement. The way she comported herself with these people this evening added to her allure. She was the total package: beauty, brains, and class, all wrapped up in a deliciously sexy body. Her dark hair cascaded down her back, and the sparkle of her eyes this evening transfixed me every time I caught her looking in my direction. I had lucked into the perfect woman for this——even better than Melinda.

"Liam," Hue said.

I had missed his question. "I'm sorry. I was somewhere else for a moment."

"You seemed quite lost in thought," Felicia told me.

"I was," I answered. "I was just thinking how lucky I am to have met Amy."

Felicia's face melted into the most kind smile. "Tell us how you won her over."

"Sunshine, why don't you tell the story. You do it so much better than I do."

Amy gasped. "You want me to tell it, really?"

"Sure," I told her, filling my mouth with another bite of my meat.

Hue feigned being busy with his steak, but I could tell he was listening intently.

Felicia put her fork down to hang on every word.

Amy took a sip of her wine. "He started sending me flowers at work."

"Nice flowers, I hope," Felicia said.

"Oh, yes. A dozen roses. First once a week, and then once a day," Amy answered with a smile.

Felicia turned to me. "That sounds so romantic, Liam."

Hue kept quiet, probably worried again about Felicia holding him to a new standard after this.

"Then twice a day," I added, smiling at my date.

"Is that what won you over?" Felicia asked Amy.

"No. Not at all," Amy said, smiling wickedly at me. She'd gone off script. We'd agreed last night that the story would be she gave in after I started sending flowers. Now she was punishing me for embarrassing her.

"You see," Amy said, "he sent them to the wrong person. He didn't even get my name right."

Hue laughed.

It was my turn to get in on this twist to the story if Amy was going to bugger it up. "That's because at the Christmas party, she had told me where she worked, but she gave me the wrong name.

She said her name was Vivienne, but that's her sister. So when I sent the flowers, of course I had no way of knowing they'd deliver them to the wrong person."

Felicia's eyes narrowed. "You sly girl, Amy. So you really didn't like him at Christmastime at all?"

"No, not until later," Amy replied.

I put my glass down. "And that wasn't all I sent."

Felicia's eyes twinkled. "What else?"

Amy's eye narrowed. Now she was trapped. "Why don't you tell them, honey."

I smiled. "A CD each time of our song."

Felicia could barely contain herself. "I'm dying to know what song."

Amy didn't answer. She forked food into her mouth and looked at me.

"Why 'Sunny', of course, because she's my Sunshine. The Marvin Gaye recording of the song," I said, leaning over to kiss Amy on the cheek.

"That's so romantic. That would have done it for me." Felicia said.

"Not me," Amy said. "I kept ignoring him. But finally he called."

I finished my bite of potato. "But you left out a part."

Amy took my comment in stride. "What did I forget?" She gave me the evil eye.

"You called the police on me for the flowers," I said. Two could play this game.

Felicia gasped.

Hue kept after his steak, letting Felicia do the grilling.

"Oh, yes, I had to call the police on him, but it wasn't the flowers. He had taken to waiting for me outside work," Amy told them.

I had to think fast. "I needed to talk to her, so I would wait by the front door to her office, but she avoided me by going out the back or side doors," I said.

"He was getting creepy," Amy said.

"Sounds quite persistent to me," Hue noted, coming to my defense.

Felicia nodded, seeming to agree with her husband.

"It certainly was embarrassing. I explained to the cops I was waiting for my girlfriend. But they insisted I couldn't stay." I hoped we were done with this excursion away from the story we had practiced.

"And just how did you get her name in the end?" Hue asked.

"I came down to apologize for the police," Amy said quickly.

"She wouldn't talk directly to me," I said. "But I got her name from the company badge she was wearing."

"I wanted to talk to him to apologize," Amy told them. "But the police insisted on keeping us apart."

"So I sent twice as many flowers the next day, and called again and again until she agreed to talk to me," I said, happy we had finally completed the story.

"Quite a journey. I guess it just shows the power of determination," Hue remarked before finishing the wine in his glass.

Felicia nodded, silently.

"She turned out to be worth every bit of the effort," I said, eliciting another blush from my girl. "And for this lady, I'd do it all over again in a heartbeat." I leaned over to offer a quick kiss, which she accepted without a fuss.

"I really do think true love stories are the best," Felicia said.

I wasn't sure if she meant true stories about love or stories about true love, but it didn't matter. We had won her over, it seemed.

Amy's glance in my direction carried a warmth I could only hope was sincere. She was a truly amazing lady, even if she wouldn't keep to a simple script.

Felicia raised her fork in Amy's direction as she finished chewing. "Where did he take you on that first date?"

"Waffle Castle," Amy answered right away. "Can you believe it? Waffle Castle for a first date. He can be sort of cheap."

This was not something we had discussed. We clearly hadn't had enough preparation time.

"Liam, you should be ashamed of yourself," Felicia scolded.

I had to defend myself and turn this around. "That's because we spent all evening talking. I was so lost in her beauty and the stories she told of growing up in Greenfield that before we knew it, everything was closed." I thought I had salvaged it reasonably. "She had wanted French for dinner, and French toast at the Waffle Castle was the closest I could come up with at that hour."

"Pretty ingenious, I'd say," Hue chimed in.

Amy put her fork down. "It was pretty cute, actually, how he tried so hard to find something French at midnight."

"We talked all night," I said before taking a sip of water. "She explained all that she and her partner, Sam, had done to start their company. She amazed me for hours. I've never met a more accomplished woman."

Her cheeks glowed red again.

"We talked almost until the sun came up," I added. I thought it was a good touch.

Hue gestured toward me. "Liam, tell us how you came up with her nickname."

I found it an easy one to answer. "I've called her Sunshine since the first day we met. She brightens up any room she enters." I looked over at her with a genuine smile. "And her being part of my life has brought warmth to my soul and brightened my outlook each and every day."

Felicia's eyes were watering.

Hue smiled at me.

Amy had been looking down, avoiding my gaze. When she met my eyes, hers were teary, soft and happy. Her blush was in full bloom, but instead of complaining, she leaned over to plant a quick kiss on me. I hoped it was a sign she might be getting over her aversion to compliments.

CHAPTER 15

AMY

WHEN WE REACHED THE GROUND FLOOR, LIAM PUT HIS ARM around me. "Thank you again." He leaned over and pressed a kiss to the top of my head as we strode through the lobby. Outside, he handed the valet his ticket.

I leaned into his warmth and didn't want to let go.

Returning with the car, the valet looked relieved to be free of the responsibility of keeping the mob boss's car safe. He beamed a megawatt smile of gratitude when Liam handed him a hundred-dollar bill for his troubles.

"That was generous," I said as he closed the door for me.

Liam settled into his seat and pushed the fob into the slot. The car awoke with a growl. "It was only fair after I scared the shit out of him."

I relaxed against the leather as he pulled into traffic. "I learned one important thing about you tonight."

"And what would that be, Sunshine?" he asked.

"You can sling bullshit with the best of them. I mean, '*She*

128

warms my soul, and she brightens up my day.' Really? That's laying it on pretty thick."

Liam gritted his teeth. He didn't say a word as he jerked the car to the right, and I was thrown forward against the seatbelt as the car came to an abrupt stop by the curb.

His eyes seared into me, sending a shiver down my back. I leaned away, toward the door.

"There was no bullshit in that line," he almost yelled. "That is absolutely how I feel."

I couldn't believe what he was telling me. I had thought it all an act. I knew he liked me, but brightening up his life each and every day? That was some pretty exaggerated bullshit, even for a real boyfriend.

His eyes were fierce, determined. "You are truly an amazing lady, Amy. But I've had it with you refusing to accept my compliments." He banged the steering wheel. "We may be pretending we've been together for months, but I can size people up quickly, and everything I've said about how wonderful you are is absolutely true. Now get over it, and stop calling me a fucking liar."

What the fuck?

"You do that one more time, and I swear I'm going to take you over my knee and you won't be able to sit for a day," he growled.

Slowly the realization dawned on me. "I didn't mean to."

His words had melted my insides. I'd thought all through dinner the comments were over-the-top hyperbole for the Schmulians' benefit. I had pictured him in salesman mode, trying to close the deal and say what the Schmulians wanted to hear to get to yes. I understood how important this was to him, how he needed to make the right impression.

Now I had to wrap my head around his angry declaration. He'd meant every unbelievably kind word.

The acceleration pinned me back in the seat as he pulled away from the curb and we approached the speed of sound.

I planted my feet on the floor and clung to the door handle as we hurtled around a corner. "Please slow down. You're scaring me."

He looked straight ahead and didn't ease up. "Soon as you're willing to behave."

"I give," I squeaked.

I wasn't sure what I was agreeing to exactly, but dying in a fiery crash because he was mad at me was not the right way to end our evening.

He let off the gas, and the screaming of the engine lowered to a loud growl. "A lady would accept honest compliments from her boyfriend. Are you ready to be a lady?"

The only catch in his statement was I wasn't really his girlfriend. This was all make-believe. I'd been brought up to be modest, and compliments had always embarrassed me. I blushed beet red with merely the slightest provocation, which didn't help.

"Yes, yes," I pleaded. Anything to avoid becoming a traffic statistic.

He braked abruptly to the speed limit, and it felt like we were crawling along, but now we were safe.

I loosened my death grip on the door. "I'll make a concerted effort to be better. Because it's important to you."

It was an honest promise because I truly meant the last part. If it was important to him, I would make it important to me. Understanding how his string of compliments had been from the heart touched me, and I would do what I could to please him——not only to secure the rest of his funding for our company, but because he deserved it and I genuinely *wanted* to please him.

My heart had raced with fear as he sped through the city. Now it beat heavily for a different reason as I contemplated what he'd said. It soon became too much to process. A man like Liam Quigley couldn't possibly see me that way. Could he? Nobody had ever said things one tenth as nice as he had tonight.

Perhaps he shouldn't have drunk the wine. Better yet, perhaps I should keep a bottle around for when I was feeling down and

wanted him to tell me how wonderful I am, and how everything
was about to get better.

He navigated the darkened streets back to my apartment in
silence. He was probably testing to see how long I could behave
myself.

I was still replaying the evening in my head when we reached
my street. I couldn't read his expression.

He parked in the loading zone out front once again and jumped
out to run around and open my door for me.

Doubtless he was right; chivalry had died in Boston. Nobody
had ever acted as gentlemanly as Liam did in my presence. Perhaps
Californians weren't all hicks.

He walked me up to my door, and we stopped outside.

I fished my key from my purse. "I had a very enjoyable
evening tonight." I fiddled with the key, unsure what his version of
a lady would say next.

"Amy, thank you for the sunshine bouquet," he said stepping
back. It was an odd line, but I was learning he had a knack for
surprising me, or I needed a California-to-New England dictionary
to translate these things.

"Liam, I apologize. I didn't mean… I just didn't——"

He moved forward and halted me with a finger to my lips. "No
apology, Sunshine. Remember to look forward, not back."

I nodded and looked up to find fire in his eyes. I waited for his
lips to replace his finger, for the kiss to begin. I closed my eyes.
Tingles ran rampant under my skin, remembering Tuesday night
and the kiss that had redefined kissing. I expected a kiss to sweep
me off my feet, the way it had our first night. When it didn't come,
I opened my eyes.

He had backed away instead. "Good night, Sunshine. I should
go. I'll call you about the next step."

I was unsure what I'd done wrong. Maybe I should have
popped a Tic Tac. "Good night."

I waved and slid my key into the lock, opening the door. I'd expected at least a kiss. Should I have been the instigator? Should I have invited him up before we got out of the car?

But this might be for the best. We could easily get carried away, and we had an agreement in place. Where would another night of passion take us? Besides, I had meant Tuesday to be a one-time event. Now it was apparent that was his plan as well.

I slipped inside and leaned against the door after closing myself inside the lonely, empty space of my shitty little apartment. I pondered my situation in the darkness. I had been apprehensive about playing the fake girlfriend, and now here I was regretting that it wasn't real.

How stupid can I be?

This was going to drive me crazy. I knew I couldn't have him. It couldn't work.

Was that his appeal? Was he my forbidden fruit? No. He wasn't forbidden; he was unattainable. A few dinners and he'd disappear in a puff of smoke. This was all just a business arrangement—— I'd insisted on it.

I flicked on the light, inhaled a deep calming breath, and vowed to take his advice.

Look forward, not back.

We'd gotten the first ten million yesterday, stabilizing Tiffany's for the time being. And tonight had been a step toward getting the second ten.

CHAPTER 16

AMY

VIVIENNE WAS WAITING FOR ME IN A BOOTH NEAR THE FRONT WHEN I arrived at Waffle Castle for our late brunch. This was her favorite location for Sunday mornings. Nothing like a good load of carbohydrates to start your day, according to her.

I slid in across from her and the cross-examination started immediately.

"So, how did your fake dinner date go?"

It'd been a *real* dinner date. "It was nice." The only thing fake was our relationship.

Eagerness showed in her eyes. "Tell me about the car. How was it? Was it as cool as in the movie?"

The car had certainly been one of the highlights and lowlights of my night. "Super cool."

"And?" she asked.

I wasn't quite sure how to describe the feeling. "It's loud, and super fast. When he opened it up, the engine screamed. The car is a fucking eye-magnet. Everywhere we went, people turned to look at us. But after a while, it's a little like driving around in a rolling zoo."

Vivienne finished a sip of her coffee. "You think he really meant it when he said he'd give me a ride?"

This was one question I could answer definitively. "He says what he means. And you don't ever want to call him a liar."

The waitress came by to ask if I wanted coffee. Vivienne had already put in our regular order: the short stack of buttermilk pancakes for me, and double blueberry pancakes for her.

"There's a story in there, I'm guessing," Vivienne said.

I nodded.

She toyed with her coffee cup. "I'm waiting."

"It's sort of a long story."

"I've got all morning," she said.

"All night long he was saying these…well, over-the-top nice things about me."

Vivienne cocked an eyebrow. "Like?"

I'd forgotten all of his exact wording. "First he said he got me the jewelry because he thought it would complement the beauty of my eyes."

"That's nice."

The waitress returned with our pancakes and my coffee.

Vivienne loaded up her fork. "Must've been more than that."

I smoothed the butter on top of my pancakes. "There was. He told the other couple he called me Sunshine because I brought warmth to his soul, and I brightened his outlook every day. You believe that shit?"

"I wish a guy would say that about me," Vivienne replied. "He definitely gets an A for effort."

"The scary part," I continued, "was in the car later. I told him it was pretty good bullshit he was slinging. He got so mad we nearly crashed."

Vivienne jerked upright, her mouth open.

"He told me to never call him a liar again. He said he meant every word."

Vivienne finished chewing her bite of pancake. "Now that's a grade-A, number-one boyfriend."

I put my coffee down. "He's not my boyfriend, got it?"

"First he fucks your socks off, and then he takes you to dinner and says romantic shit like that. We need to get you a new dictionary, Amy. That's the fucking definition of boyfriend——make that *great* boyfriend."

"But it's all fake."

Vivienne leaned forward. "If it's so fake, why did he get mad at you for calling him a bullshitter?"

That was a question I couldn't answer. It was supposed to be fake, but last night it had certainly seemed real——right up until I didn't get a good night kiss.

Vivienne put her fork down. "If you don't appreciate him, I'll let him park his shoes under my bed any day. My God, the man is gorgeous and richer than Midas. How can you not be doing everything you can to be the best girlfriend possible? Convince him to be your real boyfriend, if you insist that's not what he is already. If you don't, we need to send you in for some kind of brain scan."

Liam was someone I didn't ever intend to share with my sister. He was unpredictable, and could be annoying, but the more I thought about last night, the more I looked forward to spending time with him, lots of time. I'd said I would try to please him, and I was planning on it.

A blueberry escaped Vivienne's plate and stopped when it hit my coffee cup. I stuffed my mouth full of pancake to avoid talking.

"I say you have shit for brains," Vivienne informed me.

She might be right.

I was certainly confused. Liam wasn't an easy man to understand. He'd said all those wonderful things to me, and insisted it was how he felt. So why didn't he kiss me at the end of the night, even if he wouldn't sleep with me?

I finished chewing. "He didn't kiss me good night," I blurted.

Vivienne's brow furrowed. "Hello, Amy, this is the new millennium. If he doesn't kiss you, you go right ahead and kiss him. You don't need anybody's permission to show him how you feel. I swear, I shouldn't have to tell you this stuff. Every girl in Cambridge would be envious of your situation."

My phone rang. When I pulled it out of my purse, Liam's name was on the screen. I tilted it toward Vivienne. "It's him." I shouldn't have held it anywhere near her. She grabbed it.

She answered the call. "Amy Hudson's line, may I help you?"

I kicked her under the table.

She yelped. "No, that was just your girlfriend kicking me for answering her phone... Yeah, she's like that sometimes."

I scowled at her and held out my hand. "Give me that back."

"Yes, she's here, but first, Liam, I have a question. Did you mean it when you said you'd give me a ride in that cool car of yours?"

I lunged for the phone, but she slid sideways in the booth, out of reach.

"Sounds great. Nice talking to you." She handed the phone to me finally.

"Hi, Liam, I apologize for my sister's lack of manners."

"Not at all. You need to text me her number later. I promised to be in touch when I could schedule a ride for her, and..."

I got up to walk outside. I wanted to talk to him without my sister in my face. "And you always keep your promises. I get it."

Vivienne made a move to follow me.

I pointed a finger at her, warning her to stay. It might not work, but it was worth a try.

She didn't follow me outside, probably only because we hadn't paid yet. She couldn't have them thinking she was stiffing the restaurant.

"How's your morning?" I asked, pushing open the door and moving to the sidewalk.

"Good so far."

I pressed the phone harder to my ear. It was loud out here. "I'm glad you called. I wanted to say I'm sorry———"

"*Stop right there, Sunshine,*" he interrupted. "*What did I tell you last night?*"

"That you meant what you said," I answered.

"*Later. When I was leaving.*"

My brain went blank.

"*Look forward, not back. No more apologies necessary,*" he said.

I nodded, which was stupid, because he couldn't see it. "Okay, but I feel bad about——"

"*Maybe in your family you needed to apologize multiple times, but that's not how I was raised. You're better than that. Once is all you need with me.*"

"Okay, I'll try… It's good to hear your voice." I'd longed to call and talk to him this morning, but had decided to hold off until tonight or tomorrow. The clingy, demanding woman was not a good look for me.

"*When you say that, now I feel ten feet tall,*" he responded.

I smiled, even if I didn't understand him.

"*The reason I'm calling, besides that I just wanted to hear* your *sweet voice, is that I need you to move in with me.*"

He said it like we were discussing the weather. It was a simple statement——not a demand, or even a request. Just that was how it was going to be.

I was too dumbfounded to respond.

"*Pack what you need for the first two weeks, and we'll figure the rest out later. I'll collect you at your place. What time can you be ready?*"

Unpredictable didn't begin to describe Liam. Tuesday night he had fucked me into next month. Wednesday he had tried to take my company away, and Thursday he had offered to save it. Last night he had said the most unbelievable things about me and then declined to even kiss me. My head was spinning.

"*Sunshine,*" he said through the phone. "*What time works for you?*"

"Four," I told him. "What about four?"

"That's a little late. Can we make it three?" he asked.

Late for what? "I guess," I responded.

"Three it is. See you then, and don't forget about Viv's number. Bye now." Then he was gone.

I leaned against the glass of the restaurant on wobbly legs. *What just happened?*

After taking a minute to regain my bearings, I returned to the booth.

Vivienne was practically bouncing in her seat. "What's the news on the Liam front?"

"Just a sec," I told her as I located her contact in my phone. "I need to send him your number so he can call you later about the ride."

"Super cool. I can't wait."

I sent the contact and pushed away my plate. My appetite had disappeared.

"Amy, what's wrong?"

I leaned forward. I didn't want to announce this to the whole restaurant. "He wants me to move in with him," I whispered.

Vivienne's eyes lit up. "Hot shit. Now that's my sister. I knew you could turn it around if you tried."

What am I doing?

~

LIAM

I PULLED UP IN FRONT OF AMY'S APARTMENT BUILDING TEN minutes early. Locking the car, I trotted inside and up the stairs. It seemed dingy, even in today's bright sunshine. A stain on the wall up the stairs looked like a tenant had upchucked on the way home some night not too long ago. The carpeting in the hallway should have been replaced years ago.

I knocked on her door and waited.

"Just a moment" came from inside.

The door opened, and Amy stood in front of me, as beautiful as ever, with a smile that melted me.

Her presence instantly lifted my spirits. "You smile at me and really ease my pain," I told her.

She cocked her head. "What? How 'bout we use English from now on?" She moved forward and embraced me.

I pulled her into a tight hug. "Just saying I'm glad to see you and your smiling face, Sunshine." I rubbed her back. "Ready to go?"

She released me. "No." She turned around, walked to her couch, and sat down.

I closed the door behind me, unsure what had changed since we talked. "Sunshine?"

"Don't *Sunshine* me. And you can't just tell me what to do like that."

I approached the couch and settled in next to her. She didn't complain when I took her hand. "Let's start again. Clearly I've upset you, and that's the last thing I want to do."

"You call me up out of the blue and tell me you want me to move in with you, and last night, you didn't even kiss me. You can't just..." She started to sob.

I pulled her into me, her head on my chest. My cock started to stir with her soft warmth up against me again. Even with the fabric separating us, I recalled how she'd felt in my arms, how she'd made me feel, made me soar.

I forced the memories aside, rubbed her back, and stroked her hair. I'd screwed this up royally. I should have taken the time to explain things to her. I'd thought I would do that tonight, but clearly it had been a fucked-up plan. I didn't have any experience with this.

"I should have explained," I told her.

I was at a loss for words after that. I'd never dealt with women's emotions much in the past. I'd gone from a college rela-tionship with Roberta, where we'd grown up together and never had to go through the growing pains of meeting and learning about each other, to no relationship after she left, to coming out and marrying her. We'd picked up where we'd left off until one day she was gone, and with her my world.

Amy looked at me expectantly before burying her head against my chest again.

I'd bedded dozens, well, dozens of dozens of women, but only ever had one relationship in my life. I had virtually no experience dealing with women's emotions.

"I'm not just a blowup doll you can use and discard and then pick up again," she mumbled into my shirt.

I pulled her chin up to look into her eyes——wet, hurt eyes. "Sunshine, I know I've behaved badly. Can you forgive me and let me make it up to you?"

"No," she said curtly before pulling away, rushing into her bedroom, and slamming the door.

Shit.

CHAPTER 17

AMY

I LEANED AGAINST THE DOOR I'D JUST SLAMMED IN HIS FACE.

"No?" he asked through the wood after a moment.

"Not until you apologize three times."

He laughed. "I'm sorry I didn't explain things on the phone."

That made two. He'd thought he was going to train me, but two could play that game.

"And?" I asked, still leaning against the door.

"And I'm sorry I didn't kiss you last night," he added. "I wanted to…"

My heart leaped at his admission.

"But I didn't want to take advantage of the situation, given the agreement we have. I thought you'd let me know if you wanted a kiss, and I didn't get that vibe."

Obviously I had been too coy. Agreement or no, I couldn't help myself. I opened the door.

I placed a hand behind his neck and pulled myself to him, inches from his lips. "And what about now?" I murmured, matching the fire in his eyes.

"You know us Californians; we're pretty dense."

I pulled myself the rest of the way to him and our lips met.

He snaked a hand behind me, pulling me in tighter, pressing my breasts against him, and taking control of the kiss.

This was the kiss I'd longed for last night, the kiss that told me how he desired me, as I desired him. My mouth opened to him as our tongues sought to reacquaint themselves after five days apart.

I threaded my fingers through his hair, holding him close.

He reciprocated by finding his way to my breasts, stroking my nipple with his thumb through the fabric separating us, lighting a fire in my chest as I longed to strip his clothes off.

His hands continued to trace the outlines of my body through my clothing as our tongues sparred for position.

He smelled of old leather and manliness and tasted like pure sex, all power and need.

As we traded breath, I fell under his spell, the same one he'd used on me our first night. At every spot he touched, my nerves lit up like a pinball machine, sparks bouncing from one side of my body to the other.

He broke this kiss and let me go. "Sorry, I didn't mean to overdo it. We shouldn't..."

I looked down. "Yeah, boundaries." My chest tightened. I'd been the one to insist on them, and now I'd pushed him to break the rules. "My fault. I shouldn't have said anything. It won't happen again." I had to stick to the rules I'd requested.

He sighed. "No, it's my fault." He walked past me. "We should get going."

"What's your hurry? And you said you'd explain first. That's going to cost you another apology."

"You're right, Amy. I'm sorry I still haven't explained." He took another step back.

I waited.

"Schmulian called today. He wants to have dinner tonight, at our place."

"Our place?"

"Well, my place," he said. "He assumed we lived together, naturally."

"But we just had dinner with them last night. What's the deal?"

"I've got no idea. My only guess is that it's a test to see if we're really living together."

"Who said we were?" I asked.

"After seven months?"

"Five," I corrected him.

He took my hand. "I think this is just part of the testing."

"You think? That's what this is all about?"

"It's important," he said. "It'll make a better impression, don't you think?"

He was probably right. We would look more committed that way.

I had to acknowledge the logic. "Okay, I guess, but I'll need to bring a lot of stuff if it's going to look like I live there." I had already assembled several boxes of clothes before I had decided I wasn't going to be jerked around by him and stopped.

He followed me into the bedroom.

I went to the closet and pulled several more tops out, laying the hangers on the bed. I added a few more skirts, and when I turned around to lay them on the bed, I found him examining pairs of my panties.

"Stop that."

He had decided to help himself to my underwear drawer.

"Just trying to help——picking out the ones my girlfriend would wear."

"Sorry to disappoint you, Romeo, but I don't have any crotch-less underwear." I'd thrown out the pair of Hot Love Crotchless panties Vivienne had given me last Christmas.

He held up a pair of matching red and black thongs. "These are nice." He gave me a wicked smile.

They were sheer thongs, which Vivienne had also gotten me. A reminder to be more adventurous, she'd said.

I hadn't dared to wear them yet. They didn't hide anything, not a thing.

He added them to the open box on my bed.

I didn't have the energy to object right now. They could sit in a drawer at his place as easily as they could sit in a drawer here.

After fifteen minutes, we had quite a large pile between the clothes on hangers and the boxes and bags of T-shirts and sweatshirts, underwear and jeans.

I went to the bathroom and finished packing up the essentials I'd need. They didn't all fit in one bag. I went out to get another grocery bag from the kitchen.

Liam carried the clothes to the front door.

It took us several trips to get everything downstairs to street level. Since it obviously wouldn't all fit in his sleek little car, he called an Uber, which we loaded to the gills with my clothes.

HIS DOORMAN WATCHED THE CARS WHILE THE UBER DRIVER AND Liam's concierge helped us get everything upstairs. Two trips was all it took.

Liam left me alone in his place while he went to park his car.

The night I'd been here I hadn't paid attention to the space. Now I noticed how stunning it was. Calling it spacious didn't do it justice. With a full wall of windows, the view of the Common and the city beyond was spectacular. The Charles River wended its way by in the distance, separating Boston from Cambridge.

I wandered into the kitchen, running my fingers over the smooth coolness of the dark granite countertops. His kitchen area was almost as large as my whole apartment. A wide Subzero fridge, two ovens, an eight-burner Viking range, and a gas barbecue with a huge stainless hood over it lined one side. The cabinets were a warm cherrywood with etched glass inserts, and the granite-topped island was almost as long and wide as my car had been——the car Matt got in the divorce. Three sinks, two inset butcher block cutting boards, two dishwashers, and a stack of three warming drawers——the place was equipped to cook for a few dozen, and he lived here alone.

I peered through a doorway to an elegant formal dining room with a fireplace at one end and a window looking out on the city at the other. The table was far and away the largest I'd ever seen, long enough to seat at least twenty. Oil paintings in elaborate frames graced the walls.

I exited through the sliding glass door to a rooftop patio. Venturing to the edge, I peered over looking down on the Common.

"Like the view?" Liam asked, surprising me.

I backed away from the edge. "It's nice, but heights aren't my thing." I walked past him back into the main room.

He followed me and closed the door behind us, sealing out the slight road noise from below.

He placed a hand on the small of my back, guiding me toward the pile of clothes by the front door. "Let's get your things put away. We don't have a lot of time."

His touch was warm, and more than a little bit distracting.

"Lead the way." I couldn't control the way my body reacted.

We gathered up armfuls of clothes, and I followed him into the bedroom.

This was his room, the same room we'd used Tuesday night.

"Just a minute," I said stopping inside the door. "You don't really want me in here, do you?"

He turned to me with a quizzical look.

I stayed at the door. "I mean, we said we were going to keep this professional, right?"

He nodded his head toward the closet. "Wouldn't we expect my girlfriend's things to be in here?"

I followed him to the closet. "You don't expect me to——"

He placed a gentle hand on my shoulder. "Amy, trust me. You're safe here."

I let out a breath I didn't realize I'd been holding.

He made space in one side of the closet and started hanging the skirts he had carried. "Sunshine, for appearance's sake, I think we have to stash your clothes here."

"Let's talk about this for a moment," I said. "What's the plan? I don't really understand how this is going to work."

Liam finished hanging up the clothes and turned to me. "If you are living with me as my girlfriend, where would your clothes be?"

"I thought I'd be using the guest bedroom."

"Yes, but to be safe," he continued, "you should keep any bathroom articles over there hidden in a drawer, and same thing with clothes. It needs to appear that we're sharing this bedroom and bathroom." With that, he walked around me to get some more clothes from the hallway.

It made sense, of course, but having all my clothes in here where I had to go by him to get dressed would be awkward. I hung the blouses I was carrying beside the skirts.

When he had first proposed my being his fake girlfriend, it had sounded so easy. I hadn't contemplated these complications. This job was becoming harder by the day. But I owed it to Samantha and everybody else at Tiffany's to make the best effort I could.

"You okay, Amy?" he asked softly as he came up behind me. "I know this isn't what you signed up for, and I appreciate it. If this is too much, we can take these things back. I'll make some excuse to Schmulian."

I shook my head. I couldn't do that and put the project in jeopardy. "No, but thank you for understanding. I'll deal with it."

He took my hand. "I promise to respect your boundaries. I won't compromise you in any way. You are a guest here, and I'll treat you with the respect you deserve. I'll keep this professional, I promise. And one thing you'll learn about me, I always keep my promises. Always." His eyes and his voice carried nothing but sincerity. His touch and his manner were completely disarming.

I'd be living in the den of the lion. Was my unease because I didn't trust him, or didn't trust myself?

We finished putting my things away. I ended up with a toothbrush, toothpaste, some face-cleansing wipes, and a hairbrush in the bathroom across the hall, along with some underwear, T-shirts, a pair of sweatpants, and a nightgown in two drawers in the other bedroom.

"What time did you say he's coming over?" I asked.

"Seven o'clock," he yelled from the other room.

That didn't give us a lot of time. I opened up the large refrigerator. "You know if you're going to cook dinner for somebody you have to have something to cook," I called.

The fridge was even emptier than I'd expected for a bachelor: no vegetables, no fruit save three apples and some moldy strawberries, and no meat. The freezer section had the real stash. It was chock full of frozen pizzas and ice cream.

Liam joined me to view the disaster. "Pretty pathetic, huh?"

I frowned at him. "You can't seriously eat this shit on a regular basis."

He pulled out a package of Green Giant frozen broccoli and cheese. "At least I have my vegetables every day."

Pathetic is right.

"Where's the nearest market?" I asked.

"Lambert's is a few blocks north."

"You're coming with me."

His phone rang as I collected my purse. He answered it and waved me over.

"I'm so sorry to hear that, Hue," he said into the phone. "Amy and I would love to have you over another time… Okay, I'll wait to hear from you." He ended the call with a simple goodbye and smiled at me. "You're off the hook. No chef duty tonight. Hue said something came up and they couldn't make it. He'll reschedule later."

"But we still need groceries," I told him. "I'm not eating frozen pizza, and neither are you. If I'm spending time over here, we're eating fresh food."

His smirk telegraphed a wise-ass comment. "We can order out for fresh pizza."

I placed my hand on his chest and pushed him back. "Really? As your girlfriend, I won't let you eat crap. We're cooking, and not this frozen shit. Maybe keep the veggies and the ice cream, but everything else goes. And you can start by joining me at the market. We're going to need more than I can carry back by myself."

CHAPTER 18

(NINE DAYS LATER)

LIAM

IT HAD BEEN JUST OVER A WEEK SINCE I MOVED AMY INTO THE penthouse with me.

We were still on high alert, expecting a visit from Schmulian at any moment. He had called every two days or so, apologizing for having to delay and asking me to be patient. So, we had been careful to keep the evidence of Amy's stay in the guest bedroom to a minimum.

And I'd survived a whole week in close proximity to Amy every evening and morning without violating her boundaries.

I woke first each day and was showered before she came in to use the shower and get dressed. I gave her the privacy she deserved and pitched in by making her bed for her while she was showering in the master bath.

We left together in the morning.

Twice I had spied a girl across the street on the Common who might have been my shadow, but she was too far away to be sure. It was more likely that I had gotten paranoid since catching a glimpse of her taking my picture at the opera that night. Now most redheads looked suspicious to me.

I also drove Amy in and dropped her at work each morning. She made her own way back as our end-of-day schedules didn't mesh.

This morning I'd jumped in the shower early. Waking up to thoughts of Amy across the hall, my morning wood was stiff as ever, and persistent. As I finished soaping up, I had to take things further. I steadied myself against the wall with one arm and with my other hand began to stroke. I closed my eyes. The memory of her undressing and slowly turning for me that first night sent my hand into overdrive.

The sound wasn't loud, but it was definitely a knock.

Shit.

"Liam, I need to get into work early. Can I come in?"

I faced away from the glass shower door. "Sure. But no peeking." I willed my hard-on to go down with no luck. It never worked when I needed it to.

I heard Amy start the water at the sink. A quick peek revealed she was brushing her teeth——and leaning over in only a T-shirt, which rode up almost to her ass cheeks. The view only made my problem worse. Imagining the view with the shirt up another two inches almost did me in. She had the cutest ass and the sweetest pussy. She had no idea what she did to me walking around in the morning with a T-shirt shorter than a miniskirt.

I smiled at her in the mirror, and she smiled back with toothpaste escaping her lips. I turned the water cold and put my head under the spray, a move I instantly regretted. The shivering followed quickly.

"I found it hard waking up this morning. What about you?" she asked.

Of course I'd found my dick hard this morning, but that wasn't what she meant. "No worse than any other day," I said over my shoulder. My dick had been screaming for release, and this

morning was the worst yet, but I had promised to obey her boundaries, and a promise was a promise no matter how ill conceived.

What had I been thinking?

"I'll be back when you're done," she said.

I waved without looking. When I turned, she had gone. The
cold water was slowly having the desired effect and things were
shrinking. I turned off the water, grabbed a towel, and dried off as I
walked around the corner into my closet. Gooseflesh had erupted
all over my body. I was ready to nominate hot water as man's
greatest invention.

"Shower's all yours," I called.

Living here with her mere feet away, yet untouchable tortured
me. Every glance in her direction brought a smile to my face and a
jerk to my cock. Every word out of her mouth enchanted me.

I'd kept my promise to respect her boundaries, but this had
become more than that. Talking with her each evening was now
something I looked forward to. For her I'd broken my rule about
bringing a woman to the penthouse. Now she had me questioning
my no-relationship rule as well.

Could there be an *us* after the Springbok deal? Or was this
merely a job, a work milestone to be reached so she could go back
to her normal life——one where I was only a memory? I couldn't
read her.

She had been good natured about this arrangement, only joking
occasionally about my idiosyncrasies and even tolerating my total
lack of cooking or cleaning skills. That's why they'd invented
pizza delivery, right?

Moseying into the kitchen, I pulled out the frying pan and
sprayed it with oil. I had learned French toast was one of her
favorites, and that's what I would surprise her with today.

I'd managed a dry run yesterday afternoon while she made a
trip back to her apartment for more clothes. The pieces had come
out too dark on my first try, and better, but not good enough, on my
second. I could remedy it this morning with a lower setting on the

stove. The disposal in the sink had eaten the evidence of yesterday's attempts without complaint, and a thorough cleanup of my mess, plus opening the windows to air the place out had kept my cooking experiment a secret.

She hadn't suspected a thing when she returned. We'd spent the evening watching back-to-back Bond flicks. She chose *Casino Royale* in deference to my car, and I chose *Never Say Never Again*. Sean Connery regretted the decision he'd made to quit the Bond character and came back to make that movie, and I regretted agreeing to Amy's boundaries. I wanted a do-over.

~

AMY

THIS ROLE AS LIAM'S GIRLFRIEND SHOULD HAVE BEEN EASY, BUT IT was proving to be the opposite. I'd seen him in the mirror this morning as I approached the bathroom——cock in hand, jerking off while leaning against the shower wall. Luckily he'd faced the wall once I entered and hadn't invited me to join him under the water.

If he had, I wasn't sure I would have been able to say no. My nipples had peaked as I'd rinsed my mouth and caught his nice ass in the mirror. Had it been a mistake to insist on keeping this professional and platonic? The memories of our first and only night together hadn't faded. If anything, they had gotten more vivid with his daily closeness. My big mistake had been agreeing to move into his penthouse, but once I'd accepted the challenge, how could I back out? And how could I explain it to Samantha if I did?

I chose the sapphire earrings for today. Liam had bought two more pairs for me since I'd moved in with him, sapphire and diamond. Each set came in a small, red Cartier box. Refusing them had become impossible, and his taste was excellent. I could get used to this fake kept-woman role with all these presents.

I found him out on the patio after I finished dressing.

He turned as I opened the sliding glass door. The lion was back. His eyes appraised me from head to toe and back again, stopping perceptibly at my chest. His warm, genuine smile grew as I approached. I had yet to catch him on a bad day. He was like something out of an old-time movie. He stood when I reached the table ——a table set with a cooked breakfast instead of his usual cold cereal.

I took my seat, and he retook his. I still had trouble acclimating to his sense of manners.

"French toast? You didn't tell me you knew how to make this."

He hadn't seemed capable of anything beyond microwave dinners a week ago, and I hadn't seen him eat anything but cereal in the morning.

"Only the best for you, Sunshine. You're my spark of nature's fire. Amazing what you can learn on YouTube these days."

I couldn't always understand his compliments…spark of nature's fire?

"What's the hurry to get into work this morning?" he asked.

I helped myself to a bit of maple syrup. "An investor meeting, actually two."

His eyes narrowed. "Keeping your options open, eh?"

"You only gave us ten of the twenty we were looking for. I need to keep working on the other half until it's in the bank." I cut into my French toast and forked a piece into my mouth. It was delicious.

He took a sip of his green smoothie.

I was making him eat better, and kale smoothies in the morning were part of that.

"Not confident in your ability? Or in my fairness?" he asked.

I couldn't tell if he was truly hurt or merely curious. "I couldn't live with myself if I didn't cover all the bases and have a backup plan. Would you do any less?"

He considered his answer for a moment. "No, probably not. Who is today's prospect?"

I contemplated whether it was proper to tell him who the competition was. Although, they weren't actually competition. He'd put his money in and was a shareholder in our company now. He would also benefit if we brought in more capital.

"Two, actually," I told him. "Winterbourne Group in the morning and Lighthouse Funding in the afternoon."

"First meeting or third for Winterbourne?" he asked, spearing a strawberry with his fork.

I finished chewing. "First. Why?"

"Just judging how much time we have together," he said sipping more smoothie. "They'll cancel this meeting, so we have plenty of time."

I didn't understand the comment and let it slide.

We finished our breakfast, with him filling me in on more of his family's history. We were slowly learning about each other.

He pointed to the bridge of his nose. "You see this?" It was the almost imperceptible flaw that had made his face seem so attractive that first night. "I got my nose broken defending my sister's honor back in high school."

I laughed. "Defending her honor? What does that mean? Did somebody call her a bad name?"

"No. Nothing like that. She was hanging out with this bad sort; his name was Nick. I came around the corner and he had his hand up her shirt. I just lost it. That was my baby sister he was getting handsy with."

"And?"

"And he was a better fighter than me. I ended up on the ground with blood pouring out of my nose and my sister screaming at me. Pretty humiliating actually, but I got even. I got him kicked out of school the next day."

"Ever the gentleman, I see, protecting your little sister."

He smiled. "Yeah, after that I took self-defense training a lot more seriously, I can tell you that."

He cleared the table.

I checked the guest bedroom.

He had made the bed again for me. A man who didn't mind helping with the dishes, made beds, and gave out compliments like Halloween candy——how much more perfect could he be?

"I'll meet you out front," he told me as he left to get the car.

My phone dinged with an incoming text as I reached the street.

SAM: Morning meeting off – they just texted

Containing my amusement to a smile, I slid into the passenger seat and showed Liam the phone after his doorman closed the door for me.

He read the screen and chuckled. "I told you. It's just their style. They'll cancel the first two meetings."

"But why?" I asked.

He pulled into traffic with a quick blip of the throttle. Having Liam drive me to work every day in this car was a treat. Going back to riding the Red Line in was going to be an adjustment when this ended.

"It's a power play on their part." Liam was clearly not a fan. "I've dealt with them before, and I've learned to check my wallet after every meeting."

I laughed. "They can't be that bad."

"They're worse. Those guys are snakes in suits. It's as close as you'll ever get to meeting two-legged reptiles."

I'd been warned, and it was worth paying attention to the warning if it came from Liam. I hadn't heard a mean comment out of him about anybody until this. "I'll be careful."

Another text arrived.

SAM: Meeting rescheduled to after lunch

"I guess you were wrong," I told Liam. "The meeting's not canceled; they moved it to the afternoon. They're not playing the games you thought."

He sucked in a loud breath, and his brow creased. "Lighthouse is your only choice. Winterbourne can't be trusted." He accelerated as the light turned green.

~

LIAM

ONCE I DROPPED AMY OFF, THOUGHTS OF WINTERBOURNE GOT MY blood boiling. I didn't have her as a distraction anymore, so I stewed about her meeting with them instead. Somehow they were in on every deal I even approached. And for the last two quarters, Damien Winterbourne had totally screwed up my life.

Once in the elevator up to my office, I forced myself to focus on other things by texting my Uncle Garth.

ME: Any progress?

My uncle was being unusually non-communicative.

I exited the elevator, and Veronica nodded toward my office as I approached.

"He's only been waiting for ten minutes," she whispered. "If he tells you anything else, don't believe him."

I found Josh inside as I entered. He turned, making an exaggerated show of checking his watch. "You're late."

I double checked my watch. "Bullshit. I'm ten minutes early."

"To the office maybe. But you missed our court time."

Shit.

I sighed. "I'm sorry, Josh. I fucked up."

We'd scheduled a squash court for this morning, and it had completely slipped my mind.

He got out of his chair. "You fucked something this morning, all right, and I'll bet it was that pretty little brunette you got yourself shacked up with."

"It's not that," I told him. "I just forgot. Sorry."

"Yeah, right," he said with obvious disbelief. He made his way toward the door. "You were probably afraid I'd whip your ass."

I grabbed my little red squeeze ball and threw it at him. "That'll be the day."

He caught the ball and threw it back harder, but his aim sucked. The ball bounced off the window behind me.

"I can see this girl has you all fucked up," he said.

"Blow me," I said.

He'd already left.

I didn't need to agree with him, but he was only half wrong. Amy did have me off balance. I hadn't had a woman in my penthouse, or my life for that matter, since Roberta passed. It hadn't seemed right.

I rubbed my ring finger absentmindedly.

Somehow Amy had changed that. She had eased her way into my world, and it all seemed so natural.

Veronica ventured in now that Josh had gone. She generally avoided my office when Josh was visiting. I couldn't put my finger on it, but for some reason she didn't care for him, and I hadn't challenged her on it.

"Mr. Schmulian requested you call him when you got in."

Now we were getting somewhere. "Thanks. I'll call him right away."

He could've texted me directly and asked me to call him, but Hue was old school. He'd told me he preferred the old-fashioned way of talking to people like Veronica. There were times I agreed with him.

I reached his voicemail and left a message.

I turned to face the window. Two racing shells were competing in the distance on the Charles, each trying to out-row the other, both teams trying to reach the finish line first. The epitome of competition, but the equally matched boats were almost dead even. What determined the winner was ninety percent raw effort, but ten percent strategy.

In our competition, Winterbourne was doing something I wasn't. I just couldn't figure out what.

CHAPTER 19

AMY

IT HAD BEEN TWO DAYS SINCE THE DUAL MEETINGS WITH
Lighthouse and Winterbourne. Lighthouse had been a bust, but I'd
just finished an unexpected third meeting with Winterbourne.

Samantha strode into my office without so much as a knock.
"When were you going to tell me about this new money?"

I'd only gotten out of the meeting five minutes ago. "I was just
on my way to tell you. I didn't want to get your hopes up unneces-
sarily. Hell, the lawyers only sent one person over."

"I'm listening," she said as she took a seat.

"I met with them Monday afternoon, and the lawyer showed up
yesterday. Today they told me they'll have papers ready
tomorrow."

"And it's eleven million?" she asked.

That figure had only come up in the meeting I'd just returned
from. Obviously Grace had gone straight to Samantha and told her
the good news, stealing my thunder.

"Like I said, I was just coming to see you. Yup. That's the

deal." I tried to keep myself from giggling as I said it. It had turned out so well.

"Are they for real?" Samantha asked.

"I had my doubts until today." I pulled a piece of paper out of my folder and handed it to her. "The money arrived in escrow yesterday, so it's just waiting on paperwork with us tomorrow."

Samantha read the paper carefully, her eyes bulging as she did. "Holy shit, you did it, girl." She ran around the desk to hug me.

We released each other. "We did it," I told her. "Remember, it's all about your recipes." That was certainly the truth. Without Samantha's knack in the kitchen, the whole company would still be just a dream.

"There is a small hitch," I told her. "They want two seats on the board."

Samantha face turned sour. "Is that wise?"

"I fought it, but given their position, I don't see we have a choice. And, we don't have any other alternatives right now either."

Samantha relaxed. "You know what this means, right?"

"It means I can relax for a change," I responded.

With a smirk, Samantha pointed at me. "It also means you can quit that prostitution gig."

"It's not like that, and you know it." I rolled my eyes.

She floated to the door. "Anything you say, but we really need you back here full time, Amy."

Samantha's jab laid bare my choice. Now I had to face my situation with Liam and make a decision. Her quip about full time had only been partly a joke. Since moving to Liam's, I hadn't spent any of my normal evening hours at work. I'd tried to make up for it with some laptop time at the penthouse, but it wasn't the same. Clearly Samantha felt short-changed.

I turned to face the window and stared out.

So far my time with Liam had shown me how similar life was for the uber-wealthy, and yet how different. After a few days, I'd asked him if he needed anything washed. Naturally, he had a washer and dryer in the penthouse, but unlike the rest of us, he didn't use them. His cleaning lady gathered up his dirty clothes twice a week and sent them out to the cleaners. She used his laundry room to wash towels and sheets for him. It was almost like living in a hotel, with a maid service that came in twice a week to clean and change the linens.

We would pocket a million more with this deal than through Liam. But the more I thought about the prospect of walking away from him, the less I liked it.

Taking breakfast on his patio every morning with a view of the city had been a treat, not to mention the nighttime lights, and the five-million thread count or whatever sheets. Everything about his place was platinum-plated luxury.

I didn't want to go back to squeezing onto the Red Line trains again in the morning, sandwiched between smelly commuters. I would miss arriving at work in his million-horsepower James Bond magic carpet.

My duty seemed clear enough. I'd promised to give him my best effort. I had learned that, to him, promises were sacrosanct. Would I be able to forgive myself if I let him down now? We hadn't even had our second dinner with the Schmulians yet. It wasn't asking much to be his fake girlfriend for a few dinners. And living at his condo offered an interesting glimpse at how the one percent lived——the one percent of the one percent would actually be more accurate.

The buzz of my phone vibrating on the desk forced me back to reality, and I swung my chair around to get it. The screen lit up with a message.

LIAM: How is your day?

It was decision time. Did I tell him about the money now or over dinner and champagne?

ME: Same old same old

I had committed to his project. He deserved my best, and that's what he was going to get. I was all-in now——not because it was the least-objectionable choice, not because he'd forced me, but because it was the right thing to do, the honorable thing. Liam had taught me the value of courtesy and honor. I couldn't replicate adherence to his code of conduct, but I could certainly learn from it.

It had nothing to do with his hotness, or how he made me feel with every overly kind word.

No, not at all.

The money news could wait until he got home and we could celebrate together.

Home. That has a nice ring to it.

*L*IAM

I had just finished my four o'clock meeting with Martin when my phone rang. It was Hue Schmulian getting back to me.

"Liam, I hope I'm not calling too late, but Felicia and I were wondering if you and Amy were free for dinner again tonight."

"Not at all," I assured him. "We'd love to. Why don't you come by our place this evening? I bet you'll enjoy Amy's cooking as much as I do."

"No doubt. That sounds wonderful. What time works for you? We don't want to impose."

We set the time as seven, and I gave him the address.

I dialed Amy.

She picked up quickly. "Hey, handsome." The mere sound of her voice put a smile on my face.

"Schmulian just called, and we're on for dinner again tonight at seven. I hope you don't mind, but I committed you to cook for us."

"Sure. Part of the service. I'll head out now, and I'll text you a list of things to get at the market on your way," she replied.

"Works for me. See you soon," I told her, without adding the part I was thinking——that I couldn't wait to see her again.

We make a good team.

~

AMY

TEARS CLOUDED MY EYES. TWO STEPS TO MY RIGHT I LOCATED A tissue. After a few dabs, I blinked and could see again.

The sound of a key in the door startled me. I wasn't ready.

I went back to chopping the onions.

"The market was a zoo," Liam said putting down the grocery bags.

I put down the knife. "Usually is after work." I couldn't resist the impulse to hug him.

He squeezed me back tightly. "And why do I deserve this treatment?"

I held him close, not wanting to give up the warmth of his chest against mine. "Just because."

"Okay," he said stroking my back.

I reluctantly released him. "I have good news, and better news. Which do you want to hear first?"

He opened the fridge. "Let's start with the good news, then move on to the really good stuff." He pulled a bottle of champagne out and started removing the foil wrapper.

My enthusiasm bubbled over. "We're going to land another investor," I squeaked. "Eleven million. Can you believe it?"

His brow creased. "Another investor? That's nice." His tone didn't convey the happiness the news deserved. He stopped working on the champagne bottle. "Who?"

"And the better news," I continued, hoping he would like what I had to say. "Is that with this much, you won't have to put in your other ten if you don't want to."

Naturally he would see the upside to this; he'd been reluctant to invest in us without having control, and now he could minimize the investment since it didn't fit his agenda.

His eyes bore down on me. "Who?" he demanded coldly.

I cut another slice off the onion. "The Winterbourne Group."

The last semblance of a smile washed off his face. The champagne bottle made a loud clank as he put it down on the island's granite. "No."

His reaction caught me off guard. "What do you mean *no?*"

He glowered at me. "I won't allow it. Not them. Anybody but them." A dangerous undercurrent shrouded his voice. His demeanor was as frosty as his words.

A shiver ran through me. "You can't tell us that." I hadn't seen this side of the man before. It was scary. "It…it's our company. If you're jealous of them, just get over it." I stomped my foot. I, too, could be mad. "You don't get a say."

"Check your paperwork," he said. "I have to approve any other investors."

He approached and grabbed my arm. "Anybody else and I would let you, but not them. They're dangerous."

I pulled away. "That's not fair." My legs trembled. "That's it? No discussion?"

"We just had the discussion."

This can't be happening. I backed away. "How silly of me to think you'd be happy for me," I yelled.

He moved forward.

I backed farther away, still with the knife in my hand. Bile rose in my throat. "I hate you." I threw the knife on the counter and ran for the door. "I hate you." I screamed back at him.

"Amy, let me explain," he called after me.

I slammed the door on my way out, trying unsuccessfully to control the tears, which were no longer caused by the onion.

How could I be so stupid?

He saw everything as a competition between himself and Winterbourne. Tiffany's was just a pawn in his overall game.

∿

LIAM

MY STOMACH HAD TURNED THE MOMENT SHE MENTIONED THE Winterbourne Group. I'd tried to warn her, but she hadn't listened.

The door slammed, and she was gone.

I was so fucked.

She had no idea who she was dealing with. Getting in bed with Damien Winterbourne was suicidal.

It was the one thing I couldn't allow her to do. I had to protect her from him.

But I had another pressing problem. I dialed Hue Schmulian. "Hue, I'm afraid we're not going to be able to do dinner tonight," I told him as he got on the line.

"*Just a moment. Let me check with Felicia,*" he said before I could stop him. When he returned he said, "*Felicia says tomorrow night works as well.*"

"I'm not so sure that'll work either," I said cautiously.

"*Is there some problem?*"

"Amy can't make it," I admitted.

He paused. "*Stop me if I'm overstepping my bounds here, Liam. But if you're having some issue with Amy, that needs to take priority over having dinner with us.*"

He had guessed the issue without me having to say anything, but he didn't understand the severity of the problem.

"Thanks, Hue. Let me get back to you when I can."

"*Just one more piece of unsolicited advice, young man. That woman of yours is quite special.*"

He didn't know the half of it. *Special* barely began to describe Amy. "That she is."

He finished the call by telling me I should take whatever time I needed. I appreciated his thoughtfulness.

Now I had to question whether my Winterbourne paranoia

might be getting the better of me. It was a good thing we still had the Sanders footwear deal running, or we might lose control of the company by the end of the quarter——and somehow I still needed to close the Springbok deal. Wouldn't that be a way to royally fuck things up?

I poured myself a glass of scotch. It didn't last long.

How could this have gotten fucked up so quickly?

What choice did I have? Let Amy get caught in Winterbourne's spider web and be devoured like all the others?

I poured myself another scotch and downed half the glass immediately.

There was no way I could live with myself if I allowed Amy to get tied up with Winterbourne to save my Springbok deal. Sure, it would keep her company afloat for now, but Winterbourne would take over in the end, and their dreams would be shattered. That was the way he did business. Why hadn't I warned her more clearly? There needed to be a better word in the dictionary than *ruthless* to describe a man like him.

I should try to reason with her, explain to her who Damien Winterbourne was, how he operated, and how things would end up for her. That tack made the most sense, although tonight was certainly not the time to talk to her about it.

As she'd left, she'd made her feelings about it——and about me ——clear enough. My gut tightened. I'd brought this on myself by not discussing him with her in more detail, by not warning her how ruthless he was. I'd thought she and Samantha would be able to see The Winterbourne Group for what they were. I'd been wrong. I slammed my hand down on the granite in frustration.

I really fucked this up.

Her bitterness was the hardest thing to bear. It was the first time in a long time I'd cared about anybody else's opinion of me. In this business I needed to have a thick skin and be immune to other's reactions to me. Somehow Amy had pierced my shield. Her opinion shouldn't matter——her company was merely another investment——but it did. The hurt was real, and the scotch wasn't making it go away. I took another swig, emptying the glass.

Still, surely I could fix this. Amy was a smart girl and there had to be a way for me to get her to understand the truth about Winterbourne.

After another glass, the room looked hazier, but my options just as bad. I found myself fingering dad's coin. I flipped open my laptop and composed an email to the bank.

The bottle of scotch drew me, and I poured another glass.

CHAPTER 20

AMY

I'D CRIED MYSELF TO SLEEP LAST NIGHT. MY APARTMENT HAD seemed so foreign when I got back to Somerville, and I'd gulped down most of a bottle of wine before I knew it. It was all I had available to quell the hurt. Liam hadn't ever cared about me; he only wanted to control me, control our company. I should have known better.

I'd double checked our paperwork on Liam's investment. He'd been right——the clause requiring his permission for any other investors in the next six months was on the second page. It wasn't unusual, and I hadn't thought it significant at the time. The wording was straightforward, and we didn't have any way around it.

This morning I was wearing jeans and a T-shirt and sandwiched between two guys on the Red Line headed to work. All my work clothes were at Liam's. I'd have to make time later to retrieve them.

I knew I needed to call my sister, but how to explain what had happened eluded me. Vivienne thought Liam was damned James

Bond incarnate. She wouldn't understand how demeaning it had been for him to tell me I couldn't do what was right for our company, what was right for our team and their families.

I wished I'd never met him that night at the bar. He had seemed so nice, but last night he'd showed his true colors. He had put the clause in the contract that gave him veto power over other investors, and he'd intentionally given us only half the money we needed, so we'd be at his mercy when it ran out. He'd been two steps ahead of me the whole time.

I'd been gullible, swayed by those eyes, that smile, and his smooth talk. I was such an idiot.

I reached the office a little later than normal and headed straight for Samantha's office.

Lucy at the front desk wasn't the only one to give me a sideways glance. I never wore jeans to work, not even on Fridays. Getting my clothes out of Liam's place was moving up my priority list.

"We have to talk," I told Samantha as I closed the door.

"Not until we get some coffee in you," she said, giggling. "You look like shit, and this isn't Saturday," She eyed my sloppy attire.

I could always count on Samantha to be brutally honest, but I didn't need it today.

I sat down. "We have a problem."

Samantha leaned forward, waiting for me to continue. "I fucked up, and we can't take the Winterbourne money."

Shock wrote itself across her face. "I don't understand. Yesterday you told me it was a go."

"That was yesterday," I said. I wasn't sure how to explain how stupid I'd been. "I missed that we had to run any future investors by Quigley. I checked——it was on the papers we signed, it just didn't sink in at the time."

"And?" Samantha asked. "This is a problem because?"

I slumped down in my seat. "It's my fault. He won't approve Winterbourne, not ever."

"Why not?"

"I didn't realize how bad things are between them. It's like a blood feud, a Hatfield and McCoy thing. I can't get him to agree."

Samantha cocked her head. "Even with your relationship with him?"

What relationship?

I'd only ever been the fake girlfriend. Samantha obviously thought it had gone further.

I stood. "There is no relationship, and after last night there never will be." I took a deep breath. "I don't think we're likely to get the second ten million from him now either."

Samantha's eyebrows shot up. She was nice enough not to ask for details. "What do we tell the troops now? You know the grapevine in this place. Everybody knew about the money by the end of the day. Lucy in reception even asked me about it. Maybe we can keep the update on Quigley's money under wraps until we know for sure?"

I felt faint. I'd let the team down. "I guess... I don't know what to do yet," I told her. I had no fucking idea. I retreated to my office to figure out what to do next.

After an hour of avoiding it, I dialed Vivienne to tell her what had happened.

"*You what?*" my sister yelled through the phone after I got to the part where I'd walked out. Her reaction was an order of magnitude worse than I'd expected.

"But don't you see what he was trying to do?" I spat back at her. "He's using *my* company, *my* hard work, my *employees'* lives to get ahead in his own game. He won't let us do what's right for Tiffany's."

"*You may be older than me, Amy, but you sure as shit are not smarter,*" Vivienne said angrily.

It was too insulting to let it go by. "And what makes you so smart?"

"*I have eyeballs and brains in my head. That guy knows the business of investing. He's in the business of investing, and you have him wrapped around your little finger, so why don't you trust what he tells you? He's trying to help——"*

I interrupted her. "I what?"

"I saw how he looked at you when I was over for dinner the other night. That man is head over heels for you, big sister, and if you can't see it, you're fucking blind. I'm glad you kept Hudson as your last name. I don't want anybody knowing I'm related to someone so dumb."

That hurt. "You don't understand what he did, and you're being mean."

"You just explained what he did, and I'm only being mean because you're not listening. You're not even thinking. You need a brain transplant if you think he's trying to screw you over. It's clear as day the man would do anything for you."

She didn't get it. "No, all that was just him pretending to be a gentleman or some fucking thing."

"So it's you and your compliment hang-up again, is it?" she asked.

"So now this is my fault?"

"Sure as shit is," she hissed. *"He says something nice to you, and you go ballistic and miss how he's saying that shit with his tongue hanging out he's so into you. You're getting good advice ——for free——but you're too hung up on yourself to even consider it."* Vivienne laughed into the phone. *"There's only one thing for you to do now."*

"And what's that?" I asked.

"He's the best thing that ever happened to you, so you get your sorry ass back over there and eat crow, or suck dick, or whatever you have to do to get back to being his girlfriend. Then listen to what he has to say. Otherwise you don't deserve him. And if you're not smart enough to see it, I'm heading over there to volunteer for the job."

"You're welcome to him," I shot back. "I'm sorry I called." I hung up.

So much for sisterly love and sound advice.

I took my purse and walked out the front door, turning left toward Starbucks. A short walk often cleared my head and helped me solve a knotty problem. Thirty minutes later, I'd made several laps around the block, downed a grande mocha extra shot, and was no closer to unraveling my troubles.

The text that arrived was short and sweet.

LIAM: You are released from your consulting

Great. Now it was officially over.

Reentering the building, I walked past Sonya, a single mother with two kids, and I knew the family situations of the next three people I saw as well. Every employee I passed added to my guilt. I'd let them all down. We couldn't take the Winterbourne money, and I'd personally screwed up our chance to get the second half of Liam's money. It was exactly as bad as I'd thought it was.

Back at my desk, I closed the door and plopped my ass back in my chair. I had no fucking idea what to do.

No fucking idea.

～

LIAM

STUMBLING OUT OF BED, I HEADED FOR THE COFFEE MACHINE. THE clock on the oven said eleven o'clock.

I loaded a pod and started the machine.

It had taken forever to fall asleep last night. At four in the morning, I had finally given in and taken one of the sleeping pills I'd relied on after losing Roberta. That did the trick.

I put an ice cube into the coffee cup. In a few seconds this would cool it enough for me to chug and start a second.

My phone powered up with missed calls from Josh and Veronica, no doubt wondering why I wasn't in yet. I didn't bother to listen; instead I punched out a text to Veronica saying I'd be in after lunch.

Then I composed the harder one; the one to Amy.

ME: You are released from your consulting

I washed down two Advil from the cupboard with the last of my coffee. It was a bright, sunny day outside, opposite my disposition. I prepared a second cup of coffee and took it out on the patio.

Yesterday's sports section was still open on the table. The top story was some idiot sportswriter wanting to rehash the Patriots *spygate* scandal from a few years ago, as if it was the ultimate unfairness. Our team had been caught spying on another in 2007, learning their defensive signals for a competitive advantage. It was clearly illegal, but Boston, being such a sports-crazy town, was full of people who didn't believe it really happened, like this jerk in the paper. It'd been over a decade ago, and he still couldn't let it go. The idiot probably thought the moon landings were faked as well.

The gears in my head turned slowly this morning. It took me several minutes to realize the parallel. I slowly sipped my coffee and mulled the possibility.

What if Team Winterbourne was spying on us? It could explain everything. I'd personally fucked up our Springbok chances by fighting with Amy, but each of our other failures in the last six months could be explained if Winterbourne was bugging us.

At first I'd thought we were just operating in a crowded space and losing the deals by cautiously underbidding. But losing every one to Winterbourne didn't stack up with that hypothesis. The odds were too great.

That little redhead who followed me around was probably part of it. It could be more elaborate corporate espionage. They might have put a tracker on my car.

Shit.

Our phones could be bugged. It had happened to a firm in New York almost a decade ago, and that kind of surveillance had only

become easier since then with miniature cameras and microphones
——all the new techno-wizardry.

A half-year ago, we'd been out of our offices for a week around
the holidays, having new carpeting installed. It would've been the
perfect opportunity for them to install bugs in our building, and the
timeline matched up as well. That was right when things had
started to go south.

I need an expert for this.

~

AMY

THE PROBLEM WAS INTRACTABLE. I'D LOOKED AT IT ELEVEN
different ways, and nothing worked. We couldn't take the Winterbourne money——Liam would sue us and win. Lighthouse wasn't
interested, and we'd exhausted our list of other potential investors.
Woolsey at the bank was no help.

Tiffany's would run out of money before long if we didn't cut
back our orders for raw materials, but that would cripple our
growth. And the halted growth would doom our chances to raise
additional capital with any reasonable terms.

A little before lunch, the knock came on my door. I wished I
could hide for the rest of the day, but I wasn't going to be so lucky.

"Come in," I said reluctantly.

Grace bounded into my office. "You won't believe the call I
just got from the bank," she said, her eyes twinkling. Grace was
easily excited, so it didn't mean much.

I wasn't up for games this morning. "What?"

She waited for me to guess, but gave up after a short pause.
"The money arrived at the bank."

"Come again? We were supposed to sign the papers at the
escrow office later today, right?"

It didn't make sense that they would send the money before

we'd signed, and now we *couldn't* legally sign without Liam's approval, which clearly wasn't coming. So we couldn't accept the money.

Grace giggled. "The other half of the *Quigley* money came in." She bounced off to give the good news to Samantha.

I slumped in my chair. The world was upside down.

It took me a minute to process. Liam had sent the money *and* released me from my consulting obligation. He did care about me. Vivienne had been right, and I'd been too pig-headed to see it.

My heart raced as I dialed. Liam's cell phone went straight to voicemail. I dialed the other number I knew by heart. His assistant, Veronica, answered.

"Sorry, Ms. Hudson, I haven't seen Mr. Quigley yet this morning."

I'd tried to get her to call me Amy, but it hadn't worked. Liam swore she was efficient, but to me she just seemed cold. The lady could use some counseling to lighten up a little.

We ended the call after she either wouldn't tell me where he was or honestly didn't know. I couldn't tell which.

Everything was so screwed up with Liam and me and the company. I couldn't just sit in this office. This was an untenable situation.

I marched to Samantha's office. I needed to leave. I couldn't stay another minute.

CHAPTER 21

LIAM

AN ELECTRONIC BUG EXTERMINATOR, THAT'S WHAT I NEEDED. I wandered back in from the patio. After starting another cup of coffee, I headed to the master bath and turned on the shower. Feeling sorry for myself wouldn't fix the situation I'd put myself and Josh in, and I definitely needed some help.

Vincent Benson had taken over for me running Covington East, and he would be my first call. He probably knew someone who could sweep for bugs.

Finally I had something concrete to do.

The water was warm and soothing as it flowed over my head and drowned out both sound and thought. I needed to clear my mind before I got in to work. And I did need to show up there today.

The bug sweep of our offices would need to be top of my list. I realized I couldn't make the call from our offices, or my phone. It would risk alerting the other side. I didn't know where any payphones were off the top of my head... Maybe I could borrow our doorman's phone for a few minutes; that should be safe enough.

I got the faintest whiff of cherry and turned to see Amy leaning against the bathroom counter, watching me through the steamed glass. I covered up. "A little privacy, please."

She didn't budge. She came forward and lifted the coffee cup she was holding over the glass. "I brought you Starbucks."

I took the coffee with one hand, covering myself with the other. "Thanks. You didn't need to."

"I know, but I wanted to."

Her words warmed me more than they should have.

"I need your help getting a job," she said matter-of-factly.

I'd never meant to hurt her, or cause her a problem at her business——and I certainly hadn't meant for her to lose her job. I thought I'd prevented any trouble by sending along the remainder of the money I'd promised her.

I set the coffee on the ledge. "Look, I didn't mean——"

"Just hear me out," she said, interrupting me. "I quit my job. I wasn't quite cut out for it." She looked down at the floor. "The situation became untenable. It wasn't right for me."

Her words destroyed me.

∾

AMY

"I WANT A BETTER JOB," I EXPLAINED, LEANING AGAINST THE counter.

"What was wrong with the one you had?" Liam asked, still covering himself with his hands.

I moved toward the shower. "Not enough responsibility."

"What kind of better job are you looking for?"

I pulled open the shower door and entered. The water quickly soaked my T-shirt. "Girlfriend," I said, placing a hand on his muscled chest.

"Didn't you walk out on that job?" he asked, removing my hand.

I closed my eyes against the spray of the water. "I want the *real* position, the one with all the benefits and none of the boundaries."

"Blow me," he responded.

I sunk to my knees and took him instantly in my mouth. Vivienne had told me it might come to this.

He reached down and hauled me up with a jerk. "That was just a figure of speech, Amy."

I kept my hand on his growing cock. I wasn't going to let go without a fight.

His face softened, and his arms encircled me. "I couldn't bear that I hurt you last night," he said into my ear, squeezing me tightly.

"I'm sorry, too. What I said was mean," I replied. The water was the only thing keeping me from combusting in his arms.

He pulled at my T-shirt and wrestled the wet cotton over my head as I raised my arms. "I told you, no need to apologize, lovely lady."

I pushed at his chest. "If I have to listen to your cheesy compliments, you have to listen to my apologies."

He reached around me and unclasped my bra. "We'll have enough time for talking later. He pulled my bra off and flung it and my shirt over the glass. He palmed my breasts, kneading them lightly. "Has anyone told you you have the most marvelous breasts?"

Lucky for me, my blush was less obvious under the hot water. "Is this a yes?" I pulled on his fully erect cock.

"It's part of the interview process."

I wanted——no *needed*——to pass this interview, so my next step was to go back to my knees and return him to my mouth. I closed my eyes against the water cascading from above and sucked in unison with the movements of both my hands——the way Vivienne had shown me on a banana. She had a lot more experience than I did at these things. Matt had said he liked my technique, but his cheating said otherwise.

I needed this. I needed Liam to want me around more than I could explain. Being around him——even just eating meals with him——had filled a void in my life I hadn't realized was there until I'd left last night.

The moans emanating from my would-be boyfriend guided me as I pulled and twisted, taking him in and out and circling the crown with my tongue.

He backed up and braced himself against the wall. He tried to pull me up again, but I resisted.

"It's been too long. I'm not going to last if you keep that up," he said.

I hadn't brought a condom, so this was the only thing I could do in here. I hadn't ever gone so far as to swallow before. I hoped I didn't screw it up. "Hand me the soap," I said, urging him to slide over so his back shielded me from the water.

I took the bar and lathered him up, making his cock super slippery. I wrapped my thumb and forefinger tightly around the base and slid up all the way over the crown and down again, repeating it with two fingers and then again with one, over and over, adding more soap to keep him slippery.

He groaned every time my fingers slid over the tip, off, and back on again. After a while, his legs started to tremble and his moans increased. He was getting close, so I urged him to turn and rinse off.

I went back to my mouth action on him, looking up at his eyes as I did——another tip from Viv.

The words started cascading out of his mouth with every pull as his breath hitched.

"I can't take it."

"Oh shit."

"My God."

"Fuck."

He stiffened, and I got a spurt, followed by another, and another.

I managed to swallow, pull up on his cock, and suck a few more drops onto my tongue. I opened my mouth and showed him his cum on my tongue, which I swallowed before licking my lips.

His O-face blossomed into a gigantic smile.

Vivienne had been right; licking my lips to show I liked it was the icing on the cake for him.

I mentally reminded myself to thank her for her tips as I stood, my knees sore from the marble floor.

Liam took me into his arms and whispered into my ear. "Your turn, Sunshine."

He made quick work of unbuttoning my jeans, but getting fully out of wet skinny jeans wasn't so easy. I sat on the ledge as he worked them off, and my shoes and panties as well. They all ended up a sloppy, wet pile on the floor as he flung them over the glass.

I stood and shivered with anticipation.

"Put your foot here." He lifted my leg to rest my foot up on the ledge. "Now close your eyes."

I didn't close them fast enough.

"Close your eyes," he repeated in that commanding tone of his.

I could no longer see him, but I sensed the return of the lion. He was back in king-of-the-jungle mode. The tip of his cock brushed my inner thigh. "Protection," I mumbled.

He placed a hand on my shoulder as his other hand palmed a breast. "Do you trust your boyfriend or not?" he asked softly.

I nodded.

"I want to hear it."

"I trust my boyfriend." I giggled.

I was apprehensive, but a proper girlfriend would trust him. I let out a gasp as a soapy finger traced my folds and slid the length of me back and forth slowly, tantalizingly. Goosebumps grew as he brought more slippery soap to the party and continued to slip up to and around my clit and down to my opening, darting a finger in and out and repeating the trip back to my clit, where he circled some more.

I kept my eyes closed and reached instinctively for his cock. He was hard again, or still hard.

He pulled my hand away. "No. This is your turn." He put my hands up on his shoulders, where at least I could touch him, even if I couldn't hold him the way I wanted to.

He leaned over to kiss my breast, sucking and nibbling my nipples while his fingers kept up the assault on my clit.

A fire built within me. If we weren't in the shower, my juices would've been dribbling between my thighs now. My legs trembled as every circle and stab at my clit sent jolts through me. I shifted my foot and arched my hips into his hand, aching for more pressure, and more…more of everything.

He pulled away, an unspoken command to stay still. He was in charge, and I was to obey, or else.

I relented and shifted back.

His hand returned with more slippery soap, this time to my breasts as he gave me a two-handed boob massage. This was great, but I ached for more action down south.

"Just making sure you get clean," he told me.

I laughed. "I think they're clean…" A spark raced through me and cut off my voice as the tip of his cock found my clit.

He used his hand to work the tip over me, circling and pressing on my little nub, while another finger found its way inside me, teasing my entrance. The cock was replaced by soapy fingers as he rubbed me harder, giving me the pressure I needed on my swollen bud. My God, did this man have my number.

The tension built in my muscles, and I had trouble controlling my breathing as each stroke of his fingers pushed me closer to the edge.

With a surprise pinch of my nipple and hard rubbing of my clit, my blood boiled over and the spasms overtook me. All my nerve endings fired at once, and I fell over the cliff into a pool of bliss.

As my body dissolved into mush, my man grabbed me and held

me up, cradling me in his arms. Like a good girl, I'd managed to keep my eyes closed the entire time, and he'd saved me from having to explain to an ER nurse how I'd managed to hit my head in a shower the size of an average bedroom.

As I regained my footing and my strength, I opened my eyes and took in the magnificence of his body: the breadth of the shoulders I could now lean on when I needed support, my boyfriend's shoulders. Vivienne had been right; he'd been looking out for me all along. Now I knew I could depend on him for whatever I needed.

He'd invested in Tiffany's without any strings.

I'd totally misjudged the situation.

He rotated us in the warm water and rinsed us off, still cradling me in his strong arms.

He turned off the water and led me out.

We toweled each other off.

I had the fun of drying his still-stiff cock and balls while he attended to my chest. My boobs had never been rubbed so dry.

I yelped as he picked me up.

He carried me to the bed and set me down like I was a fragile doll, with the care of a true boyfriend.

"The job is yours, if you still want it," he said.

"I'll tell you after we finish *your* interview."

He pulled a condom out of the nightstand. We slipped under the covers and interviewed each other again before getting dressed for a late lunch on the patio.

He insisted on ordering a pizza, so I made a salad to go with it.

He got his pizza, and I got the job I hadn't been smart enough to realize I wanted——and needed.

After lunch we went to our respective offices.

I couldn't wait to get home this evening.

LIAM

. . .

A HINT OF SUNRISE FILTERED THROUGH THE SHADES AS I SLID OUT of bed quietly, so as not to wake Amy. I grabbed a bathrobe before closing the door behind me.

She appeared as I was finishing the second batch of pancakes. "You left me," she complained.

The sight of her braless in that short T-shirt woke my cock. "Just wanted to surprise you with breakfast this morning." I adjusted my bathrobe to keep it from showing.

I offered her one of the kale smoothies I had made. They tasted like shit, but if she wanted it, I could make the sacrifice.

She jiggled her way over to me, her nipples bouncing seductively behind the thin fabric. "That's so thoughtful of you," she said, running a finger from my throat down to the middle of my bare chest in the opening of my bathrobe. She was provoking me intentionally for sure. She accepted the glass with a wicked grin.

I averted my eyes and turned around to flip the pancakes, but the damage had been done. My cock was now tenting the bathrobe in front of me.

"You can set the table," I told her over my shoulder, trying to will my arousal down. I finished the cakes in the pan and stacked them on the plate with the others.

When I turned around, she was bent over, checking the drawers in the island. Her T-shirt had ridden up, showing me she was panty-less and making my cock even harder.

"I can't find the silverware anywhere," she complained innocently.

There was nothing innocent about her this morning. She'd been here long enough to know exactly where the silverware was. She was trying to taunt me, and quite successfully.

I spanked her ass as I walked by, eliciting a delicious little squeal. "If you keep tempting me like that, naughty girl, you're gonna get exactly what you're asking for." I set the food on the table.

She grinned at me from the other side of the island. "And what is it I'm asking for?"

"If you don't cover up a bit, I will not be held responsible for what happens to you."

She turned and went to the actual silverware drawer, returning with knives and forks for each of us. "And what might that be?" she asked, sitting down and shooting me a sly smirk.

She was going to be the death of me. "I don't have time this morning. I have a conference call in just a bit. I'll take you in to work when it's over, if that's okay." I poured syrup on my pancakes.

She fixed a pout on her face. "You're no fun."

I took a moment to finish chewing. "Tempt me again, young lady, and I'll bend you over this table and fuck you so hard you can't walk straight."

She smiled. "Promises, promises."

I took a sip of my smoothie and followed the wretched green gunk with some orange juice. "Careful what you wish for, you little hussy. And what's got you so full of spunk this morning, anyway?"

She straightened up. "I want my boyfriend to remember what he's coming home to, so he doesn't stay too late at work."

I nearly choked on my food laughing. "Awfully demanding, aren't we? I'll make sure Veronica pushes me out the door earlier, okay?"

Her smile disappeared. She pushed her food around on her plate with her fork. "What's her story, anyway? I don't think she likes me."

"It's not you. She's just not terribly sociable in her protect-the-boss mode. But she's extremely organized, and that's what I need. I hired her when my previous assistant was hit by a car."

Amy gasped. "That's terrible. Is she okay?"

"Banged up pretty good. She's fine now, but she decided she didn't want to come in to work in the city anymore. So we changed her job so she could work for us from home."

"That's much nicer…" Amy stuffed a piece of pancake in her mouth and didn't finish her sentence. "We should have Josh and his girlfriend over for dinner. What's her name?" she mumbled.

"Brinna," I told her. "You try to get him to bring her to dinner. I've tried twice. I'll bet you a thousand bucks she doesn't exist."

She put her glass down after a sip. "That's not a nice thing to say about your friend."

"Either that or he's ashamed because she's not as beautiful as you."

She threw a blueberry in my direction and missed. "Stop that. You're just trying to make me blush."

It worked; she was turning a warm pink.

"Don't think I didn't catch that you just changed the topic," I said. "What did you mean? Nicer than what?"

She fiddled with her food for a moment. "It's just that those online articles painted your company as such a bad place to work."

I nodded. I'd seen them too. Some woman named Merry Poppins, obviously an alias, had posted three online hit pieces about us recently on various blogs. I couldn't figure out why. Nobody even admitted to knowing her real name.

I put my fork down. "You shouldn't believe a word of it. That blogger has some agenda, and we can't even figure out who she is or what her problem is."

"That's not fair."

"You got that right." I stood, checked my watch, and took a last sip of juice. I didn't finish all of the green smoothie, but I'd put a decent dent in it. "I've got to take this call now… Oh, before I forget, is it okay if I call Schmulian and re-invite them over for dinner?"

"Absutively." She blew me a kiss as I walked to my office and closed the door before dialing Josh.

This morning's call was important, and that made me skittish about our potential bugging situation. I hadn't had a chance to arrange the sweep yet. At least calling from my house line to Josh's house bypassed the office phones. We needed to settle some nervousness on the part of the Sanders family before we could close their transaction and add shoes to our assortment of companies.

Josh picked up right away. *"Liam, I got a text that the call is off, and I can't reach them. This doesn't seem like them. Something is wrong."*

I scrubbed my hands over my face.

"I hope it's not Winterbourne again," he said, putting words to my fear.

CHAPTER 22

(ONE WEEK LATER)

LIAM

THE LAST WEEK WITH AMY HERE AS MY TRUE GIRLFRIEND HAD
been miraculous. I relished waking up beside her more each day.
Saying she made my spirits soar sounded trite, but felt so true. I
hadn't realized what I had been missing by refusing to date.

The second Schmulian dinner had gone quite well. Amy had
cooked a delicious lamb dish I couldn't even pronounce, and the
evening had been enjoyable——a bit like having old friends over.
We were making good progress with them, I thought. With the
Sanders deal getting shaky, Springbok was even more important.

Today Amy had left early to meet her sister for breakfast
before she went to work.

I'd offered to have Vivienne join us here, but Amy wanted to
make it easier on her sister by meeting in Cambridge.

After she'd gone, I poured the green glop in my glass down the
sink and rinsed it clean. Anybody who claimed to truly like a kale
smoothie had to be certifiable. I suspected Amy just forced herself
to drink them because she'd read somewhere that they were good

for her. I laughed to myself, realizing what I needed now was a scientific study proving the opposite.

The coffee machine beeped, indicating my cup was ready, and I carried it and my pancakes out to the patio. My patio was my favorite feature of the penthouse this time of year. There was no better way to start off the morning than breakfast, sunshine, and a good view of the activity on the Charles River.

I'd called Vincent Benson as planned, and he'd provided the name of a company he trusted to do a competent bug sweep.

It had taken a little while to arrange an evening where I was sure nobody would be around so they could complete their work in private. They'd spent most of last night scouring our workspace, and to my inexperienced eye, they'd seemed quite thorough. The results, however, were disappointing. They found no listening devices. They'd also checked my car and the penthouse without finding anything anywhere.

The sun warmed me as I leaned back in my chair with my breakfast in front of me. I reread the summary email on my phone. "No electronic surveillance devices detected at the subject premises listed in appendix one on this date. Additional sweeps recommended monthly. Procedures used included…" The rest was just techno-babble to justify their fee. Maybe it was paranoia on my part, but something still didn't feel right.

The rowers were out again this morning, running their heats up and down the Charles. From this distance they were small and slow, but having seen them up close, I knew they were anything but. Eight rowers could whisk one of those shells at an incredible speed. They were faster than anyone but an Olympic sprinter.

I had tried rowing once in college, but got bounced by the coach after showing up late to practice twice. The sport required daily, early-morning practice sessions. Seven days a week had seemed too extreme for me at the time.

The teamwork of the eight-man shells on the water this morning was impressive as usual. I wasn't an expert, but I'd bet

MIT had a winning rowing season this year. They looked fast——
and most of all, smooth.

Naturally, I couldn't and wouldn't place a bet on them. Only a
fool bet on sports; it was too easy for one man on the team to
throw the game.

Throw the game. The phrase rattled around in my brain for a
moment.

Slowly, I realized my problem at work. I hadn't wanted to
consider the possibility, but the facts were piling up too quickly to be
coincidence. If we weren't being bugged, we were failing because
somebody on my team was throwing the game. We had someone
working against us——a mole for Winterbourne, inside the company.

A fucking traitor. That has to be it.

I closed my eyes and went through a series of faces in my
mind. I knew everybody in the company, I thought. Hell, I'd hired
a lot of them. Nobody seemed the type, if there was such a thing.
But that's what it took to be a successful spy——you fit in and
nobody suspected you.

Another quick call to Vincent yielded a suggestion to call my
older brother, Bill.

A groggy Bill answered after a few rings. *"Hi, shorty. Is everything okay? What has you calling this early? You know it's...before
five out here."*

In my haste, I'd forgotten to take the time difference into
account. *Oops.*

"Sorry, Bill. Everything's fine. I'll call back later."

"No," he said, yawning. *"You've got me up. We're family.
Anything you need, name it."* His voice indicated the cobwebs were
clearing.

"What's wrong?" I heard his wife, Lauren, ask in the
background.

"Bill," I started, "I think I have a spy in my organization."

"That's not good," he said.

"What's not good?" I heard Lauren ask.

"*I don't know yet, SP. Now just hold on,*" Bill told his wife.

"I need some help rooting out whoever it is. Have any suggestions?" I asked.

"*Around here I'd say the Hanson firm, but since you're out there, no names come to mind. But I'm not the best person to ask. You should try Uncle Garth. His list of contacts is ten times the size of mine.*"

I knew his suggestion was solid as soon as I heard it. "Yeah, I should have thought of him." Our uncle had contacts spanning the country and the globe. He was my usual go-to helper.

"*Two pieces of advice.*"

"Yeah?" I asked.

"*One, don't trust anyone. Don't tell a soul at your company that you're looking into this. If it leaks out, the guy will go underground and you'll never find him.*"

"Not even Josh?" I asked. This was a big deal. I told Josh everything and always had.

"*Not a soul,*" he said firmly. "*You can't risk an accidental leak.*"

"*Except,*" I heard Lauren say in the background.

"*Except Amy,*" he added. "*Never keep anything from your girl.*"

Uncle Garth had been the only one I'd told about Amy. It seemed he'd decided to broadcast the news to the family.

"*That's right,*" Lauren said loudly.

"And the second?" I asked.

"*Wait a few hours for the sun to come up out here in California before you call Garth, or you'll regret it.*"

I stifled a laugh. "Sure thing, and sorry I woke you. My best to Lauren."

We hung up, and I checked my watch. I would not repeat my stupid move.

Three hours later, after going in to work for meetings with Josh and HR, I reached Uncle Garth, and he spent the first few minutes telling me the latest family news.

"Anything yet on Matt Hudson?" I asked.

"I told you it would take some time, Liam. Nothing useful yet. You need to give the Hanson people a chance to do their work."

I had hoped for something by now. "Just checking. I really called on a different matter," I told him.

"Yes, Liam, how may I help?"

I lowered my voice. "I need help locating a leak in my organization. Someone here may be giving information to the competition, and I need to catch him."

My uncle was silent for a moment. *"Liam, I only have one contact that can help you with that kind of problem."*

I relaxed a bit. If anybody could help me, it would be my Uncle Garth. "Yes?"

"Your brother-in-law, Nick."

"Who else?" I asked. There had to be somebody else. I couldn't ask Nick Knowlton for help——not after what we'd been through.

"Nick is not only good," Uncle Garth said, *"he is quite possibly the best in the country at what you need. I am afraid he is my one and only recommendation. I suggest you swallow your pride and call him."*

"He won't help me, not after what happened," I said.

Uncle Garth exhaled a loud breath. *"You might be surprised how far a sincere apology can take you. He is family now, after all."*

Nick had married my little sister, Katie, and I owed it to her to patch things up with him. I'd attended the wedding, but somehow the time had never seemed right to pull him aside and make things right with everybody else around. Before I'd gotten a chance, they were gone, and my opportunity had evaporated.

"Do you need the number?" my uncle asked.

"No. I'll call Katie. Thanks, Uncle Garth. Thanks for everything."

"I will be in touch when we have something on that other matter. And my best to Amy." he said, before we wrapped up the call.

My finger hovered over the phone, but I couldn't bring myself to dial. I'd rather lick the bottom of a birdcage than ask Nick Knowlton for help. I decided to wander over to Josh's office instead to see if he was back yet.

~

AMY

IT WAS A NICE EVENING———ONLY MODERATELY MUGGY BY BOSTON standards. I'd decided to walk home from work. I'd taken Liam's suggestion and had been bringing a set of flats to the office with me so I had the option when I wanted it. But the third bottle of Snapple this afternoon was taking its toll, and I wasn't going to make it without a pee stop.

I entered the Subway shop and purchased my obligatory item after using the restroom. I chose a bag of chips. I was stashing them in my purse when I spied someone I recognized across the street.

It was Liam's partner, Josh, hailing a cab with a girl in tow. I waved, but he didn't see me. I pulled out my phone and snapped a picture seconds before they entered the cab. If she was the "imaginary" girlfriend, Brinna, this picture was going to earn me a quick thousand dollars from Liam, and maybe a backrub to go with it. And, it appeared Liam's guess that Josh might be ashamed of her looks had been wrong. From this distance at least, she had looked quite pretty. Good for Josh. He deserved it.

Arriving home at the Tremont Street building, the cool air in our lobby was a relief after all the blocks of walking. It was odd how I now considered this my home now———not only Liam's place, but our place. It had become my refuge from the hustle and bustle of the city, and the pressures of work.

Coming home to a meal with my man and an evening on the couch was an elixir to my soul. Liam could make me laugh, and he could drive me crazy in the bedroom, but most of all, I could relax in his arms in a way I'd never been able to with Matt, or anyone else for that matter.

I finally knew the meaning of someone having my back. Liam always supported me. The blowup over the Winterbourne money had been him trying to protect me. He had shared the details of their history, and now I understood how I had misjudged the situation and Liam's intentions. Even his constant insistence on complimenting me had slowly become more endearing than the obnoxious habit I had first taken it for.

Living here felt so comfortable now.

I turned the key and opened the door upstairs. After a quick reapplication of deodorant, I changed into shorts and a Brown University T-shirt. I'd planned rosemary chicken with homemade fries for dinner tonight.

The oven was warming when Liam walked in with his usual *Hello, gorgeous* greeting. It didn't seem to matter if I was dolled up for work or wearing the equivalent of a potato sack like tonight, he was intent on making me feel good about myself, and it was working.

I snapped a dish towel at him and caught him square on the ass.

"Keep that up, and I'll punish you," he said, scooting out of range.

Music to my ears. He'd been threatening to tie me up one of these nights, and since I hadn't ever done that before, it was sounding sexier and sexier.

"And what kind of punishment did you have in mind?" Maybe a tongue lashing on the dining table? Tying me up? Or fucking against the window for everybody to see.

"I'll make you eat brussels sprouts for a week."

I put down the dish towel. "That's just plain mean." I went back to slicing the potatoes. I could sulk as well as the next girl.

But it didn't faze him. Something was amiss in his world today, and I didn't know what. With my wall-to-wall meetings, we hadn't talked since this morning.

He sat silently on the couch and closed his eyes.

After loading up the oven with dinner, I joined him.

"You can talk to me, you know." I snuggled up against him.

"I'm always talking to you."

An evasive answer if ever there was one.

I needed a different approach. "Lie down. You need a back rub."

He grumbled, but took off his shirt and complied a few moments later.

I straddled him and started working on his shoulders. The tension in his muscles was obvious. "So what's bothering you today?"

"Nothing you need to worry about," he said softly.

I gave him a quick smack between the shoulder blades. "You can't be that way. If I'm gonna do a proper job of being your girlfriend, you need to reciprocate and let me help you."

He moaned lightly as I increased the pressure. "It's nothing you can help with."

"You can still tell me about it," I encouraged. After a half minute of silence, I'd had enough. I went to the kitchen.

"Don't stop. That felt good," he said.

I poured myself a glass of wine. "Be right back." I grabbed a few ice cubes in a bowl and returned to the couch. I lifted his pants and stuffed an ice cube down his butt crack and sat on him again.

"Hey," he complained.

I smacked him on the back again. "I've got a lot more where that came from," I told him. "Now are you going to talk to me, or am I going to have to freeze your balls off?"

"That's cold," he complained.

"That's not an answer." I resumed kneading the tight muscles of his shoulders.

He moaned and relaxed his shoulders. "You're right. I just didn't want you to worry."

I moved to his neck. "Listening is in the job description, remember?"

"It's work… I've got a big problem."

"Is this about Winterbourne again?" I moved back to his shoulders.

"Yes and no. Winterbourne is still the issue, but I'm afraid the big problem is they've got a spy in my company. For the life of me, I can't think who it might be."

I started to move down his back. "So you need to do a mole hunt, like in the movies."

"Something like that."

"Maybe your brother or that guy Vincent can help."

He groaned as I pressed my knuckles in harder. "Keep that up. I called Bill, and he referred me to my Uncle Garth."

I moved down to his lower back. "And what did your uncle say?" Liam was avoiding telling me the hard truth about what was bothering him, which was very un-Liam.

A long silence ensued. "He told me to call my brother-in-law, Nick."

"And what did Nick say?" I asked as I moved back up to his middle back.

"No. Lower, more down low."

I shifted my weight down to his thighs and moved to work his lower back. I waited for an answer that didn't come. "You didn't call him, did you?"

"No," he mumbled.

"You need to call him."

He turned his head slightly. "I know what I need to do. I'm just trying to think of anything else I can do instead."

This was unlike my Liam, to put off a simple call to start a fix on his problem, especially a problem this major. The Winterbourne Group had become his private nemesis.

"You're scared," I challenged him.

"I am not scared; I'm concerned," he said.

I pressed harder. "A distinction without a difference. Is this the brother-in-law you had the run-in with?"

"The same," he admitted.

I spanked his ass hard. I realized the problem now: his phobia, his stupid rule about never saying you're sorry.

"You big wimp, you. You're scared to apologize and admit you were wrong. That's it, isn't it?"

"I'm... I just don't think he'll help me."

I resumed my back rub, farther up. "Get over your little apology phobia, say you're sorry a few dozen times, and ask. He's family. He'll help."

"You don't know him. He's not much on helping."

I moved between his shoulder blades. "Is your sister, Katie, an idiot?"

"Of course not."

I pressed my thumbs in harder. "He must be okay if she married him, right?"

"Everybody makes mistakes."

"He's married to your sister, for Christ's sake. Make the call. If he doesn't help you, I'll call Katie, and he won't be getting any for a month. That'll change his mind."

That made him laugh. "Okay, I'll call tomorrow."

He didn't realize I was deadly serious about calling his sister if he didn't get the help he needed. Us women needed to stick together to get our men to be reasonable sometimes.

"Don't wimp out on me, Liam Quigley. It's three hours earlier out there. Give him a call now."

The timer went off for our dinner.

"Saved by the bell," I told him. "After dinner, okay?" I got up to tend to the food.

"You're awfully bossy tonight."

"It's in the job description. If you don't like bossy, stop being a pussy and do what you have to do."

He came over to kiss me. "Thank you for the truth you helped me see."

His words sometimes sounded more like poetry than conversation. During dinner, his demeanor was somewhat improved, but he still wasn't completely back to the old Liam, king of the jungle.

~

LIAM

AFTER DINNER, I CLOSED THE DOOR TO MY OFFICE AND STARED AT the contact I had pulled up on my phone. Taking a deep breath, I dialed Katie.

"Liam, it's so good to hear from you. I hear you have a new girl?" she said when she answered.

"What girl?" I asked, trying to sound surprised.

"Amy, of course. Uncle Garth told me a little about her. I'm so happy for you."

I rolled my eyes. "Thanks, but more on that later. Right now I need your help."

"Sure," she said. *"What do you need?"*

"I need..." I paused to put the right words together. "I need your help convincing Nick to help me with something." Since I'd gotten him kicked out of high school, I was likely the last person Nick wanted to help.

"Don't be silly. Nick's right here. You ask him yourself."

"Katie," I pleaded, but she didn't hear me.

"Nick, it's Liam for you," I heard her say.

"Hi, douchebag," Nick said, taking the phone. *"Whatever you have to say, make it quick."*

"I called to say I'm sorry," I told him.

"And what else?" he asked.

"And I need your help."

"You're a piece of shit, ya know that?"

"Yeah," I answered.

"Say it," he demanded.

"I know I wasn't——"

He hung up. The fucker hung up on me.

I dialed back. I clearly needed Katie's help with this.

"Say it, douchebag," Nick said, answering the phone.

"*Be nice,*" I heard Katie say in the background.

"*I am being nice,*" Nick told her.

"Say what?" I asked.

"*Bite me.*" He hung up again.

I was losing at this game. I hit redial again.

"*I'm listening,*" he said.

I guessed at the magic words. "I'm a piece of shit."

"*Now we have something we can agree on,*" Nick said, laughing. "*Now what was that apology again?*"

"I apologize for getting you kicked out of school."

"*And?*" he asked.

I thought for a moment and drew a blank.

"*Call back when you figure it out, you piece of shit.*"

He hung up on me again.

I redialed after concocting a more thorough apology.

"*I'm listening,*" he said.

"I'm sorry for starting the fight. I'm sorry for lying to the principal about it, and I'm sorry that it caused you to get kicked out of school."

I hoped that was complete enough to pass the test.

"*I didn't quite catch all that.*"

I repeated my spiel.

"*I'll think about it,*" Nick responded.

I let out a breath.

"*Now, what would you like to ask?*" Nick said.

I explained the situation to him.

"*I don't give a fuck. I'm fresh out of fucks today. Fix it yourself.*"

"*Nick, cut it out. He's family,*" I heard Katie say in the background.

Nick huffed audibly over the phone. "*Okay, what's the time frame on this?*" he asked.

"I need to know right away," I told him. I made a mental note to send Katie a thank you with some chocolate.

"*Then this is what I'll need,*" he said and began laying out the information he needed: names, emails, phone numbers, an org chart, and a contact at our payroll service.

"And this is what I want you to do when I call you to say I'm ready," he said. He went on to detail the plan. It was simple enough.

I agreed.

"And, douchebag, this is going to cost you."

That was not good news. I dreaded what the payment might be, given our history. "Sure, what?"

"You can buy me a keg next time you're out here," he said before handing the phone back to Katie.

"I still want to hear about your girlfriend," Katie said as soon as she got the phone back.

"Later, Katie, I promise."

I hung up and found Amy on the couch in the great room.

She looked at me expectantly as I sat next to her. "Well?"

I pulled her close. "You were right. He's going to help."

She slapped my thigh. "Told you. You're family now."

I kissed the top of her head. With Nick's help lined up, and my woman by my side, things looked better already.

CHAPTER 23

AMY

IT HAD BEEN A HECTIC DAY AT WORK, AND I'D GOTTEN A STRANGE
phone call from an old friend. My mind was swirling, and I was
five minutes late and still two blocks away from where I was
supposed to meet my former college roommate. I didn't like it
when other people were late, and I *hated* it when I was the one
holding someone else up.

I pushed open the door and entered the restaurant's darkened
interior. My first scan came up empty. I hoped I wouldn't embarrass myself by not recognizing her after all these years.

"Amy." The call came from a booth near the back.

I started over and recognized Natalie as I got closer. She and I
had been freshman- and sophomore-year roommates at Brown. Her
face hadn't changed, but everything else about her had.

We hugged briefly.

"It's been so long," she said. "You look great."

"You too," I answered.

Her hair was longer, and her clothes and jewelry were elegant.
She wore large diamond earrings. In college she'd been adamant

about not wearing anything but the small gold ball studs she told me she'd gotten when she first had her ears pierced.

"I hear you're a bigwig at a successful company now," she said.

She had done some research on me, because our little company wasn't front-page news, or easy to find.

"We're trying to make a go of it. You remember Samantha Tiffany?"

"Sure, she was two floors up right?"

"Yeah, that's right. She and I started a chocolates company a while ago, and we're slowly growing it." *Slowly* wasn't the right word, but I didn't want to brag.

"That sounds so fun. I wish I could do something like that."

The waitress came by to get our orders.

I asked for a glass of Chablis, and Natalie ordered the same.

The waitress stood and looked at us expectantly.

We took a quick look at the appetizer menu and added an order of fried calamari.

She left satisfied.

"You look quite successful," I told her. "What are you up to? As I recall you were heading off to law school when we graduated."

"That's right. You have such a good memory. I went to Columbia for two years."

I didn't want to ask an embarrassing question, so I nodded and waited for her to continue.

"I got married," she added.

"Congratulations. That's great."

The waitress brought our wine.

Natalie took a sip. "That put an end to law school."

"Maybe you could finish up later," I offered.

She looked down and shook her head. "My husband wouldn't approve."

I immediately felt sorry for her. "Maybe you could change his mind."

She took down some more wine and shook her head. "No. We live here, and a year at Columbia is just too much time away."

It was a problem I could understand. "Maybe transfer to Harvard or BU to finish up," I suggested. There ought to be a way to finish without having to go back to Columbia.

"Just not in the cards right now. Maybe later."

The silence encouraged us to both attack the calamari the moment it arrived. It tasted quite good, and the dipping sauce was spicy.

"I heard you married Matt after graduation. How's he doing?" she asked.

It was my turn to introduce bad news. "We divorced, so right now I don't know or care how he's doing."

She reached across to touch my hand lightly. "I'm sorry to hear that. I thought you made a cute couple. What happened?"

"I got a job up here, but he went back to school——Duke, actually." I sipped my wine for a break. "The distance became a problem. It just didn't work for us."

I shuddered thinking about Matt's cheating.

"I'm sorry," she repeated.

"I'm not," I told her, deciding to let it all hang out. "I found out he was cheating on me, and so it was never going to work long term, you know?"

"Yeah, that can be hard," she lamented.

Her wording made it seem like my story hit closer to home for her than I'd realized. Her glass was empty, and she waved our waitress over for another.

I shook my head when the waitress asked if I wanted another as well. "I suppose maybe I didn't try hard enough early on," I told Natalie. "I took him too much for granted."

"Oh no," she said, flicking her hand. "Don't put it on you. It's his fault. Sometimes I wonder if they're not all like that——you know, horndogs just waiting for the opportunity."

Clearly she had been hurt by a cheater. I wasn't the only one.

But I didn't want to buy into her all-men-are-jerks narrative. I never had.

"No, it was the distance that broke us up. I wasn't there when I should have been." But I didn't completely buy my own line of bullshit; it wasn't *only* my fault.

Natalie forked a piece of calamari. "You're still putting it on you. Look, he could have stayed in town. There are plenty of schools here. Who says the woman has to follow the man, anyway?"

She had that point right. I'd tried to talk Matt into applying to a local school, but he'd said it would delay him a year to do it.

She gulped down more of her Chablis. At this rate she'd need *another* soon. "It's the one who leaves that's at fault, not the one who doesn't follow."

My phone buzzed in my purse, and Natalie paused while I retrieved it.

LIAM: Finishing up want to walk home with me?

She eyed me curiously.

"My boyfriend wants to walk me home," I explained.

"That's so cute. We can get together another time if you have to go."

Her mention of getting together another time——not to mention her call out of the blue to set up this meeting——indicated we weren't just catching up. She had something in particular she wanted to discuss, which we hadn't gotten to yet. I hoped it wasn't marital advice.

"Or you could have him join us," she suggested.

"Okay." I composed my reply to Liam.

ME: at the seafood place on Beacon with a friend want to join?

"I asked him to come here," I said.

"Great," she said, leaning forward. "I've got a favor to ask."

She wasn't wasting any more time now that Liam was heading our way.

"Sure."

As she paused, formulating her words, and I worried maybe I should have couched my answer a little more hesitantly.

"I need to find a job," she blurted.

She seemed to think it was an odd request, but it wasn't.

"Sure. How can I help? Do you need a reference or something?" This wasn't a big ask. We had been quite close at Brown, and she was a good girl at heart.

"It's sort of odd." She finished her wine and waved our waitress down again. "My husband doesn't want me to work, but I can't just stay at home and do nothing. I'm going crazy."

"What do you mean he doesn't want you working? Do you have kids?" Her situation sounded odd. Most couples these days were two-income households, at least until children came into the picture.

"No," she answered after the waitress brought her a third Chablis. "No, no kids, but he won't let me."

"I don't see what I can do to change that for you." There was no way I was becoming a marriage counselor.

"I thought I could do a little work from home without him knowing and show him it didn't interfere with anything. Then go from there."

Interfere with what? His nookie time?

"I was hoping," she said, leaning forward, "that you might need a little paralegal work on the side. Or maybe you know someone who does? You see, I can't go on a bunch of interviews. He'd find out about that."

Her husband was sounding more and more like a controlling jerk, but it wasn't my place to tell her.

"I can talk to Celia——she's our in-house lawyer——and have her talk to you, but I'm not sure if she'll know anybody who needs help or not." I lifted my glass. "It's a plus that you have boobs."

She jerked back.

I smiled. "What I mean is we're a women-run business——not quite a testosterone-free workplace, but almost——and Celia's pretty hard core about it."

Natalie giggled. "So your building is a penis-free zone?"

"Not quite, but close." For a moment I considered how we might want to get signs for the doors that said that. It was a good line. *Caution - entering penis-free zone*, or maybe *Caution - entering low testosterone zone*. The second sounded a little more acceptable. We did have male visitors, after all.

Natalie slid a card across to me with a phone number on it. "That's my number, and she can reach me between nine and eleven in the morning."

I put the card in my purse and grabbed another calamari ring.

"Thanks so much, Amy. I'm going nuts at home."

The door to the street opened, and even backlit by the afternoon light, I could tell it was my Liam. I waved him over.

"Liam," I said as he strode up with his usual swagger. "This is my friend Natalie. Natalie, this is my boyfriend, Liam."

It seemed quite normal to be able to introduce Liam as *my boyfriend*, and a warmth spread through me as I uttered the words.

Natalie offered her hand, and Liam surprised her by kissing it instead of shaking.

"Natalie," he said slowly. "You wouldn't happen to have a birthday in December, would you?"

Natalie nodded. "Yes, the fifteenth. How did you guess?"

"Natalie is such a beautiful name," he said. Liam was in charisma mode again. "It comes from the word for Christmas, if I'm not mistaken. I like it. A very pretty name for a very pretty woman."

Natalie's smile was about to break her face, as Liam's charm took its usual effect.

"Nat and I were roommates in college," I told him.

He nodded and waved for the waitress. "What are we drinking?"

"Chablis," Natalie told him, raising her glass. She wasn't slurring her words yet, but I hoped she didn't order another one.

Liam ordered another round for all of us before I could stop him.

"Natalie was wondering if I knew anybody who needed paralegal-type work done that she could do from home——you know, contracts and that sort of thing," I told Liam.

Natalie leaned forward and speared another calamari ring.

I touched Liam's arm. "Maybe you guys have a little work you could steer her way? Don't you need some contract help sometimes?"

"Sure," Liam said without hesitation. "We're always looking for good help, and you couldn't have a better recommendation than this beautiful woman here."

He embarrassed me with a sloppy kiss. How was I ever going to break him of this?

"You're hired," he said to Natalie.

His hand found my leg under the table and started its naughty rise up my thigh.

"Really? That would be perfect, Liam. I finished two years of law at Columbia," she said. "Almost got my degree before we moved here. I hope to finish it one day. You won't be disappointed."

It was a shame how close she'd been to finishing when her husband had pulled her out of school.

She slid another card across the table to Liam, who took it. "My number is right there. I can be reached in the mornings."

He pocketed the card with his free hand as the other inched up my thigh.

I halted Liam's advance before he reached his objective, smiling at Natalie all the time.

A text arrived on Natalie's phone. She read it and blew out a breath. "That's my husband. He's on the way to pick me up." She reached for her wallet.

Liam quickly pulled out his. "I've got it."

"No," Natalie protested. "I invited Amy. It's my treat. God knows I can afford it."

Liam whipped out a hundred-dollar bill. "A gentleman always pays for a lady's drink."

"But——" Natalie objected.

I stood. "Give it up, Nat. It's not an argument you're going to win."

I'd never yet won an argument with Liam once he'd brought out the gentleman card.

"Then thank you, Liam," Natalie said, taking my advice.

We walked out together, Liam's hand at the small of my back, sending my hormone levels rising in anticipation of what awaited me when we got home.

A man climbed out of the back of a black town car. "There you are, my darling," he said.

So her husband was rich enough to have a driver. Good for Natalie.

Liam grabbed my arm and jerked me back. He turned us away from them and started walking.

"Bye now," I called out over my shoulder. "That was rude," I told Liam softly.

"Do you know who that was?" he asked, pulling me along at a rapid pace.

I struggled to keep up. "Her husband, I'm guessing."

"That's Damien Winterbourne. If she's married to him, this was a setup, and you can't see her again."

∽

LIAM

WINTERBOURNE HADN'T LOOKED OUR WAY. I WAS PRETTY SURE HE hadn't seen me before we turned around, so he might still think his plan had worked.

"The nerve of that asshole," I said as we crossed over to follow the path on the Common across from Tremont Street. I couldn't believe it. Winterbourne was trying to sneak his wife into the contract flow at our company by going through Amy. If I hadn't crashed the girls' meeting, I might never have known.

What a snake.

Amy didn't say a thing, obviously just as much in shock as I was.

"The audacity is just unbelievable," I said, putting my arm around her.

She pulled away. "That was just plain rude of you."

I stopped. "What was?" I thought I'd been quite nice to the spy trying to infiltrate my company.

Amy kept walking, and I hurried to catch up to her.

A tear showed in her eye. "She's my friend."

"I didn't mean to offend you, Amy, but do you realize who that was?"

She stopped and fixed me with a glare. "Yes! She's a friend I haven't seen in a long time, and you embarrassed me by being so rude to her, just because you have a problem with her husband. Do you have any idea how that makes me feel?"

I pulled her to a stop and encircled her with my arms. "I didn't mean to make you look bad," I said as I stroked her back.

"That's not good enough." She pushed me away.

I was in deep shit. "I'm sorry I made you look bad." It was the best apology I could think of.

She was quiet for a moment. "And?"

I had no idea what I'd missed, or what else she wanted me to add.

She moved toward a bench in the shade by the side of the path. "And?" she asked, taking a seat.

I was still lost. "I don't know what else you want me to say." I sat next to her.

"For a big shot with a gentleman complex, you sure suck at

basic etiquette. You're going to call Natalie and apologize to her. She's the one you insulted back there. And…"

I waited for the explanation, but it didn't come. "And what?"

"Figure it out."

I was still lost.

"She's my friend," she continued after a moment. "You promised to do something for her. You need to follow through."

She didn't understand what she was asking.

"I can't hire a Winterbourne. I can't jeopardize the company that way."

She shot to her feet, walked a few paces, and turned around. "But you feel okay insulting my friend and making me look like a jerk, is that it? There's no way I can possibly explain this to her." She stormed off in the direction of home.

I started after her, wondering how this had gotten so complicated.

Women.

CHAPTER 24

LIAM

AMY HAD REACHED THE CONDO AHEAD OF ME. I FOUND HER IN THE kitchen, pouring a glass of water.

"You win. I'll hire her," I said with a hopeful smile.

I had officially passed the threshold to certifiable. I had to be nuts to hire Natalie Winterbourne, and if Josh found out he'd probably throw me through the window. But I had to make things right with Amy.

I'd decided I could find a way to give Natalie work that wouldn't compromise us with Winterbourne, or maybe I'd even give her false information to feed her husband. I wasn't sure how to implement this approach yet, but perhaps it could work to my advantage to have Damien's wife as a conduit for misinformation. And then I could keep my promise——even though I'd made it without having all the information I needed.

Amy turned to face me. "Her husband didn't even know about our meeting——he doesn't even want her to work. She's not trying to pull one over on me——or you. She wouldn't do that."

"Stop." I shushed her with a raised finger. "I should have been more considerate."

"Ya think?" she shot back.

"Hold on," I told her. "I'm not sorry for looking out for my company, but I admit I didn't think of how it would affect you." I pulled her into a hug. "I'll find a way to make it work for you and your friend." Her warmth comforted me.

She hugged me tightly, her head on my shoulder. "Thank you. And I didn't know who her husband was. Maybe we should find some work for her at Tiffany's."

"No need. I'll call her tomorrow," I said, rubbing Amy's back. "I can make it work——maybe even to my advantage." I waggled my eyebrows.

She rolled her eyes, but rose up to kiss me, our lips meeting and expressing our regrets in the physical way only an intimate kiss can. The scent of cherry in her hair calmed me as she deepened the kiss and let me back into her heart.

Our hands moved over one another.

She threaded her fingers into my hair.

I grabbed a handful of ass and pulled her into the growing bulge in my pants. I traced the underside of her breast.

She broke away. "I'm starving. Dinner first, please."

My hunger ran in a different direction. There would be plenty of time for dinner after I quenched my thirst for her. Ate my fill, as it were. I tried unsuccessfully to stifle a chuckle at the thought.

"What's so funny?" she asked with a quizzical look.

"Just thinking about the menu." I glanced down to her crotch.

"You're incorrigible." She swatted me on the shoulder. "Your lady said please."

I couldn't argue with that. "Okay, dinner first."

The corners of her mouth turned up with that disarming smile of hers. "And thank you for helping my friend."

I took her hand and led her into the kitchen. "No thanks needed. It's the gentlemanly thing to do. Wine?"

She giggled. "Not without pizza."

This was a twist. "Sure you wouldn't rather have real food?"

"I don't feel like cooking tonight. I just want to sit with you and talk. Could you call and get us the meatiest one they have? I didn't have anything substantial for lunch."

"Pizza. You sure are lowering your standards for me."

"A girl's got a right to change her mind now and then. I'll be back on the straight and narrow tomorrow."

I called for the pizza, and she went to change, returning in a T-shirt and running shorts.

"Can we take an evening stroll on the Common while we're waiting?"

Seeing her legs, I was more interested in diving between them than walking across to the Common, and my cock had its own thoughts as well.

"You look lovely tonight. Did I tell you that?"

She slapped my shoulder. "Cut that out. I asked if we could take a walk."

"Sure, if that's what you'd like."

"Now?" she asked.

I took her hand. "Whatever the lady desires."

We took the elevator down, and I handed our concierge a hundred to pay for the pizza and hold it for us if the delivery came before we got back.

After crossing the street into the Common, Amy snaked her arm around my waist, and I reciprocated, trying to match our strides.

"Can we talk?" she asked.

"Sure."

"What was it about Josh that you didn't want to tell me at our first dinner?"

She really did want to get into sensitive subjects tonight.

I'd kept this from her. Hell, I'd kept it from everybody, including my family.

"It's something I'm not very proud of."

"We all have those things," she responded. "I just want you to let me in, so I can help."

"I told you I had a really rough time after Roberta passed away."

She nodded, but didn't respond or prod me. We walked in silence for a moment.

I turned us right to follow a path toward the center of the Common. "Josh played a bigger part in helping me with that than I told you before."

"He sounds like a really good friend," she said.

Josh was much more than just a good friend. "One day he was trying to get me sober. I got super pissed at him and kicked him out, after which I tried to drown my troubles with even more alcohol." I paused. "The stubborn son of a bitch wouldn't take no for an answer. He came by again that night. He made the manager let him in when I didn't answer the door. I was more than passed out. They tell me I was comatose. He called 9-1-1 and got me to the hospital."

I took a deep breath before continuing to the hard part. "When I woke up in the hospital, the doctors told me that if Josh hadn't brought me in when he did, I would have died of alcohol poisoning. I had no idea you could actually drink yourself to death, but the statistics are that six people a day in this country drink so much that they don't ever wake up. If it weren't for Josh…" I paused. "I would've been one of those six that day."

"I'm glad he helped you," she said as we took a turn past the bandstand.

We walked a ways before I continued. "Anyway, he spent the next week with me, twenty-four seven, and got me turned around. So you see, I owe Josh more than I can ever repay. Both our jobs are on the line with these deals Winterbourne is messing up, and it's the only thing Josh has. That's why it's so important to me. That's why I don't want anything to do with Winterbourne and why I resisted hiring your friend."

"That makes sense. I'm really glad Josh took care of you,"

Amy said kindly. "He sounds like the kind of friend I wish I had. I know it was hard to share this, and you can count on me to do my best for you and for Josh."

"Sometimes he can be a real pain in the ass." I chuckled. "But to say he's one in a million is understating it."

I had confided in Amy something no one besides Josh and I knew, but I felt relieved now that I'd told her. It didn't feel right to keep things from her.

"Your family doesn't know about this?" she asked.

"It's painful to admit, but no. I guess I was just too ashamed to share it with anybody. Outside of Josh, you're the only one who knows my secret shame."

She squeezed my hand. We turned right again back along the edge of the Common toward my building.

"You should tell your brothers and your sister sometime. I think it would help," she offered.

We continued in silence. I stopped us across from our building. "Maybe later. Right now it's just too fresh."

When we reached the lobby, the concierge had our pizza safe behind his counter. "I already had to turn down two offers to buy it from me, Mr. Quigley," he said.

"Thanks for not giving in, Carl." I took the pizza, but declined the change and told him to keep it.

Upstairs, we had finished half the pizza when my phone rang.

Amy went to get it from the counter. "It's Josh," she said handing me the phone. "Don't forget to ask them over for dinner."

I shook my head and took the phone. "Hey, Josh, before we start, Amy and I would like to have you and Brinna over for dinner this Saturday."

"*Sure, I'll check with her*," he said. "*But first, I have some bad news.*"

I braced myself for whatever he was about to say. None of our news recently had been good.

"Don't tell me another article."

"*No,*" he said. "*Worse. I still haven't heard back from Sanders*

*after they canceled our last call, but the scuttlebutt from our
lawyers is that they signed with those Winterbourne assholes."*

I closed my eyes, willing myself to be calm and not throw the
phone across the room. "How did that happen?" I asked him.

*"Somehow they got a last look and outbid us. That's all I
know."* He let the impact of the news settle in for a moment. *"You
know what this means, right?"* he asked dejectedly.

"Yeah," I replied.

*"Closing the Springbok deal is now the only avenue to making
the quarter's numbers."*

We had one make-or-break deal now, and no wiggle room.
Without Springbok, it was game over. Game, set, match. Hang-
man's noose.

"Anything you need me to do on that?" he asked.

"No," I said firmly. "Amy and I will have to work that one."

"Okay, see you tomorrow."

I hung up. My life just got more complicated. A lot more
complicated.

"What did he say about dinner?" Amy asked.

"He said he had to check with the invisible Brinna. I told you
she's just an imaginary friend."

Amy went to her purse and pulled out her phone. "I want to
have them over for dinner and collect my thousand dollars. I got a
picture of them together. I forgot to tell you. She's real——at least
I think it's her." She held out her phone.

"The bet was dinner, not a random picture," I said, taking the
phone. "Fuck me," I added loudly as I checked the picture and
expanded it to examine the face of the woman with Josh. Now I
was totally screwed. "I need a drink."

Amy sat down next to me. "What's the problem?"

"Her," I said, pointing at the girl in the picture. "She's the
fucking Winterbourne spy who's been following me around."

The short redhead who had been taking pictures of me everywhere was Josh's girlfriend, Brinna.

CHAPTER 25

AMY

THE NEXT MORNING I FOUND LIAM HAD GOTTEN UP EARLY AGAIN
and slipped out of bed without waking me. I wandered into the
hall. The kitchen was quiet, and the light was off in his office. I
found him slumped on the couch in his bathrobe, staring at the
wall.

He'd been disturbed by yesterday's phone call with Josh, when
he learned another of his deals had been stolen by Winterbourne.
The tougher part, though, had been discovering that Josh's girlfriend was apparently a Winterbourne spy. Everything seemed to
be crumbling down around him, and he'd been restless all night.

I slipped back into the bedroom and started my shower. I
wanted to help him, but he had to be able to help himself first.
He'd drunk heavily last night, so heavily I'd had to help him to
bed. He didn't look like himself this morning either. He needed to
get his groove back if he was going to solve his problems.

After drying off, I could hear him cooking in the kitchen. I had
to decide what to wear for breakfast. I chose one of his button-up
shirts with a single button fastened at my navel, nothing else. I slid

216

a condom into the pocket, but stopped at the door and went back to put on the red heels I'd worn our first night——the ones he referred to as my "fuck-me" shoes. My ensemble was now complete.

He faced the stove as I entered.

"I don't think you should drink so much," I told him as I walked up. "It's not good for you,"

"Don't get your panties in a twist," he said without turning around to look.

"Who says I'm wearing any?" I swatted his ass as I walked past him to the silverware drawer. I looked back.

As he turned to see me, I leaned over, hiking the shirt up to give him a good eyeful.

"I warned you to cover up for breakfast," he said.

I turned around. "Or what?"

"I'm warning you," he growled before he turned back to the stove.

I walked by him again. "I can do what I want." I trailed a finger across his ass as I passed.

He didn't respond.

I leaned against the island and undid the single button. "And I can dress the way I want." I crossed my arms.

He turned. His eyes became predatory, and the bulge in his bathrobe gave him away.

I stood and uncrossed my arms. The shirt fell open.

He turned off the stove and lunged for me. "You're being naughty," he said as he hoisted me over his shoulder. "Do you have any idea what happens to naughty girls?"

I shrieked as he carried me to the couch and placed me on the edge. "You promised to make it so I couldn't walk straight," I said with a giggle. I slid the shirt off.

He pushed my legs apart and stood back. His eyes feasted on my body; he took in all of me with the eyes of the lion.

"You are the most beautiful woman I have ever seen." He dropped the robe that had been tented over his cock.

His words were an aphrodisiac, water to my parched libido. My nipples pebbled, and my juices flowed as my eyes moved over his naked physique, relishing its raw power.

His gaze darted between my breasts and my open pussy. "Suck me," he commanded, moving forward.

It wasn't what I'd expected, but it was a start. I grabbed him and stroked and sucked with my two-handed Vivienne technique. It had worked the other day, and I hoped I could satisfy him this morning.

"Tell me what you want, you naughty hussy."

I continued with my hands as I took my mouth off to answer him. "This is a good start." I licked the length of his underside as I cupped his balls in one hand.

He pulled away. "Tell me what you want, naughty hussy," he repeated.

I reached for his cock, but he backed out of reach. "I want you to do what you want," I told him.

"A naughty girl never gets what she won't ask for," he said, stroking himself in front of me and licking his lips. He continued to pump.

I tried to grab for his cock again, but he swatted my hand away once more. I pulled the condom out of the shirt pocket and offered it to him.

He didn't take it. He didn't say a word. His breathing was heavy as his eyes bore down on me. He stroked himself faster.

"I want you to take me," I said breathlessly. I needed him inside me so badly it hurt.

"You have to be clear, naughty girl."

I stood and grabbed his cock. "I want you to fuck me, hard."

With that, he backed away and tore open the condom packet. He handed it to me to sheath him.

I'd learned it was a turn-on for him when I rolled the latex over his length. I knelt before him and rolled it down, stopping a few times to lick his balls and look up into those predatory eyes.

When I finished, he pulled me up off the floor with a jerk

and walked me to the table. He cleared the tabletop with one swipe of his arm. Plates and silverware clattered loudly to the floor.

I was going to get my wish. He pushed me over, forcing my chest down to the wooden table.

The cherrywood felt cold against the heat of my breasts as I spread my legs, my arms sprawled on the wood.

He positioned himself behind me and grabbed my arms, pulling them behind me. He clasped them together with one hand, pushing me hard against the table. He positioned his cock at my pussy and teased me, running it the length of my saturated slit, smoothing the tip over my sensitive bud.

I was soaking wet.

"You were naughty, so you don't get what you want."

What the fuck?

I squirmed to pull loose, but he was too strong, forcing my chest down and my hips up against the edge of the table. "You said I could get what I asked for," I complained.

"You have to obey first. You're going to get wet for me before you get what you want, naughty girl." He gave me a hard spank on the ass.

I jerked. It hurt.

My ass stung. "I am wet."

"Not wet enough."

Squirming did no good, so I gave up. He pushed the tip of his cock against my clit and rubbed it forward and back, increasing the pressure and shifting between the tip of his cock and the fingers of the hand he held it with. He quickly worked me into a frenzy, parting my folds and strumming my swollen clit like an instrument. My legs started to tremble.

I couldn't reach him as he clamped my hands behind me, holding my chest to the table so I couldn't move.

The pressure built within me as he teased me with the tip of his cock. I needed him. I ached to have him fill me.

"You don't want it enough," he said.

I jerked as he spanked me again. "Please. I want you to fuck me, fuck me hard," I pleaded. "So hard I can't walk straight."

He released my wrists and pulled back. He pulled my hips back, urged my legs farther apart, and in one movement, he entered me.

I was still not accustomed to the size of him, but he'd made me so wet, he slid in easily.

He started to thrust. The loud slap of flesh against flesh filled the room as he pulled out and rammed into me again and again, grunting each time. Each thrust seemed harder than the last. He gripped my hips and pulled me against him as he slammed into me, finally taking me as I'd asked, as I'd wanted, as he needed.

"More, more," I groaned as he thrust harder, filling me fully to my end, painfully at first. Surges of pleasure quickly blotted out the pain.

He slid an arm around in front of me, and his fingers found my clit again. The combination of his thrusting and his fingers on my sensitive nub brought me quickly right up the mountain, to the brink and over as the waves of bliss crashed over me and my veins caught fire. I clamped down hard around his cock as he growled my name.

He grabbed my hair and pulled me back into him as he slammed into me over and over, the slapping sounds of our meeting bodies seeming loud enough to wake the neighbors.

With a final thrust, he went stiff and roared. The lion was back. The animal in him took me, claiming me as his mate. It was the connection I needed this morning. His cock pulsed inside me several more times before he collapsed on my back, pressing me against the wood, his breathing heavy in my ear.

I was wonderfully exhausted. My man had claimed me in his most primal way. I was his, and he was mine. In allowing him to take me, I hoped I'd given him what he needed——the resurrection of the animal in him to combat his enemies.

The king of the jungle was back in charge.

He took care of the condom and put his robe back on while I

slid the shirt back over my arms. I ate with no buttons secured, teasing him with my cleavage. Our breakfast had gotten cold, but it was still the most delicious meal I had eaten in weeks.

"Thank you," he said between bites.

I grinned. I was the luckiest girl in town, sitting across from my man, looking at the grin I had put on his face. We couldn't do this every morning, but I didn't plan on waiting too long to try it again.

We showered quickly and were only a little late to work. As he had predicted, I had a hitch in my walk this morning.

Sometimes, being a naughty hussy is nice.

∿

LIAM

I SAT BACK, CLOSED MY EYES, AND SMILED. I COULD STILL FEEL Amy clamped around my cock this morning. She'd made me feel so alive today. How had I gotten so lucky?

I turned my chair and looked out my office window. Alive or not, I had one hell of a problem now. With Josh dating the competition, it made him or his girlfriend, Brinna, the most likely leak. I couldn't imagine Josh would be trying to sabotage us on purpose, but I couldn't figure out why he was dating her.

He was smart enough to figure out if she was using him——at least I hoped he was.

A possibility, of course, was that she was pumping him for information and he didn't know. He might even be talking in his sleep; some people did that.

The door opened behind me. I spun around to find Josh standing behind his customary chair rather than inviting himself to sit as he usually did. "Sorry to say Brinna can't make it this Saturday. She's going to be out of town."

I checked his eyes for any signs of deception, without success. "That's too bad. Maybe next time."

Josh started for the door. "Yeah, I hope so."

I called after him before he disappeared. "Hey, Josh?"

He stopped at the doorway.

"What's Brinna's last name, anyway?" I was going to need this information.

"Turcott. Brinna Turcott," he said.

It wouldn't be wise for me to ask him too many questions at this point. "Can you close the door on your way out, please?"

He left, and I picked up my phone.

I dialed the number Katie had given me.

"Hey *douchebag. What do you have to say for yourself today?*" Nick answered.

"Not much. How are you?" I asked.

The line went dead. He hung up on me again, the asshole.

I redialed, and Nick answered the phone. "*What do you have to say for yourself today?*" he repeated.

"I'm a piece of shit," I said, hoping this was the correct answer.

"*That is something we can agree on,*" he said, laughing.

"When are we gonna stop this?"

"*When I get tired of it.*"

I needed to get down to business. "I've got a new piece of data that might help."

"*I'm listening,*" he replied.

"One of the guys here, Josh Fulton, has a girlfriend I'm suspicious of." Suspicious didn't begin to describe it.

"*What's her name?*" He asked.

"Brinna Turcott, that's spelled B-R-I-N-N-A, and Turcott with two Ts."

He didn't say anything.

"Do I need to repeat that?" I asked.

"*What? You think I can't handle something so simple as taking down a name?*"

"Not what I meant, Nick," I said, trying to dial it back a notch.

"*Sure, douchebag,*" he responded.

"How much longer is this gonna take?"

"*It takes until I'm ready.*"

"How do I translate that into days?" I asked.

"*Look, Liam, I told you I'd call you when I was ready. I haven't called yet. Even a college weenie like you should be able to figure out that means I'm not ready yet. You have two choices here. We can do it quickly, or we can do it right. I thought you wanted it done right.*"

I took in a calming breath. "Nick, I'm sorry. I didn't mean to imply anything." The last thing I wanted to do was inflame my relationship with Nick right now. I'd lose the company and my sister would kill me the next time she saw me.

"*Listen, I don't mean to be a jerk.*"

I didn't dare tell him that's exactly what he sounded like.

"*Katie said this is important to her, and for that reason, I'm gonna do the best job possible. That translates into not missing a single email account or phone connection before we start. I know you're in a hurry, but we may only get one chance at catching this guy when we go fishing.*"

I appreciated his thoroughness. "Thanks, Nick. I owe you one."

He laughed. "*I'll tally it up when we're done with this, but I can guarantee you, it'll be more than one.*"

I laughed. "You got it."

I thought we hung up on better terms than we'd started. My fingers were crossed.

JOSH STOMPED IN A HALF HOUR LATER WITH THE SOUREST expression he'd carried in a long time.

"You have a problem?" I asked.

He threw the tabloid paper on my desk. "No, *we* do. My contact at Springbok just called to alert me to this."

The headline blared: *Can any woman tame Boston's most notorious bachelor?* The photos were a lovely walk down memory lane with pictures of me with four women on different evenings, one-night stands all of them——Mindy, Celeste, and two others whose names escaped me at the moment.

"Old man Schmulian has seen this," he shouted. "And that means the Springbok deal is fucked, and so are we."

"Sit down," I told him sternly as I went to shut the office door.

He took a chair with an even worse frown than when he had entered.

"Look," I started. "I'll fix this." I didn't know how at the moment, but I had to.

"Didn't I fucking warn you? This is Boston. Half the business families here are members of the Daughters of the American Revolution. They vote republican in a democratic state."

I let him vent.

"They don't want modern, they don't want hip, they certainly don't want to sell their business to a Hollywood playboy type who ends up all over the fucking tabloids." He huffed. "They want understated, conservative, and un-newsworthy."

I scanned the paper again. "That fucking little bitch," I said.

"Who?" Josh asked in an annoyed tone.

The byline was Merry Poppins. "It's that same Poppins bitch from online."

"That doesn't fucking do shit for us," Josh complained.

He was right, but I was still going to find out who she was and why she seemed to be targeting me. I would figure out later whether I should threaten her or buy her off, but this had to stop. In the meantime I needed to get with Schmulian to smooth things over.

CHAPTER 26

LIAM

Hue Schmulian called me back after lunch. After a few initial pleasantries, he stated what was on his mind.

"Liam, I have to say that after this morning's article..."

My blood froze as I waited for his next words. He was going to pull the plug, and our deal would be dead. It was a good thing I didn't have anything breakable on my desk.

"...I was inclined to go a different direction," he continued. *"But Felicia likes you two and suggested we talk some more."*

I could breathe again. We weren't dead yet. Felicia liked us, probably all due to Amy impressing her at our previous dinners.

"Felicia and I would like to invite you and Amy out to our beach cottage this weekend." It seemed the bar had just been raised from dinners to a weekend.

"We'd love to," I said too quickly. "But before we put that in stone, let me check with Amy, just to be sure."

Hue laughed on his end of the phone. *"I always have to check with my boss, too, when making plans. Let me know what Amy says."*

"Will do." I told him.

"I'll fax over directions for you."

He didn't seem to realize people didn't use directions anymore. All I needed was an address and a phone to find any place in the country through the magic of GPS and Siri.

"That would be good," I answered.

He didn't stay on the phone any longer than necessary. He wasn't winning any awards for being chatty today.

I started to compose a text to Amy, but decided a phone call would be better.

"*Hi there, handsome,*" she answered.

"Hi, Sunshine. How's your day so far?"

"*It went to pretty crappy once I got here. I had another discussion with our turd of a banker, Woolsey, and he won't commit to a renewal on our line of credit until he sees next quarter's results.*" She huffed exasperatedly over the phone. "*So much for my day. What about you?*"

I needed to get back to Schmulian quickly. "I have a favor to ask you."

"*Yeah?*"

"The Schmulians would like us to join them at their beach cottage this weekend. Can you make that?"

She didn't hesitate. "*Sounds like fun. I'll do whatever you need me to.*"

"Thanks, Amy. I appreciate it. See you tonight."

"*Before you hang up, what do you want for dinner?*" Her question wasn't an odd one, but it struck me that way.

"Sunshine," I said. "Let's turn that around. What would you like *me* to cook for you tonight?"

She laughed. "*Are you going to tell me your repertoire extends beyond French toast and pancakes now?*"

"If I can spell it, I'm sure I can find a recipe and figure it out." I didn't have any experience, but that's where YouTube came in. "It's only fair. You've been doing all the dinners, so what would you like?"

I could hear fingernails tapping on her desk. "*If you insist. But I'll start you off easy. Spaghetti and meatballs for the main course,*" *and roasted asparagus with Parmesan cheese for the vegetable. Think you can handle that?"*

Since I knew how to spell both asparagus and spaghetti, my answer was pretty simple. "It'll be ready at seven."

"Are you sure you don't want me to come home early to help you boil the water?" She giggled.

"Don't be late, or it'll be cold."

I got off the phone with only one more insinuation that I couldn't figure out the kitchen. Once I hung up, I turned to my computer and typed in *roasted asparagus*. It didn't look too hard. I made a quick list of things to pick up at the market on the way home.

Five hours later, I was proud of the progress I'd made. I had meatballs in a pan with sauce I'd made myself. Tomato sauce, tomato paste, Italian seasoning, and extra basil turned out to be easy enough. I'd bought a jar of Prego as a backup, but didn't need it. I hid it in the back of the cupboard.

The meatballs had been harder. Only four made it through the process; the other four fell apart in the pan. The directions hadn't said how hard to squeeze them. But the menu was spaghetti with meatballs, not meatballs with spaghetti, so two each would have to suffice. The evidence of my mistakes went down the disposal.

The water reached a rapid boil. I put the spaghetti noodles in at ten minutes before seven and slid the baking sheet with the asparagus into the hot oven.

I opened a nice bottle of pinot and poured two glasses to celebrate. All I needed now was my girlfriend. This was clearly a night to celebrate.

Amy arrived moments later. "Hi, handsome. Miss me?"

"Naturally, but you can't steal my line."

She gave me a quick kiss. "You were going to call me handsome?"

"You know what I mean." I smiled and fingered the ring in my pocket——the latest thing I'd bought for Amy.

It was time.

"Everything okay?" she asked.

I pulled the ring from my pocket and fisted it. "Close your eyes."

"Liam, I'm starving. Can't we eat first?"

"No," I said firmly. "Now close your eyes."

She complied, reluctantly.

I took her hand.

Her eyelids fluttered, threatening to open for a peek.

"Keep your eyes closed." I said.

She huffed. "You and your rules."

"I'd like you to wear this for me," I told her.

CHAPTER 27

AMY

EVER SINCE GRADE SCHOOL, I'D DREADED THE "CLOSE YOUR EYES" surprises. In fifth grade, Tommy Powanski had me close my eyes and open my mouth. My surprise had been a grasshopper to chew on. The experience had ruined this common ritual for me.

Still, I'd closed my eyes for Liam. It was hard.

"I'd like you to wear this for me." He slid a ring onto my ring finger——the ring finger of my right hand. "You can open your eyes now."

It was a gorgeous friendship ring, with two heart-shaped stones, a ruby and a sapphire, interlocked in a circle of diamonds. The ring was stunning——Liam didn't understand the word *understated*. It probably cost more than a new car.

I pulled him into a long kiss, another of our true boyfriend-girlfriend kisses, the kind I had dreamed about as a little girl, a princess-and-Prince-Charming kiss.

I floated off the floor in his arms.

The oven timer sounded.

We ignored it. His tongue explored mine, and his hands roamed to all the right places, leaving trails of sparks that branded my skin.

Time stood still. In my bare feet, I tired of clinging to his neck and jumped up to wrap my legs around him. My skirt got in the way, and I almost sent us both to the floor trying to wrap myself around him.

He broke the kiss and laughed. "Does that mean you like it?"

I regretted the sudden loss of his body heat against me. "Liam, it's beautiful."

"A beautiful lady deserves no less," he said sweetly.

"Does this mean we're going steady?"

"Something like that," he responded. He led me to my seat at the table and pulled out the chair.

The slight smell emanating from the kitchen indicated it might not have been good to ignore the timer. "I think you might want to check the oven."

He quickly rescued the asparagus and took the spaghetti off the stove. A few minutes later, Liam lit the candles and served me spaghetti and meatballs with roasted asparagus on the side. Accented with wine and candlelight, our dinner was a simple affair, but more romantic than any dinner out could have been—— even if the asparagus was toasted beyond perfection.

My man had made the effort to learn to cook this for me, and the love in his eyes every time I glanced at him made me tear up. It was unlike any evening I could recall. We were eating together as a true couple; nothing was fake about this.

I kept looking down to admire the large ring on my finger. The blue and red hearts touched each other as I felt ours did.

The dessert was Sara Lee from the grocer, but I wasn't complaining. The effort he had already made was amazing. Sometimes the simplest things were the most significant.

"You know there's a Bogart marathon on tonight," he said between bites. "*Casablanca* and *African Queen*. How does that sound?"

"I'm not sure I feel like Bogart tonight."

"What would you like to watch then?"

"Can I have whatever I want?" I stroked his leg with my foot.

"Sure."

"Promise?"

"Of course."

I slid a foot up the inside of his leg under the table with a wink as he looked up. I licked the chocolaty goodness from my spoon in the most seductive way I could manage.

The lion emerged in his eyes, and his lips curved into a wicked smile, one that could only mean I was having the desired effect. He eyed me hungrily.

I took another spoonful and licked at it. "The lady has a better idea."

He swallowed. "I can tell."

I slid my foot up higher.

He shifted in his seat.

"I want you to take off your clothes and stand in front of the window."

He pulled back. "No way."

I pointed my finger at him. "You promised I could have whatever I wanted."

"That's not what I meant."

I got up and took my plate to the sink. "So it's okay to break a promise to me? I get it."

He huffed. "Of course not." He rose and removed his shirt.

I took his plate as well and started loading the dishwasher, pretending not to watch as he peeled off his shoes and finally his pants and boxer briefs. He walked to the window and faced me, waiting.

"Face the window, palms on the glass," I told him as I walked over. I would replay our first-night experience, only in reverse.

He did as I requested, grudgingly, and he flinched as I ran my nails down his back.

I reached around him and found my prize, growing quickly

with anticipation. I grasped him and started to stroke, rubbing my chest against his back as I did.

His moans soon started as I found the rhythm I'd learned he liked, but I only worked him up for a few minutes, hardening his cock in my grasp.

I could only hope the danger of being up against the window facing the Common enhanced his sensations as it had mine. I pulled back. "Go into the bedroom and lie down."

"But——" he started to say.

I shushed him with a finger to his lips, as he had done to me. "No talking." I admired his tight little ass as he walked to the bedroom, his cock swinging with each step. "On your back."

I waited by the door in the partial darkness as he lay down.

I entered and worked the buttons of my top, slowly, teasingly, sliding one arm out and then the other, letting the garment slide to the floor as I stepped closer.

His eyes scanned me, willing me to go faster.

I unzipped my skirt and pushed it over my hips, kicking it aside. I was down to the red lace panties and bra he'd selected for me this morning, as he liked to do. It made me feel sexy all day long to be wearing underthings he'd chosen. I turned around and unhooked the bra, easing it over one shoulder followed by the other. I turned to face him before I let it slip loose and fall.

His eyes bugged out as they always did at the sight of my breasts.

I bounced for him, getting the smile I was aiming for.

Leaning over and swinging my breasts some more, I slid the panties off and was naked before him.

His cock was hard against his abdomen, twitching slightly every few moments. It called to me.

I approached the bed.

He held his arms out, and his eyes devoured me.

"Hands behind your head and interlace your fingers," I told him. Just like the cops said on TV.

He smirked and did as I asked.

I straddled him and leaned over, my hands to either side of his head, rubbing my breasts lightly over his chest.

He strained upward to meet me, but I pushed him down.

It was my turn to be in control.

The lust in his eyes had me dripping wet.

I slid down to his legs and took his tip in my mouth. I started to suck and lick. I cupped his balls in one hand and squeezed the base of his cock with the other like a cock ring. I gazed up into his eyes as I licked the underside of his shaft, slowly arriving at the crown and taking him into my mouth again.

The look in his eyes, the smile on his face, and hitches in his breathing told me what I needed to know: this was driving him crazy.

I went to work and brought him almost to the edge. Then I stopped, rested for a moment, and began again, teasing him to near his breaking point.

"What? No stamina?" I teased.

He averted his eyes in an attempt to control himself, and I worked him harder, using his moans and his breathing as my gauge.

I loved how I could drive him crazy like this, that I could control his pleasure.

I let go of my play toy and slid up his body, scraping my nipples against his chest. I dangled my breasts over his mouth, letting him take my nipple and nip and suck the way only he could, first one and then the other. I moved down and slid my soaked folds over his length, teasing his tip against my clit, sending shocks through me. I was barely able to hold back, I wanted him so badly.

"Condom," he said.

"Not tonight. I'm on the pill," I told him, sliding down and back again.

His smile broadened. "I'm clean," he told me, still keeping his hands behind his head.

"Me too."

The gleam in his eye told me he was looking forward to the skin-to-skin contact as much as I was.

I lifted up and reached down to guide him in. I slid down on him slowly, just a little, then up a little and down farther, until I'd taken all of him in to the sound of a wondrous moan from my man.

He arched up into me, his eyes conveying raw desire.

I pushed down and leaned forward, grinding against him to get the clit pressure I sought, and I rocked as he pushed up and we found our rhythm.

"You're so good, so fucking tight, so fucking good," he said, breaking his silence.

I didn't complain; his words were a turn-on. I loved the dirty talk we sometimes engaged in. We fit so well. His cock was made for me and I for him.

I leaned forward, offering my breasts again, and we worked ourselves up to the edge. I pulled his hands from behind his head.

He took the weight of my breasts in his hands and fondled me gently before shifting to tweaking my nipples, which sent sparks through me.

"You have the greatest breasts. Have I told you that?"

"Never," I lied.

He had complimented my breasts a dozen times, along with my eyes, my lips, my hair, my butt, my legs, my pussy, and any other part you could name. He never stopped.

He shifted his hands to my hips and guided me for a few strokes, pushing deep, grinding me down against him, before he moved his thumb to my clit and quickly sent me over the precipice. The suddenness of my climax surprised me. Lights flashed behind my eyelids, and my blood sang as electricity rattled through my bones and spasms overtook me.

As I came down from my high, he guided my hips. I rocked into him as he thrust up into me, increasing his tempo. He finally reached the end of his rope and found his release, gushing into me with a roar——the roar of the king of the jungle, the sound I had come to love.

I collapsed onto his chest, panting and fulfilled. I could feel his heart beating with mine, as linked as the stones on the ring he had given me.

The pulsing of his cock inside me slowly diminished. I relished the connection we had as a true couple. We fit perfectly together, my gentleman and me. He had made me feel things I never expected to find, physically and emotionally.

Sex with Liam was more than soul-blistering orgasms; it was a deeper connection as well. It was different, better in so many ways. I'd never suspected this is what I was missing out on.

Our ragged breathing slowly returned to normal, and I slid off of him. After returning from the bathroom, I snuggled up against him, one leg over his and my head on his shoulder, listening to his heart.

He scratched my back and kissed the top of my head, conveying his tenderness. I was his and he was mine, and now I had the ring to prove it.

My real boyfriend.

CHAPTER 28

AMY

IT WAS A LOVELY MORNING, AND THE TRAFFIC WAS SATURDAY-light as we passed Plymouth on our way to the Cape.

We were headed down to Cape Cod to spend the weekend with the Schmulians at their place in Hyannis Port——naturally the same Hyannis Port where the Kennedy family compound was located. Liam hadn't batted an eye, as if it was perfectly natural for everybody to have a weekend house on the Cape. He was truly disconnected from reality in some ways.

I was looking forward to these two days at the beach. "So what do you expect this to be all about?" I asked.

Liam changed lanes to pass a VW. "Well, that tabloid article got their attention, but I expect they just want to get to know us better. For them, this is very personal. Hue and his father built the company and hired virtually everybody in it. The company is family to him, and he wants to do right by them."

I found myself empathizing. That was very much the way Samantha and I viewed Tiffany's. "So this is a character test?"

236

He nodded. "Yep, that's exactly what it is. He wants to take my measure and see how it fits with the way he's been running his company."

He reached over to place a hand on my thigh.

The touch surprised me in a welcome way. His tenderness was always welcome.

"Sunshine, there's never been a question about you measuring up," he said with a smile in my direction.

I was trying very hard to get used to his constant stream of compliments, but I couldn't control the heat rising in my cheeks again.

We motored on in silence. Here I was sitting in a car that cost as much as a house, with stitched leather on not only the seats, but the door panels and dash as well. I didn't deserve to be here, next to this hot-as-heck bazillionaire——"*Boston's most eligible bachelor*," as Vivienne had put it. This was all surreal, as if at any moment I could wake from the dream and find myself looking up at the water stain above my bed in my crummy little apartment in Somerville, listening to the yelling from my neighbors' apartment.

"Penny for your thoughts, Sunshine." Liam pulled me out of my daydream.

"Just enjoying the scenery." I turned to him and smiled. "And the company." I placed my hand over his. "But I'm still nervous that I might blow this for you."

He slowed behind a pair of trucks blocking both lanes. "For us," he corrected me. "It'll be fine; just be yourself. They won't be able to resist you. I know I can't."

I attempted in vain to control the heat rising in my cheeks. "Stop that."

"It's the truth. We're only still in the game because they like you so much. Hue said so when he called."

I smiled. A lady would know better than to argue.

Siri directed us through town and south toward the coastline. As his phone told us we had arrived, Liam turned onto a gravel-covered drive. We parked in front of the six-car garage adjacent to the huge, white-shingled, two-story house. Behind the house was the beach and the open water of Nantucket Sound.

I waited for Liam to rush around and open my door; doing it myself wasn't worth the argument.

I climbed out. "You said beach cottage."

Liam shrugged. "That's what he told me. I guess it's all in the eye of the beholder."

Beholder, my ass. Nobody in his right mind called this a cottage. It probably had more square footage than my whole apartment building.

Felicia was the first out the door to greet us, followed closely by Hue and his ever-present dog, Zeke.

Liam hefted our luggage into the house, and Felicia showed us to a bedroom on the upper floor.

It was a large room with an attached bath, a desk, a stone fireplace, and a loveseat facing the window.

I stopped at the window to take in the scene. The room looked out over a grassy meadow, the beach, and the water beyond. The rhythmic sound of the waves against the shore drifted in, along with the calls of a few shorebirds. It was hypnotically peaceful.

Liam's smile melted me. "Sunshine, marvelous view, don't you think?"

I nodded. "Your house is beautiful, Felicia. I love that you can hear the ocean from here."

A broad smile came across the older woman's face. "We find it very relaxing here after a hectic week in town."

"Perhaps we should get a place here," Liam said cheerily.

I played it up. "Good idea. Maybe we should scout around a little."

Felicia left us to unpack.

I waited until I heard her descend the stairs. "Buy a place? Really? On the beach? Just like that?"

"Sure, why not?" he answered.

I walked my cosmetic bag into the bathroom. "Maybe in your world, but not where I come from."

He followed and surprised me with a light hug. "My girlfriend deserves the best, and a proper boyfriend would notice how taken you are by this place."

Up against him, the warmth of his chest against my breasts sent unexpected tremors up my spine. I buried my face in his shoulder, wanting to stay here with him, listening to the surf.

I did think the setting was magical. Who wouldn't love a nice place to relax by the beach? In his world, wishes could become reality with the snap of his fingers and a few seconds of his pen to the checkbook.

He rocked us. "Did I tell you how lovely you are today?" He placed a quick kiss on my forehead.

"Only a few dozen times," I said, still clinging to him.

He released me.

It had been a simple hug, but the tenderness of his embrace came from a whole different dimension than the quick squeezes Matt had given me. I hadn't realized until just now how comforting it was to be enfolded in the strong arms of the right man——a man who would protect me, a man I could admire, a man I could trust, a man who cared, a man who cared what I thought.

"We should head downstairs and mingle, or do you need a minute?" he asked, pulling me from my trance.

"No. I'm fine."

After crackers and cheese in the kitchen and a tour of the grounds with a stroll down to the sand, Hue insisted on taking Liam out shooting.

I'd expected us ladies to just sit around and talk, but Felicia had other plans. We were headed to the spa.

This got more bizarre by the minute. I'd splurged to have my nails done, but never a spa day. The life of the rich and famous awaited.

But my thoughts stayed with the fact that in a few hours, Liam and I would be back in the upstairs bedroom——no audience, just the two of us together with the sound of the waves.

The bed awaited, and Liam was, well, Liam, the strong-willed warrior, the lion whose eyes could freeze me in place, the man whose touch could singe my skin. Liam, the man whose hair smelled of old leather, and whose kiss tasted like bottled lust. I couldn't wait.

"You coming?" Felicia asked, pulling me out of my daydream.

I scurried to pick up my purse on the way to the door. "Sure thing. I can't wait." I didn't mean the spa.

~

*L*IAM

W<small>E</small> ARRIVED AT THE SKEET RANGE QUICKLY THE WAY H<small>UE</small> DROVE. Speed limits seemed mere suggestions to him.

"Have you done much shooting, Liam?"

"A little," I told him. "When I was younger, with Wendell, my dad. He thought all of us should be familiar with firearms, so we shot pistols and rifles, mostly."

"Ever shoot skeet before?" he asked as we pulled into a parking spot.

I undid my seat belt. I wasn't used to being in the passenger seat, at the mercy of someone else's driving. "Four or five times is all."

Hue opened up the back, and we retrieved the guns, ammo, and our gear. He had a full complement of everything, including safety glasses and earplugs. He went to check in while I broke open both guns to check that they were unloaded, which they were. His guns were beautifully engraved, double-barrel, over-under models. The man took his shotguns seriously.

Geared up with safety glasses, earplugs, and shooting vests, we started at the first station by the high house after the previous pair had finished their round.

Hue went first and nailed the first two clays, turning them into puffs of orange dust. "Your turn, young man."

I got set up and called for the pull. I hit the one going away from the high house, but missed the crossing orange clay from the low house.

"Very good for someone who hasn't shot in a long time," Hue said with a smile.

We shot from the next two positions before coming to position four, the hardest for me on the course, because both clays would be crossing. I never managed to lead them quite well enough and had always missed both from this angle.

Hue had missed one earlier, but he hit both at this station, and I congratulated him again.

I stepped up to the box and loaded my two shells. "Hue, you make it look so easy."

"Let me show you a little trick," he said as he approached. Starting at the first station, just lead the target by one finger." He held a single finger alongside my barrel. "Visualize a finger-width at the end of the barrel, and add a finger of lead at each of the next stations. So here…" He put four fingers upright at the end of my barrel. Visualize four fingers alongside, and use that as your aim point."

It sounded simple enough. I raised the gun to my shoulder. "Thanks. I'll try that… Pull."

I missed on the first, but I got the second one——the first time I had managed to hit one from station four.

We finished the course with little talking besides compliments about each other's efforts.

Then we picked up our previous discussion of the Patriots' outlook for the season as another pair shot around the course.

I'd been nervous when I arrived, prepared for a series of questions about my lifestyle choices and a cross examination regarding the article in the tabloid, but neither happened. Out here, being with the old man was relaxing: two guys doing guy stuff while the girls were off doing girl stuff, which probably included gossiping up a storm about us.

We started another round of the course, and my score improved a bit, but was still nothing like Hue's. He almost didn't miss.

CHAPTER 29

AMY

FELICIA HAD BOOKED US AT THE SPA DI NAPOLI DOWNTOWN.

The aroma of the vanilla-scented candles filled my nostrils as we entered. Our gorgeous massage room featured a mural on one wall depicting a patio with columns and a balustrade looking out over the Mediterranean, as if we actually were in Italy.

Nikki, my masseuse, started with oil and a heavy shoulder massage as I lay on the soft towels of the table.

I'd always wanted to take a day off to pamper myself at a place like this, but had never found the right time, or the money. Today I would rather have been anywhere else. I was scared to be alone with Felicia, with Liam's deal hanging in the balance.

What if I screw it up for him?

Felicia turned her head to look over at me from her table. "I noticed you have a new ring."

The interrogation had begun.

I held my right hand up. "Yes, Liam gave it to me."

"It's lovely," she said. "I guess it means he thinks you're special."

I looked at the ring and what it represented. "I think he's special too."

Nikki was showing no mercy. Her fingers pushed ever harder, threatening to break bones.

Felicia grunted several times, as it appeared her masseuse was equally mean. "I like Liam. I think you've found a good man there."

I smiled. "Liam is a really nice guy." *Nice* was putting it too mildly; *terrific* would have been a better word.

Felicia winced under her masseuse's assault. "I should have warned you to take an Advil before we came over." She laughed. "But I forgot myself."

Her masseuse grinned.

"You're divorced. Is that right?" Felicia asked after a moment.

She and Hue had clearly been doing homework on us, or at least me, because I didn't remember mentioning it at either of our dinners.

"Yes, a little over a year now," I told her.

"If you don't mind my asking," she said, "what happened?"

I took a breath. My job was to get the deal done, and if it meant dealing with questions about Matt, so be it.

"We got married right out of college, and things were fine until he got accepted to go to school out of town for his masters degree." That was only part of the story. "And Samantha and I had just started our company, so I couldn't pick up and leave."

"Where was the school?"

"North Carolina. He got accepted at Duke." I didn't tell her he'd since left there because he couldn't hack it.

"Fine school, but too far to drive for the weekend," she said. "So you agreed to try a long-distance marriage?"

I hesitated answering this. My canned answer would have been *yes*, but it was a lie. "No, we didn't."

She looked over quizzically, waiting for me to expound.

"He hadn't told me he'd applied."

"That's not good."

Understatement of the year. We were supposed to be working as a team to make a life, and he went off on his own to apply without asking or telling me.

"Matt thought it would have started an argument," I told her. "And he was argument averse in the extreme. He was right. It would have been an argument when he applied. Postponing it only created a worse one when he finally informed me that he had been accepted and had already written them a check for registration fees." I had finally gotten it off my chest.

"You poor thing. That's terrible."

"Needless to say, long distance didn't work for us. And it is not something I would ever want to try again."

She nodded silently, and we let the ladies work us.

Her masseuse took a short break.

"Do you think Liam's ready for a second try?" Felicia asked.

I was confused by her question. "Second try?"

"Why, marriage of course," she said.

It was my turn to wince. Had Liam implied to them somehow that we were destined to be married?

"I have no idea." It was as close to a noncommittal answer as I could get.

Felicia took in a deep breath as her masseuse started again on her lower back. "It's terrible what happened with his wife. The Boston business community is a small and close-knit one. We knew he was hurting after losing her. It's terrible for a disease like that to take one so young." She clearly knew more than I'd expected about Liam's ordeal with Roberta.

I couldn't relay any of what Liam had confided in confidence. "I think what happened hit him pretty hard. I'm not sure he's over it yet."

I couldn't let her know it had nearly destroyed him. I had been living with a happy man the last few weeks, but some people were better than others at hiding their hurt beneath a mask. If he was putting on an act for me, I couldn't spot it, but I had been fooled before.

Felicia lifted her head. "I think he's finally ready to move on. I wouldn't be at all surprised if he pops the question."

Liam sure had her fooled. "I don't think that's in the cards."

"I see how he looks at you," Felicia told me. "That man is over-the-top in love with you, lady."

She sounded like Vivienne. Liam and I had put on an act for these people, and it seemed to have worked——at least it had been an act before.

Nikki stopped her kneading and prodding and started placing warm, black stones on my back.

This was my first ever hot stone treatment. The heat soothed my sore muscles as it soaked in——my reward for tolerating Nikki's attempt to tenderize me.

Felicia's eyes were closed, a smile on her face. Could she be seeing something I was missing with Liam?

The warmth growing in my chest was no longer a result of the stones. Could I dare to hope that Felicia was right about how serious he was?

~

LIAM

AFTER OUR SHOOTING, WE STOPPED FOR LUNCH AT A SMALL seafood place on the way back. We both ordered fish and chips.

"I think it was a very noble thing you did for Amy's company," he told me once the waiter departed.

This was not supposed to be on his radar——or anybody's.

"I'm not sure I follow you," I said, trying to feign ignorance.

He put down his water glass. "Liam, you should know that I have friends in all the local banks and law offices."

I sighed. "It seemed like a good investment."

"Right. It sounded to me like a very honorable thing to do."

He was being cagey about what he knew, and this was dangerous ground. I'd clearly underestimated Hue Schmulian.

"Did you know I knew your father?"

This statement also surprised me. We'd talked several times, and he'd never mentioned it before.

"Wendell?"

"Yes," he said. "Wendell and I were in the same fraternity in college and kept in contact through the years."

"I didn't know that."

"He was a good man."

"The best," I agreed.

"He would have been proud of you for helping Amy that way."

The waiter brought us our fish and chips, and we started devouring the food as he regaled me with a few of Wendell's exploits in college.

"And then there was the time we were at the beach drinking beer around the fire with these two girls. Wendell dares them to go skinny dipping with us."

He laughed. "So they start undressing and tell us to get in the water first. Naturally, we peel everything off as fast as we can. We run and dive into the surf. I was surprised by how cold the water was, but the real shock was when we looked back and the girls had thrown our clothes into the fire and were running away."

Hue and I laughed so hard, we got stares from the other customers.

After a moment, Hue composed himself enough to continue. "Needless to say, getting back to the frat house that night wasn't easy."

After that, the stories became more tame.

"I know the article in the paper is all about women you met before Amy," he said after a while.

I nodded. "There hasn't been anyone else since her."

"When do you plan to ask her?"

I took a sip of my Coke. "Ask her what?"

"Why, to marry you, of course."

This conversation had suddenly ventured into dangerous territory. "I think it's a little too early."

"It's never too early for the right woman," he said. "I took longer than I should have with Felicia, and I almost lost her."

I'd made the same mistake with Roberta and regretted it.

He put down his water glass. "I understand you haven't been with Amy long, but for the right woman, it's long enough."

I contemplated his statement. He didn't understand how short the time had been. Or did he?

"It's just some advice from an old man, and you can take it or leave it."

"Thanks," I replied.

"Felicia and I think she's a gem."

That was understandable; everybody liked Amy.

"But that's only half the reason I invited you down here," he continued.

I waited for the bombshell to drop.

"I also wanted to confess something," he said.

This conversation was getting curiouser and curiouser, as they said in *Alice in Wonderland*.

"I had a visit from Damien Winterbourne."

I set my jaw, trying to control my anger.

"Personally, I think your offer is a very fair one," he continued.

I didn't have to wait long for the *but*.

"But he's bid twenty percent over you, and that's something I just can't ignore."

I took in a deep breath. "What if we were to match his offer?"

"You could," he said. "But he assured me he would beat whatever you offer by twenty percent. I believe him, and I think it would just be an exercise in futility on your part."

There it was. Winterbourne had put a target on my back, and was determined to beat me in each and every deal.

I took another sip of my Coke as I formulated the question in my mind. "You said he outbid us by twenty percent?"

"Yes, that's right. Twenty percent to the dollar," Hue replied.

He'd just given me a very crucial piece of information.

Winterbourne had to have known our exact offering price, and that narrowed the list of possible traitors in my company. Not everyone knew the specifics of each offer.

I smiled. "Thanks, Hue. I appreciate the heads up."

"Nothing personal, Liam, but I can't ignore the difference in the offers."

"I understand," I assured him.

I appreciated his honesty, and his narrowing down my pool of suspects. But I was still left with the problem of how to satisfy Syd if I gave up on this deal.

I gritted my teeth. The problem seemed intractable. I pushed my food away; I'd lost my appetite.

"How do you think the Dolphins will stack up against our Patriots this year?" Hue asked.

With that simple question, he indicated our business discussion was over. All I could do now was go back and discuss our options, or lack of them, with Josh on Monday.

My life was turning to utter crap.

"Don't look glum, Liam. You have the love of a good woman," Hue added. "In the long run, that makes all the difference."

～

AMY

LIAM ASSURED ME HE'D HAD A GOOD TIME ON HIS SHOOTING expedition with Hue, but I knew him well enough now to know something was troubling him.

"Liar," I whispered when the Schmulians were far enough away.

The four of us spent the afternoon on the Schmulian's deck

before walking the beach again. Zeke failed to catch any of the birds he chased.

The walk didn't allow any time alone with Liam to pry loose what was troubling him.

Back at the house the Schmulians kept calling a cottage, we took our shoes off on the deck.

I turned mine upside down to empty the sand out before reentering.

"That's always a problem," Felicia said as she knocked her shoes together, loosening the sand from inside.

After I followed her example, the insides of mine were largely sand free, but I couldn't say the same for my socks.

Dinner time arrived quickly, and I offered to help Felicia in the kitchen.

She was chopping tomatoes for the salad when the men opted to drink their wine on the deck.

"You have a good man there," she said once the door closed.

I finished rinsing the lettuce. "Thank you. I think so too."

She put her knife down. "Don't let him get down about the news. It's nothing personal." She scooped the tomato pieces into the salad bowl.

"I'll do my best," I said, wondering what the bad news was, but too afraid to ask outright.

It had to be bad if it had gotten to Liam. He was always so positive with his "look forward, not back," no apologies motto.

DINNER WENT QUITE WELL, DELICIOUS FOOD, AND RELAXED conversation; none of the angst of our first dinner with the Schmulians. And hearing Hue had known Wendell Covington, Liam's dad, had been particularly encouraging news.

"And then we turned around to see the girls throwing our clothes in the fire," Hue told us all, breaking into a huge belly laugh. "And our wallets were in the jeans."

We all laughed at the vision of two drunk college boys stuck miles from their fraternity house, without clothes or money. This and the other stories Hue recounted over Felicia's berry cobbler had me laughing until it hurt.

By the time we were ready to retire to our bedroom upstairs, all the laughter had loosened Liam up, and he seemed to have gotten past whatever had bothered him earlier today.

He opened the door for me as he always did and closed it behind us.

I jumped him for the kiss I'd wanted to give him all day.

He returned my passion with his own fervor, but broke it off early.

"Now tell me what the problem is," I demanded.

"No problem," he said, averting his eyes.

I buried my head in his shoulder. "If I'm really your girlfriend, I deserve to know."

He held me quietly, rocking.

"A gentleman would confide in his lady."

That loosened his lips. "It's Winterbourne again."

I pulled back to look into his face. "How so?"

"They've outbid us."

I placed a hand on his chest and scratched lightly. "Can you match them?"

"I could try, but it won't work. They've got a spy inside, so as soon as I do, they'll know and up their offer again. Hue told me they vowed to outbid anything I come up with."

"I have an idea," I said. "What if you offer more right now, here, in private, where nobody else knows?"

He kissed me on the forehead. "That's not the way it works. We have to have a written contract and all that. And besides, twenty-percent extra isn't something they can ignore."

I couldn't believe I'd heard him correctly. At the size of this deal, twenty percent was double-digit millions. "They'd be nuts to overbid you by that much, wouldn't they?"

"Not if they think it's the knockout blow."

I hugged him again and wished I had a way to ease the disappointment.

"Don't worry, Sunshine. I'll find a way. I always do."

His voice belied his optimism. His company hung in the balance, and we both knew it.

CHAPTER 30

AMY

IT HAD BEEN THREE DAYS SINCE LIAM HAD LEARNED HUE
Schmulian intended to accept the offer from his nemesis, Damien
Winterbourne.

Liam insisted it was just another setback, but the way he had
explained it before, after losing the Sanders deal to Winterbourne,
he'd needed this one to keep his big investors from pulling out and
taking down his company. He'd stayed late last night at the office,
brainstorming things with Josh, and he was there again today.

I smiled as I pushed through the glass doors to the always-
welcome cool air of our building lobby with tonight's steak in my
shopping bag. The clack of my heels on the marble floor echoed in
the large room.

"Miss Amy," Carl, our concierge, called. "I've got a package
for you. Actually, for Mr. Quigley, if you could take it upstairs."

I walked over to retrieve the envelope Carl held out. It was one
of those FedEx letter envelopes. "Sure, Carl. No problem." The
return address was Johns Hopkins University, Baltimore, Mary-
land. I put the envelope under my arm and headed upstairs.

Once inside our home, I put Liam's envelope on the front table. It hit me how calling this *our home* seemed so natural now.

I couldn't get out of my heels quickly enough and padded across the cool floor to the kitchen. I pulled a glass from the cupboard and surveyed my choices in the refrigerator after putting the meat away. Mango juice seemed like the right thing for this evening.

I downed half the glass before going to change.

After donning a Red Sox T-shirt and a pair of jeans, I headed for the couch.

The blinking red light of the answering machine caught my eye on the way.

It showed one message. I hit play, getting ready to hit delete on what I expected to be another marketing call. There ought to be a law against those guys bothering everybody. Of course, there *was* a law already, but nobody paid attention to it.

But the voice that emanated from the speaker wasn't a marketing call. "*Liam, this is your uncle, Garth. I could not reach you on your cell phone today, so I am leaving this message on your machine. I know how much you have wanted to be admitted to medical school, and I have finally had some success on that front. I received a call today from the Dean of Admissions at Johns Hopkins. He has opened up a place for you in their school this fall. They promised to send a package of material, which should arrive today. I am sorry that it took me so long to be of help to you in this matter. I am confident you will make an excellent doctor. Please call me when you receive this message.*"

My legs went weak, and I braced myself against the table. I hit the play button again to make sure I hadn't misheard the message. When it finished, my stomach was sour.

Liam was going to Baltimore. He'd been working on this the whole time and hadn't told me.

I couldn't do a long-distance relationship. Not ever again.

I thought back to our conversation at that first dinner. He'd mentioned his goal was to be a doctor, but he'd laughed it off as impossible——or at least improbable given his test scores.

Now here it was a certainty. Yet again, his world and mine were so different. He was rich, with a powerful family behind him. They could make calls, cash in favors, and make doorways appear that were never open to the rest of us. His uncle makes a few calls, and abracadabra, he goes from rejected to accepted at medical school.

Matt had chosen his schooling over me, and the result had been a disintegrated marriage. Liam would make the same choice; he had to. He'd promised Roberta. I looked down at my ring.

It was clear where this would lead. Medical school beckoned, and his promise to his dead wife would be fulfilled. And I'd be left here in Boston.

Of course I couldn't pick up and leave, follow him. He and I had talked about it when we'd discussed my situation with Matt. He knew I wouldn't leave. I'd put so much time and effort into Tiffany's, and I owed Samantha and the rest of the team so much. I couldn't abandon them.

I went into Liam's office and located a piece of paper. I wrote a note, trying to hold back my tears. I couldn't do this any longer. I couldn't stay. I wouldn't continue down the path to another failed relationship where the more I invested, the more I lost.

Reluctantly, I went to the bedroom, took off the ring, and placed it with the note on top of the nightstand on Liam's side of the bed. Although the bed and both nightstands were his, I had come to think of the bed as ours, and the nightstand on the right as mine. How silly——there was no us. There couldn't be, not with him leaving. I couldn't, I wouldn't, make him choose between me and his promise to Roberta. Whichever way that went would rip him apart.

I gathered my purse, put on my Nikes, and made for the elevator. This was a chickenshit way to leave, but facing Liam would take more strength than I could muster right now. Maybe we could talk in a month or so.

My legs shook as I pushed the down button. The door opened, but I didn't enter. I went back to the penthouse and unlocked the door.

I took the key off my key ring and placed it next to the ring on my goodbye note. I couldn't have it. I couldn't be tempted to come back. This had to be a clean and complete break. Only by being strong could I protect my heart. I could send Vivienne back to get my things, right now I had to leave.

I closed the door one last time, and when the elevator doors opened again, I passed into the car and pressed the button to the lobby for the final time.

The shiny stainless doors closed, and the cold of the tiny cab enveloped me. It was only twenty-six floors down, but I knew I was descending from life in the clouds to the real world at street level, where people like me dwelled.

CHAPTER 31

LIAM

My phone showed missed calls from Nick and Uncle Garth.
After parking back home, I returned Nick's call.

"*It's about time, douchebag,*" he said, answering in his normal friendly manner. "*What do you have to say for yourself today?*"

"I'm a piece of shit." I hoped we would be ending this ritual soon.

"*That's for sure,*" he said.

"I'm returning your call, Nick."

"*As much as I hate to do it, I have some good news to give you,*" he announced.

Finally.

"Yes?"

"*We have a fish on the line,*" he told me.

This was the news I've been waiting for. "Who is it?" I asked anxiously.

"*Just a fish right now. Won't know who it is exactly until we reel him in.*"

"How does this work?"

He let out an exasperated breath. *"All I know right now is that the information got to Winterbourne."* He paused. *"It'll take a little time to track it back precisely, but they went for the bait. So now it's just a matter of time before I figure out what path it took."*

"Thanks, Nick." This was the best news I'd had in a long time.

"You're welcome, douchebag."

It was the first time he had said anything normal to me. Perhaps we were making progress.

"One other thing," he added. *"This guy Winterbourne's accounts are odd."*

"Right now I don't care about how he does business, just as long as he isn't doing it by spying on me."

We got off the line after I asked him to give my regards to Katie.

Next I dialed my uncle.

"Liam, I have great news," he said in greeting.

"The Matt Hudson check finished?" I asked.

"Unfortunately, no. Not yet," he said. *"Did you get my message on your answering machine?"*

"No, I'm only walking in the front door now."

Our doorman, Carl, greeted me as I passed him on the way to the elevators. "There was a delivery for you earlier. Miss Amy carried it upstairs."

"Thanks, Carl," I mouthed silently to him as I continued to listen to my uncle on the way to the elevators.

"Ah, well, I have had success on another front," Garth began. *"I received a call today from the Dean of Admissions at Johns Hopkins. He has opened up a place for you in the medical school this fall."*

The elevator door closed, and the car started its upward journey.

"That's great," I shouted into the phone. I couldn't believe it. I had given up hope for this year and already planned another set of applications next year.

"This requires that you attend the new student orientation on

the eighteenth and pay a few miscellaneous fees. They promised to send you a package of material, which should arrive today. I am sorry that it took me so long to be of help to you in this matter."

Upstairs, the deadbolt was unlocked. I picked up the FedEx envelope on the front table and ripped it open. Inside were an incoming student checklist, housing application, and first semester bill for Johns Hopkins, along with a letter telling me I had been admitted and needed to attend new student orientation.

"I just got home, and the material is here. I don't know how to thank you enough for this, Uncle Garth."

"No thanks necessary. I am certain you will become a fine doctor."

After hanging up, a quick survey of the rooms yielded no Amy. A check of the patio also came up empty. A half-empty glass of juice on the counter indicated she had been home.

She must have gone out for a walk on the Common.

The bottle of pinot grigio in the fridge was almost empty. I poured what was left into a glass and went to change. I downed the wine in celebration on the way to the bedroom.

Passing into my closet to hang up my coat, I caught a glint of light from the nightstand. Walking over, I found it was the ring I'd given Amy and a house key atop a folded piece of paper.

I opened the paper and read the note.

Liam,

I know you'll make a wonderful doctor.

I'll arrange to get my things later.

Goodbye,

Amy

Fuck.

I threw the glass across the room. It shattered against the wall, glass shards littering the carpet. What the fuck was going on? I hadn't talked to her about this because I thought med school was so far in the future———*our* future.

Now it looked like I was keeping things from her.

Dammit! I have to find my woman.

~

AMY

I CLOSED MY APARTMENT DOOR BEHIND ME AND CAME FACE TO face with the reality that was my fucked-up life.

The envelope on the table reminded me I had a court session scheduled with Matt and his attack-dog lawyer tomorrow. I hadn't confided in Liam, but I had gotten a notice last week that included a picture of me wearing the emeralds Liam had bought me. The letter claimed that I had hidden money from my cheating now-ex-husband and the court, and Matt was now entitled to half my interest in Tiffany's Fine Chocolates. Show up or be held in contempt of court, it had read.

Fucking scumbags.

Shakespeare had it right: first we kill all the lawyers.

A bottle of wine called me from the fridge. I unscrewed the cap and poured a large glass, nothing dainty and ladylike about my drinking tonight.

A few weeks ago my problem had been finding the right investors to provide the financing we needed for Tiffany's and all the people there. Now I'd fixed that, only to have my scumbag ex threatening to take it all away. He hadn't done one iota of work to make Tiffany's a success, and now he was demanding half my stake in the company Samantha and I had toiled to launch. What an asshole.

A few weeks ago I had been happy to go on dead-end dates with a string of mostly losers. Okay, not exactly happy, but at least I wasn't getting my heart broken.

Then along came Liam, and my world was turned upside down. He'd drawn me out until I'd dared to feel again. I'd felt like a desired woman, a girlfriend, even a lady. Now that was gone, snatched away from me by fate.

I poured another glass and settled in to watch *Judge Judy*. The show always made me feel better because some of the people on there were even stupider than me.

Judge Judy had just finished chastising some moron to pay his girlfriend for the damage he'd done to her car. And, no it didn't matter that he had only wrecked it because he was drunk when she threw his ass out of the apartment. It didn't make it her fault just because it was the beer in her fridge he got drunk on, and no, it didn't make a difference that she'd refused to bail him out. That only made her smart. The guy nearly blew a gasket, which I guess is why they have a bad-ass bailiff in her fake court.

A knock sounded at my door.

"Amy." It was Liam's voice from the hallway.

I approached the door. "Go away."

"We need to talk," he said.

"No, we don't. The job is done. The Springbok negotiations are over. You said so yourself. I fulfilled my part of the bargain."

He waited for me to say something more, but I didn't. "Amy, we need to talk."

"You already said that, remember? I told you I would be your fake girlfriend to get the deal done, and it's done, so now I'm done."

"As I recall," he said, "you took the job of *actual* girlfriend."

I had, and now I regretted my choice. "I was just faking it," I lied. "I thought it would increase the odds of getting the deal done if I faked being your girlfriend well enough to fool you."

"You don't mean that."

"You calling me a liar?"

"Tell me what the problem is," he said. "You owe me that much."

The request was simple enough. It wouldn't make it easier, but he was right. I needed to explain, though if he thought about it at all, it was pretty obvious.

"I saw the envelope. I heard your uncle's message. I know you're leaving."

He tried the locked door handle. "Amy, open the door so we can discuss this."

"We just had that discussion." I turned his words around on him.

"I want you to come with me," he said.

And there it was: the demand that I leave my life to follow him. He'd agreed that it had been Matt's fault when he left me, not mine that I didn't follow him. Now the shoe was on the other foot, and the logic got turned around.

"You know I can't do that. I can't abandon Samantha and everybody else and leave my company."

"Sunshine, then you stay here. I'll go to school there, and I'll see you every single weekend."

He hadn't been through it, so he didn't realize how it wouldn't work. It could never work.

"Been there, done that," I told him. "It doesn't work. It can't work."

"Then I'll tell you what, Sunshine, I'll stay here with you."

His suggestion was off-the-wall stupid.

"You can't do that. You won't do that. You know it, and I know it."

"Bullshit," he said angrily.

"You promised Roberta to become a doctor and heal people. I know how you are about your promises. You won't be able to let that one go. It will tear you up inside every day until you decide to honor the promise and leave me."

"Sunshine, I would never leave you."

I was tempted to believe him. "Liam, you forget I know you. I can't put you through that. I won't put you through that. I won't make you choose between me and your promise to her."

The hardest part was understanding that in the end, he wouldn't choose me anyway. He couldn't; the stupid coin in his pocket would drive him away.

For the longest time, he didn't say anything. "Sunshine, life is all about making choices. I choose you."

I couldn't let him tempt me. "And I don't get a choice? Liam, the answer is no. I can't and I won't let you break your promise to become a doctor. And I can't and I won't try another long-distance relationship. It can't work."

If I let myself become more attached to him, it would only be harder in the end. That would utterly destroy me.

"What would you like for dinner?" he asked, surprising me, tempting me.

"Liam, I won't fall for that. I'm not opening the door."

He spent another ten minutes trying to convince me to open the door.

Finally he sighed. "We'll talk again tomorrow. Sleep tight," he said. "Love you, Sunshine," he called just before his footsteps faded out down the hallway.

I'd understood how he felt, but this was the first time he'd said the words. So natural, so normal, as if he'd said them a million times.

He loves me.

I didn't say a thing. I didn't trust myself. Maybe he did, but did it matter? I went to the window and hid behind the curtain as I looked out. I watched him drive away, carrying my heart.

Returning to the kitchen, I spied the almost-full bottle of tequila from the last time Vivienne and I had attempted margaritas.

CHAPTER 32

LIAM

I HAD TRIED, AND I'D FAILED. I COULDN'T EVEN CONVINCE HER TO open the door and talk to me face to face. I hadn't made a single bit of progress with her.

She'd said she'd faked the whole thing, and I'd fallen for it.

I didn't believe that for a second.

I'd learned the hard way to never let myself get close to a woman, to keep myself safe. Losing Roberta had taught me that. I'd spent all the time since her death not letting a woman get into my heart, not going on dates, not sleeping over, staying safe. Until Amy.

Now Amy had taught me the lesson all over again.

How could I always pick the ones that would leave me?

I poured myself a third glass of scotch, and the bottle was now empty.

I grabbed my keys. A liquor store was only a short walk away. That I knew from experience.

$\sim$

AMY

"WAKE UP!" MY SISTER SHOUTED SO LOUD IT THREATENED TO break the windows of my little apartment.

I rolled over in my bed and put my hands to my ears. "Keep it down. You don't need to yell." The little men with jackhammers were busy trying to break out of my head.

"I'll stop yelling when you start making sense," she said, still way too loudly.

I put my head under the pillow. "Go away."

She did, and finally it was quiet.

I stumbled out of bed and found the Advil bottle in the drawer of my bathroom. My tongue had grown a fur coat. I grabbed three of the tablets and swallowed them with water from the sink. I climbed back in bed as Vivienne returned with a steaming mug.

"Here, drink this." She shoved the coffee at me.

It tasted like tar. "What the hell is this?" I only had instant in the kitchen, and this didn't taste anything like it. The little men with jackhammers liked it even less.

"Triple strength. Now drink it, or I'll have to pour it on you."

I debated for a moment if a coffee burn was really worse than drinking mud before I chose to drink her cup of shit. "You're a terrible cook."

"What the fuck?" she yelled, only slightly more quietly this time. She held up the tequila bottle I'd cozied up with last night. She flung open the curtains.

I closed my eyes against the searing light pouring in.

"This isn't like you. You don't guzzle hard liquor, especially on a weeknight."

"Go away," was all I could manage.

"And this place smells like shit." She turned on the water in the bathroom. "No wonder. You puked last night, but your aim wasn't very good."

It didn't come back to me, but the way I felt, it didn't surprise me. This morning nothing would surprise me.

"I'm going to charge extra for this," she yelled from the bathroom.

I hid under the pillow while she bitched about cleaning up my barf.

She pulled the covers off me. "Time to get up and join the living."

I pulled the covers back up. "What are you doing here, anyway?"

"Samantha called. She was worried when you didn't come into work and wouldn't answer your phone. She expected you in before court."

Fuck.

"What time is it?" I asked.

"A little before two."

I had missed it. "Fucking shit. I was supposed to be in court this morning." Now I was going to be totally fucked by Matt and his bloodsucking lawyer.

"Well, you fucked that up. Want to tell me why you got so shit-faced last night, and what you're doing here instead of in your palace in the sky?"

I retreated under the pillow again. "None of your business."

"I called Liam, and he just said you decided to sleep here. So tell your little sister what you did to get yourself banished from the castle."

I hated to admit the truth. It hurt so much. "I broke up with him."

"You what?" she yelled at a million decibels.

The Advil hadn't taken effect yet——if it ever would——and the jackhammer men told me how much they hated the yelling.

"Please, keep it down."

"I'll stop yelling when you tell me what happened."

I didn't know where to start, and some of it was fuzzy. "He's leaving town."

"Okay, that's not great, but what's the deal?"

"He promised his wife before she died that he'd become a doctor."

"And?" she asked.

"He got into medical school in Baltimore."

Vivienne put her hand on my shoulder. "What did he say about it?"

This was going to be the hard part for her to understand. "He said he wouldn't go, and he'd stay with me."

She shook me. "That's great. Problem solved. Now you can go have wild make-up sex and be back to normal."

"No," I said. "It won't work."

Vivienne stood. "Bullshit. Make-up sex always works with guys. He said he'd stay here for you. It doesn't get much better than that."

"I can't do that to him."

"You must still be drunk, sis. You're not making any sense. You don't want him to leave, and he wants to stay. Looks like a happy ending to me. Make-up sex is next on the agenda."

She didn't get who he was. "Viv, it's not so simple. He made a promise, and that's the one thing he lives by. If I ask him to break that promise, it'll eat him up. It'll end up tearing us apart. I just know it."

"Get up and take a shower. I'm taking you out to get some food. Maybe then you'll make more sense, because right now, you're just twisting things up."

I sat up too rapidly, and my head objected. "I am not."

⁓

LIAM

A SOUND SOMEWHERE WOKE ME.

I managed to get an eye open. The image was fuzzy, but I

could make out a bottle on the coffee table in front of me. I pulled myself up enough to grab it and took a swig, not bothering with a glass.

Hair of the dog.

It would help with this fucking headache.

The banging at the door roused me again.

"Liam, open up." It was Josh.

I ignored him and lay back down.

I closed my eyes.

"Liam, let me in."

After a while, the pleas stopped and peace returned.

What day was it? The answer didn't come. There had to be an easier way to get drunk that involved more drunk time and less hangover time. That was going to be my next invention. The way my head pounded this morning, it would sell like hotcakes——and at almost any price.

Sleep was what I needed.

It hurt less when I slept.

CHAPTER 33

LIAM

THE ROOM WAS SHAKING.

The earthquake wouldn't stop.

"Wake up," she said.

I struggled to get an eye open. One was welded shut with some kind of eye-crud superglue; the other wouldn't focus.

"Wake up, Liam," she repeated, shaking me more violently.

The eye I'd managed to open gave me a fuzzy image. "Katie?" My sister was here, or this was a monster fucking hallucination. "You're not real."

"I'm real, and right now I'm real serious. Get your fucking ass into the shower and get cleaned up."

I managed to sit upright and reached for my bottle again, but not quickly enough.

Katie grabbed the bottle in a blur. "No way, Jose. You're not getting any more of this."

I lunged for her, but missed and ended up on my hands and knees.

She gave the bottle to Josh.

Josh was here too. How did that happen?

"How did you get in?" I asked, getting to my feet and heading to the liquor cabinet.

Josh walked to the kitchen. "I was worried about you, so I called Katie."

Katie held up something shiny. "And I still have the key you gave me last time I visited."

He started pouring my scotch down the sink.

"Hey, that's expensive stuff."

"You can afford it," Katie said as Josh poured the last of it down the drain.

I went around my sister to my liquor cabinet and opened it. It was empty. It couldn't be empty.

"We cleared that out before we woke you," Josh told me.

"Fuck you, I needed that," I told him.

Katie offered me a cup and some tablets. "You need this more."

The coffee was hot, but would have been better with some whiskey in it. The Advil would help, I hoped.

Katie started herding me toward my bedroom. "Now off to the shower. You smell even worse than you look."

I made it to the master bath without falling. My eyesight was improving, but my head was feeling worse. I sloughed off the sweats I was wearing and stepped under the warm water.

"Here, drink this," Katie said, reappearing with a glass.

I covered up. "How about a little privacy?" My sister could be awfully damned pushy.

"I'm your sister, remember? Nothing I haven't seen before."

I took the orange juice with my free hand, covering what I could with the other.

She stood there staring at me. "I'll take the glass when you're done, and no pouring it down the drain like you used to do as a kid."

"Ha ha." I drank the cold juice, which went down easier than the hot coffee, and handed her the empty glass.

She stopped at the bathroom door. "I'll be waiting on the patio when you're done." She wasn't going to be shooed away easily.

A little while later, the kitchen smelled scrumptious as I limped through. I found her and Josh on the patio with a bacon-and-eggs breakfast Katie must have cooked, because it was beyond Josh's capabilities.

I took a seat across from them. "Thanks, Katie. Smells good." I spooned some eggs onto my plate.

"How come I have to hear about your lady friend from Uncle Garth? You should have called me."

"Sorry. I never got the time." My excuse sounded lame even to me.

"Right," Katie said. "So tell me what's special about her."

"Nothing. She's just another girl," I lied. I didn't care to rehash any of this with Katie or Josh."

"Right," Katie repeated. "That's why you were doing the drunk homeless guy imitation on the couch."

"And not coming in to work," Josh added.

"I just felt like it," I explained. "Now that you've talked to me, when is your return flight?"

She picked up her juice glass. "Fat chance. I'm not leaving until I meet this girl and kick her ass."

"She doesn't need beating up, and since when are you in charge of my dating life?"

She speared a piece of bacon. "Since you took a swing at Nick in high school and decided to interfere in my life."

"Seriously?"

She finished chewing. "If you don't start talking, I'm going to invite Nick to come out and join us."

Josh was staying remarkably quiet, but he couldn't stifle his laugh at Katie's threat. I pointed a threatening finger at him.

"I didn't say a thing," he said, putting his hands up in mock surrender.

The last thing I needed was any more time with Nick Knowlton. I had no choice now. Katie didn't indulge in idle threats.

"Her name is Amy."

Katie glared at me. "Josh told me that part. Let's skip to the fight or whatever."

I finished the piece of bacon I had started while Katie waited, glaring at me. I could drag this out and waste her time. It served her right.

"There was no fight. She left me a day or two ago."

Josh shook his head. "That was a week ago."

"What day is it?

Josh double checked his watch. "Wednesday."

I had completely lost track of time. It had been a week——a whole week. I thought back, and as much as I tried, I couldn't remember a thing after going over to see her.

"Is she okay?" I asked Josh.

He finished chewing. "This week she's going into work regularly is all I can tell you."

His words were a relief. I didn't know what else I'd expected.

"She left and said we couldn't be together anymore," I said.

Her words were still crystal clear in my memory. As much as I wanted them to change, they were the same each time I recalled them. "*It can't work*," she had said. The words had a deadly finality to them.

Katie finished her bacon. "And?"

"And that's it," I told her.

She picked up her phone. "I'm dialing Nick if you don't start talking."

I let out a breath. "Alright." I was absolutely not having Nick here. "It started when Uncle Garth called and said he got me into Johns Hopkins med school."

"That's good news. You wanted to go, right?"

I took another forkful of eggs before continuing. "Yeah, I did, but that's in Baltimore, and Amy's tied down here in Boston."

"But it's only a quick flight. You can spend every weekend together. It's not like you can't afford the flights."

"She won't go for that," I explained. "Her previous marriage was a long-distance relationship, and it ended badly. The whole thing is a nonstarter for her."

Katie wasn't buying it. "That's silly. Lots of people make it work, even cross country."

"I can't convince her of that——nobody can. So I told her I'd stay instead of going to med school."

"And that didn't sway her?" Katie asked.

I shifted in my seat. I'd thought it sounded easy as well, until Amy had reminded me of my promise.

"The problem is, she thinks my promise to Roberta would screw up our relationship." I had unconsciously brought out my Lincoln half-dollar and was rubbing it.

Katie pointed a finger at me. "Is it that damned coin again?"

"Give me a break," I shot back. "Dad gave me this."

She grabbed her purse and pulled out a dollar coin. It was a Susan B. Anthony dollar, the kind you didn't ever see around anymore.

She held it up. "Dad gave me this one. It was to be my reminder of his most important lesson. But I let it fuck up my life. I let it overrule everything else until Nick got me to see how unhealthy it was."

"Nick," I said, rolling my eyes. "I don't——"

"He's family now," she spat back, interrupting me. "What's our number-one rule?"

I knew it, and she knew I knew it.

"Say it, Liam," she demanded.

I gave in. She was right. "Family comes first."

"That's right, and now he's family, so give him a break. You would like him if you gave him half a chance. Bill does, and Lauren too."

That floored me. Bill had been as opposed to Katie having anything to do with Nick Knowlton as I was back in the day. Mentioning Lauren was the kicker. My sister-in-law was like a human scale; she could take someone's measure quicker than anyone. If Nick was the bullshitter I thought he was, Lauren should have seen through him in two seconds.

Katie sipped her juice. "Now let me finish. I fucked up by not putting Dad's lesson in perspective, and I don't want you to do the same. Don't throw out the lesson; just figure out how to work it into your life without letting it take over."

I nodded. She had a point. We could all become a little obsessive about things.

"So what exactly was your promise to Roberta?" Katie asked.

Josh sat back. He'd been quietly enjoying seeing Katie scold me, and I would get back at him later when she wasn't around.

I fingered my coin. I remembered it clear as day. "That I would become a doctor and heal people."

"Look," Katie said. "You can figure this out. There has to be a way to stay in Boston with her and still keep your word, at least well enough for you and her to feel good about it."

"I tried getting into Tufts, Harvard, and BU. They won't take me. Uncle Garth only got me into Hopkins because he knows the dean."

"What about U Mass?" Josh asked.

I ignored him. I'd tried them as well.

Katie leaned forward to touch my hand. "We'll figure it out. There has to be a way."

I nodded. I didn't see it now, but her confidence was reassuring, if misplaced. "I told you, I can't get into any of the schools here. With my scores, I can't get in anywhere."

"You have to start with a better attitude.

I nodded.

"There's the other problem," Josh said. "He's flunking relationship one-oh-one here."

"What the fuck do you know about relationships?" I shot back.

"Enough to know that you not calling for the last week is a big time fuck up."

His statement was a slap in the face. I'd crawled into a hole and fucked up by not keeping after her.

"He's right, you know," Katie said. "That doesn't send the right signal. If you want to keep her, you can't break contact like that."

"I'll claim I was in the hospital."

Katie laughed. "Grow up. We're not in middle school. At least be honest about screwing up."

"She won't even talk to me."

"You need me now," Josh said.

"How's that?"

He sat up straight. "This is a marketing problem, and I'm better at that than you are."

CHAPTER 34

AMY

THE CALL CAME FROM LUCY AT THE FRONT DESK. "*YOUR MORNING delivery is here. Gary is bringing it up.*"

"Tell him not to bother," I told her.

"*He's already on the way.*"

"Just start refusing them. I don't want them." After respecting my wish to be left alone for the first week, the flowers had started. This past week Liam had been out of control.

"*I can't do that.*" She sighed. "*Samantha would kill me.*"

I gave up.

Gary arrived in my doorway a minute later, with Samantha in tow. She had gotten back from a conference yesterday.

"These are beautiful," she gushed.

"You can put them on the credenza," I told Gary.

He walked them over and set them down. "I think he really likes you." Gary, master of the obvious.

"It's not mutual," I informed him.

He shrugged his shoulders and left.

Sam walked over to the bouquet of roses. "Lucy tells me you've been getting these every day and giving them away."

"Twice a day now."

She pulled the card from the holder. "Wow, I wish someone would send me something like this."

"You can have them."

They didn't change a thing; I'd made my decision. I knew what was best for me, and I couldn't go back on it, no matter how many flowers Liam sent me.

She fingered the envelope. "What does the card say?"

I went back to my computer screen, hoping she would get bored and leave. "Don't know, don't care."

"This is romantic."

When I looked up, she had opened the card. I couldn't complain; I'd claimed not to care.

She read the card. "Listen to the CD. It says it all. Please have dinner with me. Love, Liam." She fanned herself with the envelope. "That's what I call smokin' hot."

"Like I said, not interested."

"What's on the CD?" she asked.

"Not a clue. Like I said——"

"Yeah, not interested." She walked to my phone and dialed. "Lucy, please ask Gary to bring up that boombox he has down in shipping. Thanks."

"Can't you just leave it alone? It's my life, not yours."

She sat down. "You're my best friend, and I can't let you totally fuck up your life without at least saying something."

"I am not fucking it up," I said firmly. "I'm keeping it from getting fucked up."

"And who told you not to marry Matt?" she asked.

I had forgotten that one. "You did. But it doesn't mean you know everything. You had a fifty-fifty chance of getting it right."

Gary arrived with a dusty boombox in hand. "You wanted some music?" He punched a button and "The Gambler" by Kenny Rogers started playing.

"Thanks, Gary. We've got it from here." She took the player from him and turned Kenny's volume down.

"You do have to know when to fold 'em. He has that part right," I told Samantha.

She scowled at me, pulled the CD from the flowers, and loaded it into the player.

The music started.

I knew the song right away: "Sunny," the song he'd told the Schmulians was our song at that first dinner downtown. I teared up. The refrain kept getting to me——all that talk about love so true. I turned toward the window to hide from Samantha.

Liam had called me Sunshine from our very first meeting at the bar. As the song continued, I realized he'd interspersed snippets of the lyrics in many of our conversations. He'd told me I made him feel ten feet tall, that I was his sweet, complete desire. He'd told me I eased his pain and helped him see the truth. And that I was the spark of nature's fire——whatever that meant.

Every refrain made it harder to keep my resolve, but I had to. My sanity depended on it.

Mercifully the song ended.

I stayed facing the window.

"You really should listen to the lyrics like he said," Samantha scolded. "I don't know a woman in this building that wouldn't love a boyfriend half as romantic as the one you're throwing away."

"Are we done yet?" I asked still facing the window to hide my tears.

"Yeah, we're done," she said. "I'll leave you with it."

I heard the click as she pressed play, and the music started again.

I saw her leave in the reflection of the window.

The door closed behind her, but the music continued.

"*Sunny one so true, I love you…*"

LIAM

I HAD A MISSED CALL. I HELD MY BREATH, CLOSED MY EYES, AND wished for it to be Amy. I opened my eyes. No such luck. The screen told me Uncle Garth had called.

He picked up when I returned the call, and after filling me in on the family, he finally got to the reason for his earlier call. *"The Hanson Group has finished the background check you requested on Mr. Hudson,"* he informed me calmly.

"And?" I asked.

"It contains quite a lot of interesting material. Mr. Hudson has been a rather busy young man, it seems."

I waited for the punchline, but it didn't arrive.

His voice carried loudly over the line as the elevator doors opened. *"I will forward you their email with all the particulars. I think you will find it quite interesting. If I may be of further assistance with this matter, you need only ask."*

His statement suggested he thought there was a thread in the material worth pulling to see where it would lead. My uncle delighted in being mysterious.

I knew better than to try to get him to summarize the information over the phone for me. It had never worked in the past.

"Also," my uncle continued, *"your brother William tells me your financing is all lined up, if you would like to give him a call."*

Fantastic news.

"Great. I'll call him in a bit. And, Uncle Garth, I can't thank you enough for your help."

"There is one thing I would ask, Liam," he said.

"Anything," I responded.

"Your sister chose a good man. Find a way to make up with Nicholas. I think you will be surprised by the man beneath the surface."

I had nowhere to hide after his request. "I will. I promise."

Once we hung up, I immediately began to contemplate how long I could put off my distasteful promise to my uncle.

When I got back to my computer upstairs, the email was waiting as promised: a multi-page report on Matthew Hudson. The first two pages contained nothing substantial. The surprises started on the third page.

After a celebratory glass of wine, I dialed my older brother, Bill.

He quickly confirmed the money I'd requested was ready to go.

~

AMY

"ANOTHER NEW SUIT, I SEE," SAMANTHA NOTED.

I still hadn't retrieved any of the clothes I'd taken over to Liam's place.

"Yeah," I admitted. "You like it?"

She took a seat. "Sure… Still haven't got your stuff, huh?"

"I tried sending Vivienne, and he sent her away."

"Just tell him to send it if you refuse to go over and get it," she suggested.

I fiddled with my pen. "I tried that. You want to know what he said?"

She looked at me expectantly.

"He told me no way. I have to talk to him if I want my stuff."

She laughed. "Then go listen to him. It's better than having to buy a whole new wardrobe."

"I can't."

She pointed a finger at me. "You mean you won't."

"Same difference. He'll just try to talk me into something, and I'm not going there."

"I'd go over," she said.

"You're no help."

She twirled her pen for a second. "Sometimes a friend needs to tell you what you don't want to hear."

"Ready for the meeting?" I asked her.

"Changing the subject won't make it go away."

She was infuriatingly right.

Lucy called from reception to tell us the World Foods people were here.

"Saved by the bell," Samantha said. She got up, and we moved into the conference room for the meeting.

Celeste, the buyer from World Foods we'd been dealing with had called this meeting on short notice. A shakeup in their procurement strategies had made *The Wall Street Journal* last week. The article had said they planned to pare back their supplier list to more seasoned companies.

I dreaded this meeting, because I worried it was to tell us we no longer qualified, and to try them again in a year or two——or more. A result like that would be more than a disappointment.

Today Celeste had brought another lady from corporate with her, we'd been told.

I steeled myself for the let down as I entered the conference room. *Never let them see you vulnerable*, I reminded myself.

Samantha and I handed our business cards to the new corporate representative. Celeste introduced her as Joanna Bethel. She was a stern-looking older woman.

Joanna offered us each her card, which indicated she was from the home office in Austin. She nodded to Celeste, who began. "Thank you for meeting us on such short notice."

"It's our pleasure. We're at your disposal," Samantha replied sweetly.

She should have said at their mercy, like the mouse is always at the cat's mercy.

"You may have read a few things in the trade press about changes to our procurement strategies," Celeste continued.

Samantha and I nodded silently.

"We aren't ready to comment publicly yet," she said. "But we did want to meet with our supply chain to explain a few things before the rumors got out of hand."

I'd seen the *Journal* article. *Grocery giant cutting supplier list* had been the subtitle. It wasn't an announcement, but the *Wall Street Journal* reporter seemed to have a good source at the company. I'd gotten frantic calls from three other vendors wondering what insight we had on the changes. Everybody was worried.

I crossed my arms and prepared myself to keep a stiff upper lip when they brought the hammer down. It wasn't fair. We had prepared so well to work with them. We had made every modification to our computer linkages they'd requested, but we didn't stand a chance if they were cutting back suppliers.

"I am happy to say——" I heard Celeste begin.

My heart skipped a beat. Had I heard her right? She said happy. Was there possibly a ray of sunshine at the end of this tunnel?

"——that Tiffany's is qualified to move on to the next step in the vendor-qualification process."

I let out a long breath I'd been holding, waiting on her verdict. We'd all worked so hard to get to this point.

Samantha's face lit up. "That's wonderful."

This was a bittersweet success, however.

"Pardon me," Samantha added after a moment. "I thought the trial northeast deliveries we made last week were the final stage."

Celeste's eyes shifted to Joanna momentarily before meeting mine. "They were, and based on your success at that stage, I recommended adding you to our supplier base——starting here in the northeast before expanding to other regions."

This was fantastic news. Celeste had a reputation as a tough gatekeeper. Acquiring her recommendation had always been the key to getting on their shelves.

Celeste fiddled with her pen. "Since last week, though, corporate has added a new step." She paused.

"At the corporate level, the company has decided we need to

better evaluate the caliber of the management team behind the products," Joanna continued. "We would like to see your two- and five-year marketing and product-development plans."

"Right now?" Samantha asked, knowing full well neither of us had developed anything that far into the future.

Joanna stifled a laugh. "Oh my goodness, no."

I was able to breathe again. The task would take us days to complete, but we could get ready by next week if we worked through the weekend.

"Over dinner before I leave is my preference. I find a casual setting is better than a stuffy conference room, don't you?"

Samantha and I nodded.

Joanna turned to Celeste. "Very good. You recommended Holmby's, is that right?"

Celeste nodded. "Yes. They have some quiet rooms in the back."

Joanna rose, and Celeste followed her lead, making the pecking order clear and indicating the meeting had run its course. "Shall we say seven o'clock, then?"

"Tonight?" Samantha asked, putting my fear into words.

It was a good thing she'd spoken, as my mouth had suddenly gone too dry to form the words.

"Yes. I leave for the west coast in the morning."

Crap.

One afternoon to do a week's worth of work.

$\sim$

Liam

At the conclusion of our meeting, I shook hands with Ryan Westerly and Anton Sarkissian. Wanda, my ever-present short shadow, escorted me back to the lobby, where she returned my phone.

"Thanks, Wanda. I look forward to seeing you again."

She smiled. "You too, Mr. Quigley."

"Liam," I corrected her.

With papers in hand, I climbed into my car, started the V-12, and turned my phone back on.

It came alive with a missed call from Nick. It was about time.

I got on the road before I dialed. "Do we have news?" I asked when he answered the phone.

The line went silent. He'd hung up again.

"Fuck you, Nick," I said out loud before I redialed his number. *How much longer are we going to be playing this stupid game?*

"I'm a piece of shit" were the first words out of my mouth this time.

"You sure are," came the reply.

I was hoping he had the Winterbourne spy cornered. "Have you figured out who it is?"

"Yes and no. I'm down to a few candidates."

I turned right toward the bridge. "Who?"

"I don't work that way, Liam. No names yet."

Fucking jerk.

"Why the fuck not?" I demanded.

"I know what it's like to be accused of something you didn't do. I'll give you a name when I'm one-hundred-percent certain I have the right guy."

I huffed. "Sure."

I didn't have a goddammed choice. I was at his mercy here. I hated being so fucking helpless, reliant on *him*, of all people.

"Look, Liam," he started. *"I know what I'm fucking doing here. Do you want my help or not?"*

"Of course. I'm just…" I searched for the right word. "… anxious to find the mole."

"Well, the reason I called is I need you to put another piece of bait in the water."

Now we were getting somewhere; doing something instead of merely waiting improved my mood. "What exactly?"

He explained what he wanted me to write. *"And have Veronica give it to Josh after Martin in finance has gone home. Can you arrange that?"*

"No problem," I told him.

Martin was always in early so he could leave by five to pick up his daughter from day care before they closed. Josh never left that early.

After we hung up, I still had a ways to go before reaching my destination, so I turned the problem over and over in my mind. I couldn't come up with a reason why Martin would betray us. He'd been an early hire and had seemed so…boringly normal for a finance geek.

But then again, money could turn almost anybody, and Winter-bourne had plenty to throw around. Martin had two kids, one in school and the other about to start kindergarten. His wife worked, as I recalled, but living in Brookline could be a stretch even on two incomes.

Why did Nick have me giving the note to Josh?

Was the elusive Brinna his other suspect?

It couldn't be Josh.

Could it?

I almost puked at the thought. *Anybody but Josh.*

After two more hours of driving, I found the place down at the end of a country lane. It was more secluded than I'd expected.

My fingers found the outline of the ring in my pocket.

The man who opened the door wore coveralls and had the tanned face of someone who worked outdoors.

"Mr. Hoare?" I asked.

CHAPTER 35

AMY

SAMANTHA HAD FINISHED HER PREPARATIONS AHEAD OF ME. AND
her presentation was simpler and more elegant than mine.

I'd worked until the last minute, making changes, and had
gotten my marketing forecast into not *good*, but acceptable form.

We arrived at Holmby's a little ahead of the appointed hour. I
carried my presentation in a simple manila folder, Samantha had
found a pretty maroon one for hers——the kitchen geek showing
up the supposed marketing whiz.

My blouse was sticking to my back, and the cool air as we
passed through the doors of the restaurant was a welcome change
from the mugginess of the street. The interior immediately brought
back memories of my first dinner with Liam——a long dinner, an
enchanting dinner. I swatted the memories away as Celeste waved
to us.

I carefully avoided looking in the direction of the table Liam
and I had occupied that night, for fear he'd be sitting there staring
back at me.

Celeste and Joanna were huddled near the back with another

lady, most likely our interviewer. They hadn't given us a single clue as to how things were going to operate this evening.

We approached and greeted them, and Celeste introduced us to "Katherine with a K," before escorting us down a hallway to a set of private dining rooms.

"We'll be doing the interviews separately this evening," Katherine informed us. "Samantha, you and I will take the Greylock Room." She indicated the door on the right. The rooms had the names of local mountains etched on brass nameplates. "And Amy, you can wait in the Sugarloaf Room. My partner will be along in a moment, I'm sure." She pointed me to the door across the hall.

We nodded and said our goodbyes to Celeste and Joanna.

"I'll give you a call tomorrow," Celeste told us as she and Joanna left.

Samantha nodded to me with a smile and followed Katherine into the small dining room.

"I promise I don't bite," I heard Katherine tell Samantha as she closed the door.

I did as I was told and entered the Sugarloaf Room. I was surprised to find only a small dining table set up off to the side, with the majority of the space left open. The table was elegantly set for dinner with a white tablecloth, gleaming silverware, and wine glasses. There was no obvious place to set out my presentation, and only two chairs. Unsure what to do, I took a seat.

A knock came at the door, and a waiter entered, placing a plate of garlic shrimp on the table. His nametag read *Marvin*. He asked what I'd like to drink.

I chose iced tea.

He withdrew, and once again I was alone.

I salivated at the aroma of the garlic shrimp, which dared me to eat one before my interviewer——interrogator——arrived.

A few minutes later, the waiter returned with my iced tea.

I took a sip, and the waiter opened the door to leave, only to be stopped by a man standing in his way.

"Marvin, could you please get us a bottle of prosecco to start?" It was Liam.

Marvin nodded, and Liam closed the door, blocking my path to it.

My chair squeaked on the wooden floor as I jerked to my feet. "What are you doing here?"

"Take a seat, Ms. Hudson." His commanding tone had returned.

I took the chair and sat back down, realizing anything else would result in a shouting match I couldn't afford with the World Foods person still on the way.

I folded my hands in front of me. "I need you to leave."

Instead, he took the chair opposite me. "You look lovely tonight."

I resisted the temptation to lash out at him. "Thank you."

He scooted up to the table. "I have a proposal for you. It'll take you just a minute to hear it."

I leaned forward. "And I have one for you: Leave now, and I won't start screaming."

"How would that sound to the World Foods lady across the hall?" he asked.

Screaming was obviously off the table if I wanted to land the account. I composed myself. "Make it quick… And how did you know she's with World Foods?"

He smirked. "I recognized her. We go way back." He took his fork and speared a shrimp from the plate. "Delicious. You should try one," he said.

"Please, Liam, I'm expecting someone any minute."

Another knock at the door stopped my heart. It only started again when it turned out to be Marvin with the prosecco.

Liam was quiet until the waiter retreated after opening the bubbly and pouring us each a glass.

Liam took a sip. "I understand you're nervous. I'll be quick. I think you'll like this. Our last deal worked out pretty well for you, didn't it? A twenty-million-dollar investment with you getting the proxy for the voting rights."

It had been an exceptional deal for the company, one we couldn't have replicated with anyone else.

I smiled demurely. "Quickly?"

He was going at a snail's pace, probably just to anger me.

He smiled. "Here's the offer. You agree to spend the next two hours with me——"

"I can't," I pleaded, cutting him off.

"Patience. You haven't heard my offer yet."

I put up my hand, stopping him. "I won't go back to being your girlfriend."

"Not asking you to," he continued. "You have dinner with me now, agree to talk with me…"

I rolled my eyes.

"Honestly talk with me, and I'll ensure World Foods accepts you as a vendor."

My mouth must have dropped to the floor. The audacity of this man was off the charts, believing I would fall for such a lie.

"You want me to believe you could do that?"

"I already have. Joanna is an old family friend, and she has already agreed to add you if I suggest it."

"They wouldn't. It's so…"

He pulled a paper from his jacket and unfolded it. "She already has." He handed it to me.

It was a letter from World Foods, accepting us as a supplier and setting next month as our start date. My mouth went dry. It certainly looked real. Celeste had arranged this evening's meeting, and we knew she was a real World Foods person… It was too much to process.

"You can keep that, if you agree to my terms," he said.

"And Sam?"

He forked another shrimp. "You really should try these. She's having dinner with my sister, Katie, right now."

I speared a shrimp and checked my watch. "Okay."

I could deal with him for an hour or two if the payoff was this letter. For the moment, I had to assume it was real. Walking out was too big a risk.

"How did you...?"

His smile grew. "My family has connections, and this was important enough that we called in a few favors. I mean, how else was I going to get to talk with you? You won't return my calls, you ignore my flowers. Did you even play the CDs?"

I shook my head. "No," I lied.

I'd actually played the song a dozen times, listening to the lyrics, wishing to be the girl they were sung to.

He pulled his phone out and laid it on the table. "You should listen to the words." The song started, filling the room with the verses I knew all too well.

"Okay, already," I said. "I did listen, but that doesn't change anything."

Liam stopped the song as our waiter reappeared, this time with a tray of food.

"I took the liberty of ordering for you," Liam informed me.

Naturally my plate was the swordfish, and his was the Kona-coffee-crusted New York strip steak——the same as our first dinner.

"Let your hair down," he said after Marvin closed the door.

I hesitated; it seemed too personal a request.

"Please," he added.

I pulled the pins out one by one and shook out my hair.

"Now you look even more beautiful. You should wear it down all the time."

"You've said that before." A mild blush, by my standards at least, crept into my cheeks. "And you should stop telling me what to do." At least I didn't throw food at him.

We started our dinner as we had many evenings together at his penthouse, by rehashing our days——except tonight he wanted to be filled in on my past couple weeks.

I left out the sobbing and sleeplessness without him. I asked about his week, but he turned the questions around to ask about me again, not answering.

I have to stay strong.

Being across the table from him had become so natural, so comfortable——not at all like my evenings had been with Matt.

The thought of Matt sent a shiver through me, as I realized I was only two days from another court showdown with him——the next low point in my life after missing the last one.

"You look concerned," Liam said, bringing me back to the present.

I took a breath. "I have a court date with Matt coming up." I stopped the forkful of fish heading toward my mouth and put it down.

"In two days, I know. Don't worry. Bad things have a way of catching up with bad people."

I liked his sentiment, but Matt seemed immune to karma. I should have been surprised that Liam knew about my court date, but after everything he'd arranged tonight, nothing surprised me.

"You finished?" he asked.

"Yeah," I admitted. "I think I've lost my appetite."

He started the song again on his phone and stood.

He offered me his hand. "May I have the pleasure of this dance?"

I recoiled momentarily before giving in and taking his hand.

We swayed a slow dance to the music, his hands on my hips and mine on his shoulders, close but not touching.

"Do you want to hear about my two weeks?" he asked.

"Of course."

He sang along with the music for a moment, ending with *I love you*. He looked into my eyes. "I got to thinking about my life, and what was important to me."

I couldn't hold eye contact. I looked down at his chest.

"You were right," he said. "I take my promises pretty seriously."

"Ya think?" I giggled. There was seriously, and then there was beyond seriously, and somewhere beyond that was where Liam put his commitments.

He pulled me closer, and my breasts touched his chest lightly as we swayed. "No fair making fun."

"Sorry——I mean okay." I was forgetting my lesson about saying sorry too much.

"So I decided I needed to get my promise to Roberta out of the way before we could be together."

I blinked back a tear. Was he asking me to wait for him to finish medical school? Four whole years? "Liam, I don't——"

"Hush. This is the part where you listen, remember?"

He pulled me in closer, and I laid my head against his shoulder. He stroked my hair. "So I took care of my promise, and it's done. Now I can stay here in Boston with you."

I pulled back to look at him. "But how? You promised to become a doctor. That's not something you can just buy."

Our song began again on his phone. He'd put it on repeat.

"No, I promised to heal people," he said. "I bought a biotech company, and I'm going to devote myself to that mission, healing way more people than I could as a doctor. But I'm going to need help."

Tears welled in my eyes. Hope filled my chest. He had found a way to stay and also not have one of his stupid promises tearing him apart?

I hugged him tightly, beginning to cry. "Help?"

The old me would have demanded my girlfriend job back, but he had taught me a lady waited to be asked.

He kissed my head. "The problem, is I need someone to make me eat real food so I stay healthy enough to heal all those people."

"Like a girlfriend?" I asked with my coyest smile.

"No." He released me and pulled a box from his coat pocket.

My God, it was a red box with gold lettering. Cartier. My heart tried to pound its way out of my chest.

He opened the box and sank to one knee. "I was thinking wife." A gorgeous, monster heart-shaped diamond ring sat in the velvet. "Amy Hudson, the day I met you, my life became extraordinary. You are the joy in my heart. Will you do me the honor of taking my name?"

I gasped. "It's gorgeous." I shook my head. "But no, not unless you promise to stop with the stupid compliments."

He closed the box and stood. "That's a promise I can't make."

I jumped into his arms, and the box fell to the floor. "Okay, already. I'll marry you if you promise to drink your kale smoothies in the morning."

He lifted me off my feet and twirled me around. "Why is everything with you a negotiation?"

"Well?"

"Five days a week," he suggested.

"Six."

"Three," he countered as he spun me around again.

"Okay, five."

"Deal."

I speared my fingers in his hair and pulled myself up to kiss my man——no longer my boyfriend, now my fiancé. It had been too long.

He grabbed my ass and pulled me into his embrace. My skirt rode up, and I wrapped my legs around him. Our tongues tussled for position. He tasted of the coffee seasoning on his steak and raw desire. The faint aroma of old leather in his hair took me back to our first night at his penthouse, my first night of primal sex—— raw, lust-fueled abandon. The first night of the rest of my life.

Too soon for me, he broke the kiss. "We need to save this for later." He released me and retrieved the Cartier box from the floor. "Want to try it on?"

I offered my hand, and he slid the massive ring onto my finger.

I gathered up my World Foods letter, and Liam led me out of the room. But instead of turning toward the door, he took me to the Greylock Room.

"I think we're done here," Liam announced as we entered.

Samantha's jaw dropped. "Liam?"

"Hi, Sam. Katie, I'd like you to meet my Amy. Amy, my sister, Katie Knowlton."

The woman who had introduced herself as Katherine was up quickly to hug me. "Sorry for the bit of theater."

"Theater?" Samantha asked. But then she caught sight of the ring on the hand I held up, and she rushed to embrace me with eyes the size of saucers. "Does this mean what I think it does?"

"Yup," I told her as she released me.

Samantha's brow creased. "Wait a minute——was this all a hoax?"

I offered her the letter. "Yes and no. In black and white, we're now suppliers to World Foods."

Samantha scanned the letter, and the concern on her face melted into a wide smile. "This is real?"

"Absolutely," Liam told her.

Samantha's expression foretold another twenty questions, if we didn't leave quickly.

I stepped back. "Sam, I'll explain tomorrow. Right now, Liam and I have somewhere to be." I didn't tell her the somewhere was twenty-six floors up, with a view of the Common.

The fire in Liam's eyes told me I might need some Advil in the morning to walk straight.

CHAPTER 36

LIAM

"YOU READY?" I ASKED AGENT DIXON.

"As soon as you can verify the subject is in the building," the FBI special agent answered. His short partner, Agent Parsons, nodded but hadn't said a word all morning.

Nick had called a week ago telling me he had the goods on my mole, but it had taken since then to get the US Attorney for the district of Massachusetts to get an indictment.

Last night I'd gotten my woman back, and today I'd get my revenge. It couldn't get any better.

The news van rolled up, right on time. They were always into a good perp walk, grist for the evening news. I wanted this to be a public spectacle, lest someone else be tempted to betray me.

I made the call.

Veronica picked up right away. *"Good morning, Liam Quigley's office."*

"Veronica," I said. "I was just calling to see if Josh was in yet."

"Yes, he went to get a cup of coffee. He should be right back. Would you like me to have him call you?"

I looked up the side of our building, visualizing Josh fixing his morning cappuccino. "No thanks. I'll call back in a bit." I hung up and turned to Agent Dixon. "We're a go."

The two agents clad in navy windbreakers with FBI in large yellow letters on their backs followed me into the building. The three of us made quite a spectacle traversing the lobby to the elevators.

After a quick ride, the elevator doors opened, and I led them out.

"At the desk right there." I pointed out our mole.

The lead agent, Dixon, strode up, with his short companion following.

I stood back and watched from beside the elevator.

"Veronica Feibush," Dixon said loudly. "You are under arrest for trade secret theft and conspiracy. Please stand up and put your hands behind your back."

Her jaw dropped.

"Stand up, please," Dixon repeated.

This time she complied, her mouth a thin line as she stared daggers in my direction.

What could she possibly be angry at me about? She had betrayed me, not the other way around.

Agent Parsons rounded the desk and placed handcuffs on Veronica. She pulled out a card and began reading her Miranda rights, finishing up with, "Do you understand these rights as I have explained them to you?"

The blood had drained from Veronica's face, and a feeble "Yes" was all she said.

By now, the spectacle had drawn dozens of cubicle denizens out to watch the boss's personal assistant get arrested, humiliated, and hauled off to jail. Josh was in the gathered group, looking as surprised as the rest.

Veronica's eyes were now downcast, avoiding eye contact with any of them.

As I had racked my brain to come up with a candidate for the mole, a few names had come to mind, but never hers. It showed how easily I could be fooled.

I'd avoided my office as much as possible since I'd found out. It had been a difficult week, resisting the urge to confront her and find out why. Finding out the *why* would have to wait.

She shot me a scowl as the agents led her past and into the elevator.

I didn't join them. This evening, I would catch the news footage of the perp walk downstairs. It would add some spice to the newscast, and we'd invited a reporter from the business journal as well. I would also enjoy reviewing that coverage. I wanted everyone in town to know the cost of crossing me: humiliation and cuffs.

When Nick had called to reveal her as my mole, I'd considered everything from egging her house to slashing her tires. Luckily, he had talked me down off that particular ledge and convinced me to turn her in to the feds. Sweet revenge.

With the elevator doors now closed, I walked toward my office. "Okay, the show's over. We can get back to work now."

A multitude of whispered and mumbled reactions passed among them as the group broke up and returned to their cubicles and offices. This was certain to be the main topic of lunchtime conversation for at least a week.

Josh followed me into my office and closed the door. "You didn't tell me about this."

I took my seat behind the desk. "I didn't tell anybody, not a soul."

He took his normal chair. "What's the arrest for?"

I leaned back. "She's been passing information to Winterbourne. That's how they've been stealing our deals."

His brows shot up. "No," he said slowly. Then he nodded. "Now it makes sense." His eyes narrowed as he contemplated his coffee cup. "Why didn't you tell *me*?"

"They told me I couldn't," I lied, implying that the US Attorney had forced me to keep it from him. I cared about Josh too much to tell him the truth——that I'd suspected his girlfriend Brinna. I still didn't know why she'd been following me around with her camera, but that could wait for another day.

After Josh left, I called Nick to thank him. "I am a piece of shit," I began.

He didn't hang up on me since I'd gotten the password phrase right. "*I'm growing tired of that shit. How 'bout I give you a promotion to douchebag?*"

"Sounds good to me," I replied.

"*Is the show over?*"

I looked out the window. "Sure is. The TV crews are packing up. Thanks for telling me what to put in the last bait note." I'd argued with him, but Nick had insisted that I include a juicy trade secret.

"*That was the only way to make this a federal offense; otherwise all you could do was fire the bitch. Eighteen US code eighteen-thirty-two makes trade secret theft a ten-year federal offense, and I promise you just a month in prison will be worse for her than anything you could have come up with.*"

No doubt.

Nick had the personal experience to back up his claim. Two years in state prison had taken away a chunk of his life he would never get back.

"*I mean, egging her house? That's such a pussy move.*"

I sat down. "How about you come out here so I can show you how grateful I am?"

"Kiss my ass, college boy."

I laughed. "That wasn't what I had in mind."

"*You couldn't pay me to come out there. The weather sucks.*" He had a point. Boston weather might be good for the northeast, but it didn't compare to southern California.

"*Later, douchebag. I gotta get back to real work,*" he said.

At least I'd been promoted on the Nick scale.

CHAPTER 37

AMY

THE DAY AFTER LIAM'S SPECTACULAR VICTORY OVER THE COMPANY mole, I had to face a battle of my own. Today it would be the two of us against the two of them.

My negotiator took my phone and tucked it into his jacket pocket. "Do not worry, Amy. This will go just fine. The most important thing is to not react to whatever they say. Merely remember your lines."

I nodded. "Okay."

"Trust me."

"I do," I replied, steeling myself for the onslaught.

The elevator doors opened, and we stepped out into the sixteenth-floor lobby: glass, chrome, and mahogany, the expensive digs of Maximilian Forrester, my ex-husband's super-slimeball divorce lawyer. It hurt to think some of my money had subsidized this.

We made our way to the receptionist. The pretty young thing behind the desk put down her iPhone and smiled up at us.

"Ms. Hudson to see Mr. Forrester. I believe we have a ten

o'clock appointment," the old man intoned to the girl behind the desk.

I checked my watch; we were right on time.

"Please have a seat," she said. "I'll let him know."

We sat in the overstuffed black leather chairs——which had likely seen their fair share of nervous ex-wives——while the receptionist called back to the offices.

I crossed my legs and waited.

Pretty Young Thing went back to watching something on her phone while we waited.

Ten long minutes later, my negotiator visited the receptionist again. "Please tell Mr. Forrester that in two minutes..." He checked his wristwatch. "...we will withdraw our offer and depart."

Her chin dropped. She made a frantic, whispered call. It seemed they weren't used to being threatened here.

Less than a minute later, we were escorted into the back——all the way to the conference room adjoining the corner office, the one with Maximilian Forrester on the door in gold lettering.

I bit my tongue as we entered. Matt, my a-hole ex, was here as expected.

His attorney got up to greet us; Matt did not.

"Garth Durham, representing Ms. Hudson," Liam's Uncle Garth told the attorney. "And I believe you know Ms. Hudson."

I nodded, but didn't make a move to shake Max's hand. I'd regretted it last time I had.

Uncle Garth reached out to shake Matt's hand. "And you must be Matthew. I have read so much about you recently."

Bewilderment showed on Matt's face.

We took our seats opposite the evil duo.

Max looked at Uncle Garth with a sly smile. "I believe you said you had an offer for us?"

Uncle Garth smiled back. "That I did." He pulled two manila folders from his briefcase. The single typewritten page of the opening offer was in the first folder; the second contained much more.

Uncle Garth pulled my phone out of his pocket. "I would like to record this meeting; is that acceptable?"

"Sure," Max said.

Uncle Garth started the phone recording and passed the offer sheet across the table to Max.

The lawyer read quickly and started to chuckle. "This is a joke, right?"

"Not at all," Uncle Garth responded. "You have thirty seconds to confer with your client and respond. After that, the offer is withdrawn."

Matt grabbed for the paper and started to read. "I pay her half a million? Today? No fucking way. The bitch owes me," he said angrily.

I rose and almost jumped across the table to scratch his eyes out. Uncle Garth quickly put a hand on my arm to hold me back.

I regained my composure and sat, reminded of Uncle Garth's admonition to not react.

Uncle Garth ignored Matt's outburst and addressed his lawyer. "Accept or reject?" he asked. "The next offer you receive will not be nearly so generous." He finished his statement with a steely glare at Matt's laughing lawyer.

"Young lady, you should've gotten yourself a better lawyer," Max said to me.

"He's not my lawyer," I replied.

Max's brow creased. "Then, it's been nice meeting you, but I think we're done here." He rose from his chair.

Uncle Garth remained seated. "I think we should start by discussing Matthew's current marriage to Svetlana..." He pulled out another paper. "I believe Donkova is her maiden name. I hope I am pronouncing it correctly," he added, now addressing Matt.

Matt slumped in his chair.

Max took his seat again. "I'm sorry, Mr. Hudson hasn't remarried."

Uncle Garth slid the paper across to Max. "This marriage certificate from the Bahamas indicates otherwise."

Matt shifted in his chair. "Must be another Hudson. I'm not married."

He didn't realize yet he was struggling in quicksand.

The next grenade came out of Uncle Garth's folder. "These pictures might refresh your memory." He slid across the wedding pictures of Matt and Svetlana the Hanson firm had uncovered.

"You should have told me, Matt," Max said angrily.

Even I could tell he was lying.

Matt closed his eyes and took a deep breath, but stayed quiet.

Uncle Garth had prepared for this and now pulled out the next piece of evidence. He smiled as he passed it to the indignant attorney.

"That email chain shows you and he discussed it several times, and you advised him not to disclose it in return for half of the additional spousal support payments."

Max's face lost it's color. "Those are attorney-privileged communications."

Uncle Garth was now ready to drop the hammer on the king of late-night TV.

"Not when they pertain to criminal conspiracy and fraud," he noted. "You, Mr. Forrester, received ten thousand dollars from the account of Svetlana Donkova to arrange her marriage to Matthew here for the purpose of gaining entry to the United States. You hid Mr. Hudson's remarriage from the court, and I do believe the state bar takes a very dim view of such practices."

Max looked about ready to puke. "Perhaps we were a bit hasty in rejecting your offer."

Uncle Garth shook his head. "As I said previously, that offer is now off the table."

I squelched a giggle; we were coming to the fun part.

"Ms. Hudson will be filing a motion with the court to amend the settlement. She will demand seven hundred and fifty thousand dollars from your client, which is half of the inheritance he received six months before the divorce, which you and he also kept hidden from Ms. Hudson and the court. That is, along with recapture of all monies already paid to your client."

The evil duo was completely deflated. They had nowhere to hide.

"You may keep those," Uncle Garth said as we stood to leave. "We have additional copies for the authorities."

Pretty Young Thing was still watching her phone as we passed by her on the way to the elevator.

As soon as the doors closed, I gave Uncle Garth a quick hug. "Thank you so much for all this."

"Anything for a soon-to-be family member."

The elevator car started its descent.

"I thought that was fun," he said, handing me my phone with the recording.

I laughed, concurring with the sentiment. I couldn't wait to play the recording for Liam.

"How'd it go?" Liam asked as soon as we emerged in the lobby.

Uncle Garth had insisted he not come upstairs with us. A physical altercation might have ruined everything.

"Smashing," I said, trying to pick a word Uncle Garth might use.

Liam hugged me. "Can't wait to hear the replay."

"I expect that your court date will go quite well," Uncle Garth told me.

Liam's smile grew.

"If you two lovebirds will excuse me, I have an appointment with the State Board of Bar Overseers."

After another quick hug, Liam's uncle was gone.

Liam kissed me, surprising me.

"What was that for?"

"I just had to kiss the most beautiful woman in town," he said in a booming voice that filled the lobby.

"Why, thank you," I said softly, trying to be the lady he deserved.

I took in a deep breath of clean morning air as we exited the building. This sad chapter of my life was finally closed. I could now move on to the next. No looking back; Liam had made me promise. And I would keep that promise to my man.

My gentleman.

Liam held the door for me as we exited to the street. "What would you like for lunch? There's awesome Italian just down the block."

I gave him a quick kiss. "I can't today. I have to meet a friend."

"I can give you a lift," he suggested. "Or maybe I could join you."

"Sorry, honey. Not today. The two of us have girl stuff to discuss."

His smile drooped briefly before he recovered. "Love you. See you back home tonight then." He waved as he walked to the right.

My destination was to the left, but I didn't dare let him follow me and pop in unannounced. I waited until he turned the corner before I set out for the restaurant.

My lunch date had chosen Indian, and I looked forward to a nice curry. I located her already seated near the back.

"Amy, it's so good to see you." She gave me a hug. "Now let me see that ring."

I showed her my huge engagement ring, which had become the talk of the office.

Her eyes grew. "It's lovely. I wish I'd gotten one half as nice."

I took my seat across from her. "Thank you. Liam spoils me." An understatement of the first magnitude.

She waited patiently for me to begin.

"Felicia, I want to thank you for agreeing to meet me today."

It was time for Felicia Schmulian and me to get our men to move past stupid.

CHAPTER 38

(ONE WEEK LATER)

LIAM

SYD KOVNER STRODE INTO THE BOARDROOM LIKE HE OWNED THE place, as he surely thought he did. Based on our last status update, a month ago, we were still behind our target and right where he wanted us: at his mercy.

Craig Barnett followed behind, as he always did.

Josh, Martin, and I greeted them, and we took seats around the table. I sat at the head, with Josh and Martin on one side and our cranky investors on the other.

Syd smirked. "I think we're here to review progress against your milestones today."

He was ready to chop us off at the knees.

"That's right," Josh answered.

I adjusted my notepad. "Martin, why don't you get us started."

Martin stood and put his first foil on the projector. His presentation was quite a bit more monotone than Josh's would have been if I'd let him do it. The first three slides went by without any questions from our audience of two.

Josh shifted in his seat, preparing for the inevitable.

The shit hit the fan when Martin moved on to the foods division.

Craig zeroed in on the operating margin and overhead numbers, asking Josh numerous questions.

Josh tried valiantly to defend his baby, but the verdict was already in as far as these two were concerned.

Syd saved his ammunition and let Craig pummel Josh for several minutes. The real battle would be the next foil with the consolidated results.

Poor Martin moved on and put up the consolidated results slide.

With blood in the water, it only took Syd five seconds to paste on a devilish grin. "Liam, looking at the bottom line number there, would it be safe to say you've missed your commitments from a year ago?"

"Forecast," I corrected him. "Yes, the numbers are two percent shy of where we wanted to be, but we plan to make up that ground in the next quarter or two."

The duo exchanged glances, and Syd pulled a folded piece of paper out of his jacket pocket. He slid it over to me.

"These results are unacceptable," he said coldly.

I took a deep breath. Even though I had expected this, my hands still shook as I unfolded the paper. It was the note I had been dreading for weeks, official notice that these two wanted to pull their investments out immediately based on lack of performance according to paragraph three dah, dah, dah——it ended with a demand to wire the funds tomorrow.

Syd eyed me. "Well?"

I didn't answer.

The door opened and Hue Schmulian entered, coffee cup in hand.

I put the letter aside. "Before we deal with this, I'd like to introduce our newest board member. I think you both know Hubricht Schmulian."

Syd's brow creased. He seemed temporarily taken aback.

Craig looked to Syd, unsure what to say.

"I don't understand," Syd said, finding his voice.

"Nobody told us about a change to the board," Craig added.

"That's because it just happened yesterday," Josh told them. "And we thought it best to introduce him in person, since you were coming in today anyway."

That settled the duo for the moment.

Hue stirred his drink. "I was just freshening up my coffee. Sorry if I'm late."

"Not at all," I told him.

"Good to see you again, Syd, and you too, Craig." He shook their hands before rounding the table to sit between Josh and me.

Hue, it turned out, knew these two very well, having participated in several investments with them and sitting on another board with Craig.

"Let me explain," I told Syd and Craig. "I met Hue here while negotiating to buy his company last month."

"Didn't that fall through?" Craig asked.

"No," Hue told them. "Not at all. Young Liam here helped me get a fifty-percent premium out of that poor schmuck Damien Winterbourne. Made me a lot of money, he did." He shot them a killer smile and patted me on the shoulder.

After learning that Winterbourne was locked into outbidding me by twenty percent, I'd upped our offer by thirty percent, forcing Winterbourne to take his shot and pay Schmulian a fifty-percent markup for the company.

"Anyway," Hue continued. "After seeing how astute Liam is, and him helping me make a boatload of money, Felicia and I decided to invest some of the proceeds from our sale into Quigley-Fulton. And Liam here was kind enough to add me to the board."

Syd and Craig had just lost their leverage, and they knew it.

"I'm not sure that's very wise," Syd said after a moment. "We're here to check on progress, and frankly it's been a bit disappointing over the past year. As a matter of fact, we were planning on pulling out." He laid their cards on the table, hoping to scare Schmulian off.

"That's too bad," Josh said, laying it on thick. "We've enjoyed having the benefit of your insight."

"Have you met your forecasts or not?" Syd asked, looking at me.

"No," was my one-word answer.

"Then I'm out," Syd announced. "I'll expect a wire transfer in the morning."

Hue leaned forward. "Good news for me," he told Syd. "Liam," he said, turning to me. "I'll buy his shares."

Syd's eyes narrowed. He was cornered now.

"I'm not sure pulling out is such a good idea," Craig said softly to Syd.

The team had broken ranks.

"Remember Kirkland and Seabrook?" Craig continued. "I think maybe we should give this more time to mature."

Hue had already told me this story, and I was counting on Craig and Syd to remember it as well.

Syd and Craig had bailed early on Kirkland and taken a sixty-percent haircut, while Hue had stuck it out and rode it to a four-hundred-and-fifty-percent gain. Seabrook had turned out similarly, and Hue never let them forget it.

The blood drained from Syd's face. "You might be right. Maybe we should give this a bit more time."

His saying *a bit more time* was just theater. Based on the contract, this was their one and only chance to pull out for the next five years, and we all knew it.

Syd retrieved his letter, and we adjourned the meeting with the regular backslapping and an agreement to keep them updated quarterly.

Hue had pulled it off and gotten them to back down. We now had the freedom to run the company without worrying about meeting quarterly goals, and having Hue on the board would be helpful in the long run as well.

I took a deep breath, feeling joy well up inside me. I'd finally fulfilled my obligation to Josh.

EPILOGUE

"YOU KNOW YOU'RE IN LOVE WHEN YOU
CAN'T FALL ASLEEP BECAUSE REALITY IS
FINALLY BETTER THAN YOUR DREAMS." – DR.
SEUSS

AMY

THE NOISE WOKE ME.

I rubbed my eyes, but couldn't make anything out in the dark. I tried to control my breathing and listen.

Another noise.

My heart raced.

Someone was in the house.

"Liam, wake up," I said softly.

He wasn't as light a sleeper as I was. I turned to jostle him awake, but the bed beside me was cold and empty.

I was alone. I jerked to sitting, still groggy.

My mind went in circles as I tried to clear the cobwebs. *Gotta call 9-1-1.* My phone——where was my phone?

Shit.

Our phones were charging in the kitchen. What did we have I could defend myself with? I had to get to my phone.

I slid into a T-shirt. Liam always kept his squash racket leaned up against the bureau. I made my way silently across the bedroom.

My hand found the racket in the dark. I slid over to the door, listening for any other sound.

Slowly I turned the handle on the bedroom door and cracked it open.

The aroma of bacon surged through the crack. The light was on in the kitchen, and now I could hear the crackling of the bacon in the pan.

What a fool.

Liam was trying to make breakfast without waking me, and all I'd had playing in my head was some scene from a horror flick. We shouldn't have watched *Aliens* last night. Turning on the light in our bedroom, I squinted into the brightness. Slowly, my eyes adjusted, and I replaced the squash racket. The last thing I needed to do was greet Liam with a weapon when he was fixing me breakfast.

"Good morning, Sunshine. Ready for your big surprise?" Liam asked as I padded into the kitchen.

"Bacon and eggs?"

He stirred the pan. "That's just the beginning."

I checked the clock on the microwave. "At five ten? Why couldn't it have waited till the sun came up?"

He loaded the bacon onto two plates of eggs. "Because we have a long way to go today," he said, eyeing me. "And, I warned you about coming out here dressed like that."

He had warned me, and I occasionally enjoyed ignoring the warning and getting the punishment. Braless and panty-less in a T-shirt usually did the trick.

"I'll get dressed after breakfast." I came over and brushed a breast against his arm. "I missed you."

"I'm warning you."

"Promises, promises," I said on my way to the fridge. With luck, I might get more than one treat today.

It was too early to go out on the patio. He brought the plates over to the table. "After breakfast might be too late."

I opened the fridge, but found the vegetable drawer empty. "What happened to my kale?"

The blender startled me as it started up loudly.

"Two kale smoothies coming up," he said.

I loved that I didn't have to force him anymore. I took a seat across from him after he brought the smoothies over. The scrambled eggs didn't last long with my appetite this morning.

"So what's the surprise?"

He finished the last of his smoothie. "It wouldn't be a surprise if I told you, now would it?" He nodded toward the doorway.

Our suitcases waited near the door. "A trip?" I squeaked. This was getting better all the time. "The Cape?"

All I'd managed to get out of him all week was that he had a surprise planned for me today.

He raised his eyebrows. "Twenty questions won't get you anywhere this morning."

It had been worth a try, but I rarely got anything out of him. Guessing didn't work either; his poker face was too good.

He picked up the plates and turned to take them to the dishwasher.

I dabbed the straw from my smoothie glass on my shirt. "Oh look, I got something on my shirt. I'm going to have to wash this right away." I pulled the T-shirt over my head.

My man's eyes bulged.

I was going to get my treat after all.

He advanced on me.

I squealed and ran around the island, trying to keep the granite between us.

He soon caught me. I wasn't fast enough, and I'd learned that the sight of my boobs bouncing as I ran was his visual aphrodisiac. A turned-on Liam would not be denied. He carried me over to the door and outside to the patio. He put me down against the banister, facing the darkness of the Common. The sound of the occasional car drifted up from the street through the chilly morning air.

"Stand there," he commanded.

I did as I was told and shivered, naked in the cool air. Facing the edge, I heard the sound of his clothes coming off behind me. I knew better than to turn around. The anticipation had me wet already. Pushing him into animal mode was a special treat in itself.

He spanked me hard.

I screeched, as much with surprise as from the sting.

"Lean over and spread 'em," he said firmly.

I did as he asked, bracing myself against the banister. "Quiet, they're going to hear us," I pleaded.

"Who cares?" he growled as he reached around and found my breasts. The warmth of hands was welcome against the chill, but the feel of his hands on me was something I always welcomed. "What does the naughty girl want?"

"She wants you to take her," I said softly.

"I didn't hear you."

This was the peak of naughtiness——sex outside, almost in public, where people could hear us even if they couldn't see us in the darkness. "Fuck me. Fuck me hard," I yelled.

I made out a person walking on a path in the Common. He stopped and looked up, searching for the source of the sound.

Liam's fingers found my folds and dragged my juices forward to my clit. The danger of our position on the rooftop was palpable. His fingers started their attack, in the way he had learned brought me quickly to a peak. His recipe of delicious torture never failed to make me combust.

He pulled his fingers away and guided the tip of his cock into place, and with a quick shove, he filled me, sending tremors rattling through. His finger returned to circle and press against my clit as he pumped in and out, faster and harder. The lion took over and pushed him up to animal tempo.

"Harder," I yelled, and I watched the walker stop again and look up, searching us out in the dim light.

Our dangerous position amplified the sensations of Liam filling me, and the pressure on my clit took me higher as he pounded into me again and again. There was a loud slapping of flesh meeting flesh——the sound that couldn't be mistaken for anything other than the primal creatures we had become.

"More," I yelled. "Harder."

Liam complied, and with another press on my swollen little bud, he pushed me over the threshold. A series of twitches erupted that lit all my nerve endings on fire. I noticed the walker locate us and wave from the Common just before my climax forced my eyes shut.

My pulse pounded in my ears, and the spasms overtook me. I contracted around his cock as he found his release, gushing into me with a roar and final push.

He held my hips up as my legs went limp, and I turned to jelly in his arms. With a yank, Liam lifted me and carried me back inside.

"Next time you're naughty, it might be in the daylight."

Naughty certainly could be fun, and nothing was better than my Liam in full animal mode. I wouldn't admit it, but I was up for the daylight. The danger of being heard and seen had intensified the experience.

He carried me into the shower, with the perma-grin I had put on his face.

I slowly regained my muscle function, and before long, we were cleaned up, clothed, and downstairs getting into a town car.

"Now will you tell me?" I asked as I buckled my seatbelt.

"Nope."

THERE WERE DEFINITE ADVANTAGES TO TRAVELING WITH LIAM. First-class seats on the flight from Boston to Miami, and now we had comfortable seats in the first-class lounge waiting for our next flight.

It had been cloudy when we left Boston. At least here it was warm and sunny.

Liam still wouldn't tell me our final destination. He had

promised it would be relaxing, and I would enjoy it. Since we were in Miami waiting for our next flight, I figured it had to be somewhere in the Caribbean, or maybe South America. I had tried twenty questions again and gotten nowhere, even my hand stroking him under the coat he had lying on his lap hadn't worked.

The alarm clock on Liam's phone went off with the snippet of "Sunny" he had set it to.

He checked the time, and double-checked it. "Okay, Sunshine. It's time for us to go."

I gathered my things. "When will you tell me where we're going?" I asked for the ninety-ninth time.

He kissed me quickly. "Not yet," he replied for the fiftieth time. Half the time he ignored me.

We made our way to the gate, where I finally learned our destination.

I grabbed my man and gave him a wet kiss. "You spoil me."

It was impossible to hide where we were going when the board said this flight would take us to Belize City. He deserved more than a kiss, but it would have to wait until we were alone.

He wrapped a possessive arm around me. "It's in my job description."

I'd told him months ago that Belize was at the top of my list of places to visit. I had fallen in love with the pictures of the crystal clear water and the sea life of the world's second-longest reef system, after the Great Barrier Reef.

The flight to Belize City was boring, but short. The fun part was the last leg.

Liam had booked us a place on Ambergris Caye, and the way to get there was a small turboprop puddlejumper to the city of San Pedro.

I got to ride up front next to the pilot, with all the gauges and the control wheel. Lucky for us, I was smart enough not to touch anything.

The view outside into the shallow waters was breathtaking as we approached the island in the low-flying plane.

A little minivan that passed for the local taxi got us quickly to the resort. Our condo was in a set of buildings two miles north of the city.

A lovely woman named Mirabella checked us in. "Your unit is in the second building on that side, on the second floor." She pointed out the window to the right. "And this is the key to your golf cart, so you can get around the island." She handed Liam the key.

I looked out toward the surf. A boat zoomed by going north at high speed.

"If you prefer," Mirabella continued, "you can catch a water taxi off our pier. They can also get you into town, or up the coast to one of the restaurants."

Water taxi sounded more fun to me than a dusty ride in a golf cart. I ventured outside, taking in the multiple pools and the beach while Liam took care of the logistics with Mirabella. This was truly a magical, out-of-the-way place and stunningly beautiful, even better than the online pictures. Mirabella had mentioned that Bill Gates' compound was only a little farther up the island.

Once inside our unit, we unzipped our bags, and I started unpacking the clothes Liam had chosen for me. I hadn't gotten a vote.

My tops went in the closet and the shorts in a drawer. The overhead fan was a welcome relief as I worked. I'd traveled in Boston-appropriate attire, not the shorts and sleeveless tops that made sense in the tropics.

When I got near the bottom of my suitcase, I found he'd chosen his favorite thongs, including the two sheer ones, a racer-back sports bra, and a few push-up bras as my only underwear choices.

Although I suggested a nap, Liam insisted we eat lunch by the pools.

I pulled on some shorts.

"Only swimsuits allowed by the pool," Liam said, pulling his trunks on.

"They can't have a rule like that."

"My rule," he told me with a wink. "They have a swim-up bar, and I plan on plying you with multiple adult beverages."

I rummaged through the bottom of my suitcase. "I like the sound of that." I found three bikini bottoms, but no tops——typical Liam.

I held them up. "You have got to be kidding. I'm not going out there topless."

He grinned at me. "Personally, I think you'd look great."

I scowled. "I hope they sell suits here."

Liam opened his bag and pulled out the matching tops to my bottoms. "I must have put them in the wrong bag."

"Right."

A bottle of sunscreen, two towels, and a swim coverup over my bikini, and I was ready to relax after our three flights.

Liam picked a shaded table by the pool for us.

I took the chair next to him and held his hand. "Thank you. This is wonderful."

The waitress came by, and I decided on a Caribbean Smackdown for a drink. I had no idea what it was, but it sounded like what I needed. Liam chickened out and picked a margarita. Burgers and a nacho plate rounded out our order.

"Did I tell you I love you today?" Liam asked.

"Only a dozen times, and I love you too." It had probably been more, but I wasn't counting.

The view, the weather, and the company combined to make this a perfect afternoon. I leaned back and closed my eyes, taking in a deep breath of the warm tropical air, listening to the surf in the background.

Holding my fiancé's hand, I settled into the perfect vacation: sun, warmth, quiet, and my gentleman.

~

LIAM

. . .

"HEY, DOUCHEBAG," NICK'S VOICE CARRIED ACROSS THE POOL.

I turned to see Katie and a grown-up Nick Knowlton at the poolside swim-up bar. I hoisted my drink to them, not answering him verbally.

Amy turned to look. "Hi, Katie," she called, waving at the pair. "Wanna join us for lunch?"

She turned to me. "You didn't tell me we were meeting them here."

"Surprise, remember?"

Katie and Nick hoisted their drinks overhead and waded through the water toward us.

"Good to finally see you again, douchebag," Nick said as he approached.

I stood as Katie followed him.

Nick gave Amy a quick embrace, but didn't offer me his hand.

Amy and I each got a hug from my sister before sitting back down.

The waitress brought our nacho plate, and I added another to the order.

Nick eyed me cautiously as he ordered food for them. "So, douchebag, what do you have to say for yourself?"

Katie shot Nick a stern glance he didn't catch.

I took in a deep breath and sat forward. "I'm glad you two could make it. I wanted to apologize in person, Nick, for how I behaved in high school. I'm sorry I lied to the principal that day and cost your chance at college."

I'd gotten it out in one breath, and exactly the way I'd rehearsed. I hoped it was good enough.

Nick's face was impassive. "And?" he finally said.

Katie picked up her drink and took a sip, glancing between us.

"And I'm glad you married my sister," I told him, standing to offer my hand across the table.

"Me too, douchebag." He took my hand and proceeded to crush it as we shook.

I gave a half-hearted return grip. This was a rare contest I intended to lose.

Eventually he released me and sat back down.

I shook out the pain in my hand.

Katie gave him the evil eye. "What do you say?"

"He's got a wimpy handshake."

Katie surprised us all by pouring her drink on Nick's head.

Nick jerked back, but still got a full dose of ice and alcohol. "What'd you do that for?"

Katie glowered at him. "What do you have to say to your brother-in-law?"

Nick grimaced. "Apology accepted, Liam." He wiped himself off with a pile of napkins.

Katie winked at me while Nick wasn't looking.

I had redeemed myself and graduated from douchebag to a guy with a name.

Before lunch arrived, Nick challenged us to chicken fights in the pool.

With Amy on my shoulders, we fought them to a draw at four apiece, before Nick and Katie won the last one to beat us five to four.

We returned to the table wet and tired, but laughing like a true family.

∽

AMY

A TEXT ARRIVED ON LIAM'S PHONE AS WE WERE DRYING OFF.

"They just arrested him," he told us.

It was finally over. Liam had been waiting for this news all week.

"He deserves it," Katie said, sitting down.

I'd learned Nick had found oddities in Damien Winterbourne's accounts while helping Liam track down the spy in his company. Since financial fraud was right up their alley, Nick and Katie had continued the investigation. With a little prodding, the FBI had gotten interested. We'd known through Liam's contacts that Winterbourne was about to be arrested on tax evasion, fraud, and a list of other charges. He had become sort of a mini Bernie Madoff in Boston, and nobody had suspected——not even Natalie, who was probably even more glad to be working part-time for Liam now.

"This news deserves champagne," Liam proclaimed. His financial death match with Winterbourne was now over. He'd saved his company with the Schmulian maneuver Felicia and I had helped arrange, and Winterbourne was getting what he deserved.

The server told us they didn't serve champagne by the pool ——something about glass bottles——so we settled for a pitcher of margaritas.

"Make mine a Bud," Nick added.

Katie leaned over to me. "Nick doesn't do mixed drinks," she whispered.

"To the Network Knight," Liam proposed as a toast once we all had glasses. Katie told me that had been Nick's hacker handle.

The smile on Nick's face was priceless. My man had won him over.

I started on my burger as Nick recounted the evidence he and Katie had discovered on Winterbourne. The man was truly a skunk.

I lifted a fry to my mouth.

"There you are." The voice came from behind me——a voice out of my past.

I quickly swallowed and turned. "Mama, Daddy." I rushed to hug my parents. It couldn't be. My parents never traveled out of state, except to Vermont on occasion.

Vivienne trailed behind them.

"Liam made me promise to come," my father explained after I released him from my hug.

I couldn't believe Liam had accomplished this. In college, I'd begged them to visit me in Providence, which was only a few hours away, but it had been too far.

"When?" I asked Daddy.

"The day he came to ask for my blessing to marry you."

I gasped and turned to Liam. "You did that? You never told me that."

He smiled. "A gentleman follows certain conventions, and that's an important one. I wanted your father's blessing before proposing to you."

I was flabbergasted. I knew he took the gentleman code seriously, but I'd never even suspected he'd met my parents. We had a trip to Greenfield scheduled for next weekend, and my mother hadn't let it slip.

"I thought it was a damned decent thing to do," my father said. "Anyway, Liam here promised to always take care of you, and only asked me for one favor in return, so here I am."

"But, the cows?" I asked.

Daddy patted my fiancé on the shoulder. "Liam hired the Jones boys to come over for the week," Daddy told me.

"A week?"

Daddy put his arm around Liam's shoulder. "All week. Liam's paying 'em double what they're worth, if you ask me."

"You sneak. You knew about this and didn't tell me," I accused Vivienne, giving her a big hug. "Is that why you didn't return my calls yesterday?"

"Look, blame Liam. It was his idea. Me, I would have told you a week ago."

We pulled another table over and added chairs.

Daddy ordered his usual beer, but Mama said I should order for her. She was in for a surprise.

"Got room for one more?" Josh, Liam's partner, came strolling over.

"Sure," Liam yelled, "If you're paying."

Josh laughed and I caught my sister eyeing him hungrily as he was introduced around.

Josh had cut Brinna loose, with only a bandage on his arm now to show for the experience.

Brinna had turned out to be the one writing the blog posts and tabloid features about Liam. It seems she'd lost her job at a company Liam and Josh had acquired last year and blamed them. It didn't matter to her that she'd been let go four months before the purchase. Angry people needed someone to blame, and she'd fixated on Liam and Josh.

"What's the story with the bandage? Your girlfriend bite you?" Nick asked, laughing.

Josh patted the bandage. "That would have been better. She gave me some nasty burn marks with a stun gun."

Nick's laughing stopped.

Katie gave Nick a subtle elbow to the ribs.

"I'm just lucky she didn't get me somewhere else," Josh said looking down at his crotch.

"Hope you cut the bitch loose," Nick said.

Josh nodded. "Long gone. She's in jail now."

Nick raised his glass to Josh and took a swallow of his beer.

I'd heard the story. After her arrest for assault, it turned out Brinna had an outstanding warrant for attempted murder in New York, and she was there now awaiting trial.

"If you're down here, who's minding the store?" I asked.

Josh ran Quigley-Fulton now that Liam had gone over to Chameleon Therapeutics full time.

"I put Martin in charge for the week," Josh said.

Liam put down his margarita. "That should be *interesting*."

Vivienne had been watching this whole interchange intently. She touched my shoulder and leaned over. "Does he have another girlfriend yet?" she whispered.

I shook my head. "I don't think so."

A sly grin grew on my sister's face. Poor Josh had no idea what he was in for.

"When's Uncle Garth showing up?" Nick asked. "I've got something I want to show him."

Liam put his glass down. "Later this afternoon."

I turned to Liam. "How many people *did* you invite?"

"Less than twenty——at least I think so. Just a few more of my family members will be arriving today and tomorrow. I wanted them all to get a chance to meet the most beautiful lady in Boston."

"Thank you," I replied, trying unsuccessfully to stop my hair-trigger blushing reaction.

But I was getting better at controlling my mouth and graciously accepting his compliments, like the lady he constantly told me I was.

"Oh, and the Schmulians as well," he added.

I leaned over to whisper to him. "Josh isn't seeing anyone is he?"

Liam cocked his head. "Not so far as I know."

"I think Viv just locked on her targeting radar," I whispered.

He looked over and chuckled. "Good for her. He's a good guy."

I hugged my fiancé. "I love you. This is so special."

"I was hoping you'd like it."

My man had given me a vacation with my parents, the one thing I'd never had growing up.

I kissed him again. "Love it."

My man, my gentleman.

THE END.

SNEAK PEEK: SAVED BY THE BILLIONAIRE

Natalie

In line at the coffee shop, no one recognized me. No one gave me dirty looks or spit on me.

Finally a moment of anonymity, a moment of peace.

The clientele at this Peet's was more businessmen and fewer neurotic housewives than the one I'd been frequenting near home. The fireman at the counter was rattling off order after order at the poor barista.

"But Lucy, I don't know if I have time for that… But I can't… Okay, you win." The whiny male voice came from behind me.

I glanced back at the lengthening line, held up by the guy ordering for a dozen. Mr. Whiny on the phone to Lucy was the short, bald guy directly behind me.

The broad-shouldered man ahead of me moved up to the counter after Mr. Infinite-list finished reading his written orders. Ninety-seven dollars and change was a lot of coffee.

I closed my eyes and listened to Broad Shoulders order. I couldn't see his face, but the deep, seductive voice with a hint of gravel predicted a chiseled jawline and stubble——a high-octane man, a real man, unlike the whiny wimp jabbering on his cell phone behind me.

The sound of Broad Shoulders' voice had me visualizing a deep, dark chocolate pudding——something I could lick all day long.

He ordered a medium caffè mocha, my drink of choice as well.

"Ryan," he said when the barista asked his name.

Ryan, a very lick-worthy name.

I gulped, realizing how inappropriate my daydreams had become just four months after my divorce. I knew it was four months because the final decree had arrived yesterday. I was finally free of Damien Winterbourne.

When I opened my eyes, Broad Shoulders had paid and moved aside, making room for me to order. I'd been right about him being a high-octane man. He had the deep blue eyes, the chiseled jawline ——everything except the stubble, but that could be cured quickly. Tall and imposing, he tugged at his collar, apparently ill at ease in his expensive suit and tie.

"Miss?" the barista said, pulling me back to reality.

I advanced to the counter. "I'll have the same."

She rang me up and smiled. "And your name, miss?"

I slid my AmEx card into the reader. "Natalie."

The card machine beeped twice, and the little screen read *declined*.

The barista shot me a questioning glance. "Try it again. Sometimes it acts up."

I removed the card and shoved it back in.

The reader complained loudly again.

"Perhaps another card?" the girl behind the counter offered with a sigh.

I located my Visa card and tried that with the same embarrassing result. The line behind me was restless, and the muttering increased. Nothing nice, no doubt.

"Get a clue, lady," was the only thing I could pick out of the mumbling.

This is not my day.

I cringed as I pulled back the second card. "Something must be wrong. I'll have to call and get this straightened out."

I left the counter, looking down at the floor to avoid the stares, and scurried to the corner of the store. I dialed the number on the back of my Visa. When the annoying mechanical voice asked for it, I keyed in my card number. Instead of giving me my balance information, I was told to wait for the next available agent. I settled into a seat while the telephone hold music played.

"Caffè mocha, right?" That same one-hundred-octane male voice said.

I looked up to see Mr. Broad Shoulders, Ryan, holding two cups with an iPad tucked under one arm.

He held one out for me. The sight of this man froze me in place, now that I got a good look at the features and size of him. His deep blue eyes captured me and wouldn't let me go.

"Here, take it; I can't drink two." The voice was even deeper and more chocolaty than at the counter.

"You shouldn't have," I offered feebly, reaching for my purse to pay him back.

His brow knit, and he thrust the cup forward. "Here, I can't miss my quota."

I accepted the cup. "Quota?"

His smile returned. "When I was ten, I promised my mother to do at least one good deed a week."

My grin nearly broke my face. "Really?" A man who kept a promise to his mother couldn't be all bad. Or it was the most off-the-wall pickup line I'd ever heard.

He turned and walked toward the door.

Not a pick-up line, evidently.

"Thank you," I called after him, watching his tight ass like a pervert. Hell, it had been a long time, after all. I deserved to watch if I wanted.

My phone buzzed with an incoming text. I moved the phone from my ear and checked the screen.

BROSNAHAND: Call me - we need to talk

Another chat with Brosnahand, my ex-husband's lawyer, was not going to rise to the top of my list today, and probably not even tomorrow. Whatever information he had to pass on was unlikely to brighten my outlook. Even after agreeing to the divorce, Damien still wanted to talk to me. The feeling wasn't mutual.

Becoming Damien Winterbourne's wife had been the worst mistake of my life. He'd fooled me, along with all the people that now regretted ever having done business with him. To every one of my previous so-called friends, sharing his last name meant sharing his guilt. The Winterbourne name was now radioactive in Boston, at least until the memories faded. As soon as I sold the house, I'd get as far away from here as I could, as fast as I could.

Damien was cooling his heels in jail, awaiting trial——a good place for him to be. The judge had been perceptive enough to see him as a flight risk.

I ended the call with the credit card company. Waiting on terminal hold would be more comfortable at home. I hadn't remembered to charge my phone last night, and the notice on the screen told me I had less than twenty percent battery left. I ignored the warning. The phone went back in my purse.

I collected my free mocha, my purse, and added a packet of sweetener to my cup before heading out. Coffee wasn't the purpose of my trip to this part of town. Cartier Jewelers next door was about to open.

Turning right out of Peet's, the sight stopped me in my tracks. I stifled a laugh.

With his coffee in one hand and his iPad in the other, Ryan was trying to use his chin to scroll the text on the tablet as he read a page and chin-scrolled farther down to read some more.

I ventured closer, stretching my smirk to a smile. "Thank you for the coffee, Ryan."

He glanced momentarily in my direction. "You already said that." He went back to his reading.

Somebody has a stick up his ass today.

Thankfully I didn't mouth the words.

"You're welcome, Natalie," he added after another chin-scroll.

He'd noticed my name, a point in his favor.

I found myself glancing at his profile in the morning sun as I waited. His face was one a Roman sculptor would have chosen, I decided.

After a few minutes of silence between us, Jonas Gisler, the store manager, came to unlock the door.

As I entered behind Ryan, the time on the wall clock read ten exactly. Gisler was Swiss and proudly precise, I'd learned earlier.

Ryan went directly to the ruby counter.

I waited.

"Mrs. Winterbourne, what may I help you with today?" Gisler said with his Teutonic smile.

Surprise overcame Ryan's face. "I was here first," he announced loudly.

Gisler was unmoved as he continued to watch me for a response to his question. My status as a repeat customer seemed to trump Ryan's position in line.

I pointed toward Ryan. "It's Spencer now, Mr. Gisler, and he's right. He was first."

Gisler's smile broke down to a mild grin. "As you wish." He moved to the ruby counter. "What may I help with today, sir?"

Ryan pointed through the glass. "I'd like to see that one, please."

I shuffled closer, pretending to scan the cases for a purchase.

Gisler pulled out a ruby necklace with a huge heart-shaped stone, set in a circle of diamonds, and laid it on a velvet mat.

Ryan looked at it, perplexed. "No, that won't do." He didn't bother to check the price tag as any normal person would. "Let's see the next one over."

Gisler complied, bringing up another gorgeous necklace.

Ryan shook his head.

"Perhaps if you were to tell me your parameters, I might recommend a few pieces," Gisler offered.

Ryan ignored him and pointed to another necklace and then two more. None of them pleased him.

Gisler sighed. "Perhaps a feminine perspective might help? Mrs. Spencer here has exquisite taste."

I blushed at the compliment.

"Sure," Ryan said, casting a glance my way.

I moved next to him, but avoided eye contact, lest I freeze up. "I'll try, and it's Miss."

"I don't have a lot of time," he said. "I'm due in court soon." His body heat became perceptible as he shifted closer.

"A lawyer, huh?"

He tugged at his collar. "No," he said curtly, my hint to shut up.

That explained why he seemed uncomfortable in his expensive suit. A lawyer also would have used a page of words instead of one.

A quick peek at the tags on the necklaces he had chosen first showed prices from forty to seventy thousand. This was one lucky woman.

"Special occasion?" I asked.

"Her birthday," he replied, choosing more than a single-word answer this time.

"Mr. Gisler, those three in the back, please." I pointed out three more modest stones than he had originally chosen, a little less ostentatious, more ruby and less diamond surround.

I'd checked his left hand earlier, no wedding ring, which most likely meant special girlfriend gift. If he went too big now, he'd have a hard time topping it with the engagement ring.

"Those are too small," he said quickly.

"She must be very special. Wife? Girlfriend?"

He shook his head. "Sister."

"Right," I said, letting too much disbelief color my voice.

He turned toward me. "Yes, sister." Annoyance tinged his tone.

"Then we want to avoid these heart-shaped stones." I pointed out the first set he'd selected. "Mr. Gisler, the third from the end please."

The jeweler pulled out a beautiful cushion-cut solitaire ruby on a white gold chain. It was way too large for any normal person to give his sister, but the smile on Ryan's face said we'd found the one.

The price tag was face down, and he didn't bother to turn it over. Instead, he handed his AmEx card to Gisler. "I'd like it gift wrapped and overnighted to this address," he said, pulling a piece of paper from his wallet.

"I can take care of that for you, sir." Gisler took the card and the paper to his register.

I moved back to a more respectful distance. "What'd you do wrong?" I asked.

He cocked his head. "Pardon?"

"That's an awfully expensive birthday gift." I couldn't believe he didn't see how absurd it was.

His eyes flicked downward. "I forgot her birthday last year."

Even if I'd forgotten my sister's birthday, she'd be getting something like a scarf.

"And you think she's expecting something like this?"

The man would rate as totally clueless if he agreed with my question.

"I think she'll complain like crazy, actually, but that's just tough. She'll have to take it."

He didn't seem to understand the difference between expecting something this extravagant, and accepting such a beautiful gift.

If I opened something like this on my birthday, you wouldn't be able to pry it away from me with dynamite.

Gisler returned with the credit card and charge slip.

I couldn't resist peeking. Fifty-eight thousand dollars. If I had a brother, I would want one like Ryan, although right now my hormones were casting him for a different role than brother——way different.

He replaced the card in his wallet. "You can get it there tomorrow?"

Gisler stiffened as if that were an insult. "You can rely on me, sir."

I shocked myself by reaching over to touch Ryan briefly on the arm.

He didn't recoil. Instead, a warm smile tugged at his lips.

"Ryan," I said. "You know, flowers and a phone call go a long way as well."

He nodded. "Appreciate the advice, Miss Spencer."

"Natalie," I corrected him.

He checked his watch and collected his receipt. "Thank you again for the help." He reached the door in a few quick strides. "Natalie," he added before the door closed behind him.

Gisler huffed loudly. "Now, Miss Spencer, how may I help you?"

I opened my purse and pulled out the red velvet pouch. "I'd like to get these cleaned, if I could." I handed him the pouch. "And the post on one of them needs some looking after."

He gently opened it and slid out the earrings, my pride and joy. "My, they are even more lovely every time I see them."

"Thank you." They were the best pair of diamond earrings I would ever own, eight total carats of beautiful brilliance.

He held them up for a closer inspection. "Yes, I see. I can have these ready for you after lunch, if that's acceptable."

I nodded. "Perfect. I'll be by around one." That would give me time to pick up Murphy and also get to the gym before returning. I'd been told some cats liked car rides. Murphy was not among them, as the long scratch on my arm proved.

Once I'd gotten him to the groomer's this morning, his mood had changed, as it always did. He loved the attention. Now I just needed a Star Trek transporter to get him there without having to load him into the car.

I bid Mr. Gisler goodbye and sucked down half my mocha on the way back to the car.

As I started the engine, the radio came alive with Frank Sinatra singing "That's Life." His tune could be my theme song, a reminder to never give up.

First, there had been Damien's arrest, followed by the ridicule and shame, and then the divorce. Now I finally had my name back. Once I sold the house and left this city, I could reclaim my future, in a place where the Winterbourne stigma wouldn't follow me. Natalie Winterbourne's life was over, but Natalie Spencer's was ahead of me. I could feel it.

Like a sign of things to come, the road bent left, and the sun beat in through the windshield, lifting my spirits. I turned the music up high.

The drive home went quickly in light mid-day traffic, with fewer crazies than normal on the road.

I turned the corner onto my street, and there they were: two police cars and three black SUVs in front of my house.

I pulled up to the garage and climbed out of the car with my battle-face on. I'd had enough of these searches already. They'd been here only last week, for Christ's sake.

This one was different. Some of the windbreakers had US MARSHAL in bold yellow lettering on the back, in addition to the usual FBI jerks.

A uniformed cop held up his hand as I reached the walk. "Hold it, ma'am. You can't go in."

I started past him. "The hell I can't. This is my house." In the past, the only way to deal with these assholes had been at high volume.

He grabbed my arm. "Agent White," he called.

I wrested my arm loose, but stopped where I was. The last thing I needed was some stupid cop tasering me in the back, on my own property.

One of the agents from last week trotted over. He flipped open his badge momentarily, as they all did. They could be dime-store replicas for all the time they *didn't* give you to inspect them.

"Special Agent White," he announced like it should mean something to me. "Mrs. Winterbourne, I'll need your car keys."

This had happened each time. They wanted to search the car as well as the house.

The key fob was still in my hand. I hadn't stashed it in my purse yet. I handed it over with a huff. "It's Spencer now, and how long is this going to take? I have to go pick up my cat."

He pocketed the key. "Mrs. Winterbourne," he said, intentionally trying to piss me off for sure. "This house and automobile, and all the contents, are being seized as products of a criminal enterprise."

"That can't be right," I complained.

"For any questions about this forfeiture, you may contact the United States Attorney." He offered me a business card.

I couldn't be hearing this right.

He forced the card at me again.

I took it. *Kirk Willey, Assistant United States Attorney*, it read.

The agent pointed toward the street. "You need to step off the property now, Mrs. Winterbourne."

With my legs shaking, and my breakfast threatening to come up, tears clouded my eyes. "But this is my house."

"Not any longer," Agent White said coldly. He moved his hand to the butt of his gun.

Join Erin's mailing list and be notified when this book and others are available. WWW.ERINSWANN.COM/SUBSCRIBE